THE HINDU LAW:

BEING

A TREATISE ON THE LAW ADMINISTERED EXCLUSIVELY TO HINDUS

BY THE

BRITISH COURTS IN INDIA

THE HINDU LAW:

BEING

A TREATISE ON THE LAW ADMINISTERED EXCLUSIVELY TO HINDUS

BY THE

BRITISH COURTS IN INDIA

HERBERT COWELL

GYAN

Published by

Gyan Publishing House
5, Ansari Road
Daryaganj, New Delhi-110002
Phone: 011-47034999, 9811692060
E-mail: books@gyanbooks.com

Distribution Network
gyanbooks.com
India, USA, Canada, UK, Australia

ISBN: 978-93-6780-482-7 (PB)

First Published, 1870

2nd Impression 2024

Printed at: Gyan Press, Delhi.

THE HINDU LAW: BEING A TREATISE ON THE LAW ADMINISTERED EXCLUSIVELY TO HINDUS BY THE BRITISH COURTS IN INDIA
Author: HERBERT COWELL

TAGORE LAW LECTURES—1870.

Tagore Law Lectures—1870.

THE HINDU LAW:

BEING

A TREATISE ON THE LAW ADMINISTERED EXCLUSIVELY
TO HINDUS

BY THE

BRITISH COURTS IN INDIA.

BY

HERBERT COWELL, Esq.,

BARRISTER-AT-LAW, AND TAGORE LAW PROFESSOR.

CALCUTTA:

THACKER, SPINK AND CO.,

Bombay: THACKER, VINING & Co. London: W. THACKER & Co.

1870.

PREFACE.

THE following Lectures were delivered in Calcutta, in pursuance of the will of the late Baboo Prosonno-coomar Tagore, C. S. I., in which provision was made for the appointment of a Law Professor to be elected by the Senate of the University of Calcutta and to be called "The Tagore Law Professor," who "shall read or deliver yearly at some place within the town of Calcutta, one complete Course of Law Lectures, without charge to the students and other persons who may attend such Lectures." The will directed the Lectures to be printed, and not less than 500 copies thereof to be distributed gratuitously.

The intention apparently was to provide for the publication of text-books upon Indian law, which should be specially adapted to Indian practitioners and students.

No one can have practised or administered law in Indian Courts without recognizing the want of a law literature, the growth of which it is the object of the Founder, and of the Calcutta University, to whom the regulation and control of the Professorship were entrusted, to foster. The Indian system of jurisprudence, the system of law administered in India by the English, is of the strangest description, unparalleled in the history of the world. No government was ever called upon to legislate for so heterogeneous a community, or to combine together so many conflicting systems of law under one general administration of justice. That community includes Hindus, Mahomedans, Englishmen, Buddhists, Jews, Armenians, and Parsees. Some of these derive their law exclusively from their religion, others from the place where they are born, or where they live. Then there are classes of mixed race who are rapidly increasing in numbers; also those who belong to one race by blood, but have adopted the religion of another, who therefore form new and distinct classes which have sprung into existtence since English rule was established.

This conflict of laws under a common administration of them, a common legislature and a common political government, must gradually give place to a single system in which the purely personal law will be as limited as circumstances will permit.

Political unity tends to produce in course of time a social union, especially as regards those transactions of life of which law takes cognizance, and to necessitate a legal system which shall be, as far as possible, of general application. And the Legislature and the Courts of India established in the country have, from time to time, endeavoured to bring law into harmony with the wants of a changing society. Under such circumstances, it becomes important to review the existing state of the laws which are, for the time being, enforced. The University selected that law, which is peculiar to the race to which the Founder himself belonged, as the first subject of these Lectures. In this wide field of discussion, the Hindu family system, differing from all others within the Empire in its constitution, religion, and legal duties, appeared to be a fitting subject in which to endeavour to trace the influence upon the separate law of a particular community of its absorption into one general political society. My object, therefore, has been, while collecting and arranging the existing rules of Hindu law, as administered in British India, to shew the spirit in which they have been developed, and the character of the changes which circumstances have rendered necessary.

The second course of Lectures will be devoted to the Hindu law of inheritance and succession.

H. C.

CALCUTTA, *November* 22, 1870.

TABLE OF CONTENTS.

INTRODUCTORY LECTURE.

LECTURE II.

THE POSITION OF THE HINDUS IN THE BRITISH EMPIRE.

LECTURE III.

THE HINDU FAMILY—THE JOINT WORSHIP.

LECTURE IV.

THE HINDU FAMILY—THE JOINT ESTATE.

The Mitakshara and the Dayabhaga. PAGE

LECTURE V.

THE HINDU FAMILY—ITS MANAGEMENT, AND LIMITS.

LECTURE VI.

THE MEMBERS OF THE FAMILY—MAINTENANCE AND GUARDIANSHIP.

LECTURE VII.

THE MEMBERS OF THE FAMILY—THEIR CIVIL STATUS.

LECTURE VIII.

THE HINDU WIDOW.

LECTURE IX.

THE RITE OF ADOPTION.

LECTURE X.

THE CONTRACT OF ADOPTION.

LECTURE XI.

THE RIGHT TO ADOPT.

PAGE

LECTURE XII.

PERMISSION TO ADOPT—PLURAL ADOPTION.

LECTURE XIII.

THE RIGHT TO GIVE IN ADOPTION—THE QUALIFICATIONS FOR BEING ADOPTED.

LECTURE XIV.

THE QUALIFICATIONS FOR BEING ADOPTED.

LECTURE XV.

THE EFFECTS OF ADOPTION.

LIST OF CASES CITED.

ERRATA.

In Lecture III, in several places, for *Sapindakarana* read *Sapindikarana.*

On page 87, for the foot note there printed, repeat the foot note on page 86, and transfer the foot note on page 87 to page 88.

Page 93, line 8 from the bottom, for *the High Courts* read *some of the High Courts.*

Page 93, line 9 from the bottom, for *would* read *will.*

Page 93, line 11 from the bottom, for *assumes* read *on the assumption.*

INTRODUCTORY LECTURE.

Object of these Lectures—Divisions of the Subject—To whom Hindu Law applies—A Personal and not a Local Law—Characteristics of the Community—Castes—Present Position of Brahmins—Birth of Hindu Law—Its early Character—Its gradual Growth—The Rise of the Schools—The five Schools of the present day—The Influence on Hindu Law of its English administration—The manner in which that Influence is exercised—Its earlier and later Development compared—The Course pursued by the English—The necessity for reviewing their Administration—The Plan of this work.

In the year 1868, the late Baboo Prosunno Coomar Tagore directed, by his will, that a Law-Professorship should be founded for the purpose of delivering yearly, at some place within the town of Calcutta, and of subsequently printing and publishing one complete course of law lectures. He confided to the Senate of the University of Calcutta the duty of regulating the 'kind of law' which was to be taught. In pursuance of the wishes so expressed by the founder, the Senate resolved that some branch of Hindu, Mahomedan, or Anglo-Indian law should annually form the subject of these lectures, and that a definitive selection should be annually made by the Syndicate of the University, in consultation with the Faculty of Law and the Professor,—such selection to be made with a view to the ultimate formation of a body of Institutes of Indian Law. It is in accordance with the Resolution of the Senate that during the first year of the existence of this Chair its labors are directed to the

LECTURE I.

subject of the Hindu law, or to so much of what Mr. Macnaghten* calls that 'interminable and troubled ocean' as can be usefully dealt with in a single course, bearing in mind that 'completeness' is the object of the founder, and a 'body of Institutes' is the design of the University.

Object of these Lectures.

I may say, in the outset, that I read the will of the testator, and the resolution of the Senate as expressive of a wish that these lectures should be devoted to the treatment of the subject selected in a manner which shall be practically useful. The direction to publish given by the one, and the design adopted and announced by the other, shew that the annual production of a systematic treatise upon some branch of law, rather than the task of aiding or directing the labours of University students, is the duty imposed upon the holder of this office. And with respect to the subject of the first year's course, having regard to the intentions of the Founder and the Senate, I may define it to be the discussion of those rules or principles of law which are at the present day applicable exclusively to Hindus, and are so recognized and acted upon by the highest Courts of Justice established by the English Legislature and Government. With Hindu law, as it may have been ages ago, or as it was originally declared by the ancient authorities, we have to do only as with the ancient framework of an historic society. The early precepts of the Hindu lawgivers have been controlled by the vicissitudes of experience; and the rules of law, which at the present day govern the lives and property of Hindus, depend partly upon the doctrines received by the various schools of interpretation of the sacred text, and

* Practical Remarks, Mahomedan Law, p. 19.

partly upon the usages which have obtained in particular classes or localities and are adapted to existing habits and customs, subject to such modifications, changes and improvements, as have been, from time to time, introduced during the last century by the action of the English Legislature and the decisions of English Courts.

Perhaps, in a lecture intended to be introductory to a subject of this wide extent, it may be useful, so far only as is consistent with the special and practical object in view, to refer to the social and historical aspect of the community, which is thus bound together by its own rules of law, and marked off from the rest of the Empire. And accordingly I shall endeavour, in the first place, to point out to whom the Hindu law applies and under what circumstances a man ceases to be amenable to it; then to look at the general characteristics of the community which is governed by it; and lastly to trace the steps by which that law, as it is administered at the present day, has been developed from the primeval code.

Divisions of the subject.

With regard to the first point, it must be recollected that the Hindu law has obligatory force only upon those who are Hindus both by birth and by religion. When a Hindu is converted to Christianity or to Mahometanism, and has shown, by his course of conduct after his conversion, what rules and customs he has adopted, he is released from the trammels of Hindu law, and is thenceforth governed by the law and usage of the class with which he has associated himself.* And even within the limits of that large community which is Hindu both by birth and by religion, there is considerable scope for

To whom Hindu law applies.

* Abraham v. Abraham, 1 S. W. R., P. C., 5; and 9 Moore I. A., 227.

LECTURE I. personal choice as to the school of law by which the individual or the family is to be governed. For, as families or individuals migrate from one country to another, they may choose whether they will retain the shasters and usages prevalent in the country which they leave, or adopt those which they find to be general in the country in which they settle.

This freedom of choice, as to the particular shasters or school of law by which he was to be governed, was declared to be the right of a Hindu by an early decision* of the Privy Council. Neither the *situs* of the property, nor the domicil of the owner, determines the law which affects his rights. A Hindu may import into any country to which he migrates the particular law of his own tribe, the governing circumstance to be attended to in deciding by what law he is bound being the intention as mani-

* Rutcheputty Dutt Jha and others *v.* Rajunder Narain Rae and others, 2 Moore I. A., 132. The point at issue in this case was whether the laws, according to the shasters current in Mithila, should govern the right of succession to property derived from an ancestor who had originally emigrated from that district, and whose descendants had uniformly retained in Bengal the religious ceremonies and usages to which the family had been accustomed. It had been held by the Sudder Dewanny Adawlut (1) in 1801, that if a person of Mithila family living in Bengal continue the observance of the Mithila Shasters on occasions of marriages and mournings in his family, and have a Mithila purohit, or priest, to perform his ceremonies, his legal rights were to be determined according to the Mithila Shasters; but that if those ceremonies were performed by him according to the Bengal Shasters, his rights should be determined by the Bengal Shasters. The same doctrine was affirmed in the case of *Ranee Sreemutty Debea v. Ranee Rung Luta*, 4 Moore I. A., 292, where a family of Sutgop Brahmins migrating from Bengal to Midnapore, where the Mitakshara law prevailed, were held to be subject to Bengal law in respect to inheritance to property situated in Midnapore, they being shown to have performed their religious ceremonies according to the Bengal authorities.

(1) Rajchunder Narain Chunder Chowdhry *v.* Goculchund Goh, Reports of Select Cases, Vol. I (new edition), p. 56.

fested by the character of the purohit, ceremonies and usages, which he, or his descendants after him, retains about him. Whatever, therefore, may have been the case formerly, and whatever may be the case now, where a Hindu passes from one native territory to another, he nevertheless can move from one district to another, within the limits of British territories, and carry with him, as a personal law applicable to his family and his possessions, the rules of the shasters under which he has lived up to the time of his migration. Further than this, the doctrine* is now established, that a Hindu so migrating must be presumed, until the contrary be shewn, to have brought with him and retained all his religious ceremonies and customs, and consequently the law of succession and of property which is associated with them. This is more especially the case when the family is shewn to have brought with it its own priests who continue their ministrations. Although the presumption is in favour of a Hindu retaining the shasters of his birth, yet the principle has been definitively affirmed by the Privy Council, that a Hindu may, if he chooses, change the shasters or school of law by which he wishes to be governed.† The real test to be applied is by what shasters the customs and rites of marriages and funerals are conducted; occasional

* Nobinchunder Perdhan *v.* Janardhun Misser, Suth F. B. Rulings, 67.

† *Ranee Pudmavati* v. *Baboo Doolar Sing*, reported in 4 Moore I. A., 259, was a case of a family of Bengalee Sudras which had migrated at a remote period from the district of Burdwan to the district of Purneah. A number of customs were described which the Hindu law officer declared to be part of the Mithila law, and it was held that the family, although originally subject to Bengal law, had, since their migration, adopted and performed the religious rites and ceremonies of Mithila, and were therefore subject to its law.

LECTURE I.

or daily religious services may be changed without effecting a corresponding change in a Hindu's legal liabilities.*

A personal and not a local law.

The principle thus laid down is consistent with the theory that Hindu law is a personal law, one that applies in its various forms to individuals and families, and not to localities, and has been secured to Hindus chiefly because it is so largely (to an extent which these lectures must describe) associated with their religion. The designation of the different schools is derived from the names of provinces, and it is common to allude to Hindu law as current in a particular province. Such phraseology is no doubt sufficiently accurate for ordinary purposes, for, as a general rule, those resident in a particular locality follow the same shasters; but nevertheless it is erroneous, in so far as it conveys the notion of a law whose operation is confined to particular localities. There are at this moment numbers of Hindus resident in Calcutta who are governed by the law according to the school of Benares or of Mithila, and it is quite possible that all five schools of Hindu law may be current, in the sense of being applied, in any one province. Hindu law is personal, and not local. A Hindu may throw it from him altogether by changing his religion, and he may choose to adopt it in any one of its various forms. But so long as a Hindu by birth retains the Hindu religion, he is amenable to Hindu law in one form or other, whether he wishes it or not.

Characteristics of the community.

Now, with regard to the community, it remains at the present day what it was at the time of Menu, an aggregation of families rather than of individuals. With such a people as to some extent with the inhabitants of modern

* Koomudchunder Roy *v.* Seetakanth Roy, Suth. F. B., 75; Ranee Pudmavati *v.* Baboo Doolar Singh, 7 S. W. R., P. C., 41.

Russia, co-ownership is the normal condition of the rights of property. Commensality and co-ownership are the characteristics of Hindu family life, and the village community is a political or social expansion of the domestic institution. Individual will and energy are checked by the influences at work in a society by far the largest portion of which rests on a basis of joint responsibility for most of the duties of life, and which sinks the rights of each one in the aggregate claims of the family. Such influences, combined with those of climate and soil and of the peculiar religious observances, which fix in successive generations a sense of dependence upon those who may come after them in regard to their fate in the future world, may readily account for the stationary condition of the society. A permanent literature, however, and an original jurisprudence secure to it the respectful appreciation of the world, notwithstanding the absence of that progressive development of ideas and institutions which is the pride of western nations, and is associated with their ideas of advancing civilization. In three thousand years of Hindu history there are but few changes to be observed in their social condition. The most important one to be noted is the advance which was made in Bengal three centuries ago, by which a large population was emancipated from the worst trammels of the communal system, and the separate rights of the individuals were preserved from total dependence upon the joint right of the aggregate family.

Castes.

Besides the fact of co-ownership being the prevalent condition of the rights of property, there is the other leading feature of Hindu society which has powerfully influenced its notions of the rights of persons, and that is the particular manner in which it has divided itself into

LECTURE I. four great *castes.* There is nothing singular, so far as the ancient world is concerned, in a great community being parcelled out in divisions, by reference to the principles of religion, of war, of industry, and servitude. The singularity of the Hindu division is the wide and lasting separation between the three higher classes and the lowest, in every thing which pertains to the law, religion, manners, customs, and habits of life. Sudras have, in the course of Hindu history, risen to be kings, but their place in the social system is that they are the servants of the other classes, especially of the Brahmins. In religion they are declared to be incapable of regeneration, in the sense in which that term is understood when applied to the three twice-born classes. A Brahmin, according to Menu, may not perform sacrifice for Sudras, or read the Vedas even to himself in their presence.* Sudras, again, may not be taught the law, nor be instructed in the mode of expiating sin. Until a twice-born man is invested with the signs of his class, he must not pronounce any sacred text, except what ought to be used in obsequies to an ancestor; since he is on a level with a Sudra before his new birth from the revealed scripture†. Practices forbidden to the twice-born classes as "unfit for cattle" are afterwards expressly permitted to Sudras, to whom servile attendance is prescribed as their highest duty.‡ In the course of these lectures, I shall have to point out in what respect Sudras at the present day are actually governed by different laws from those which apply to the rest of the Hindu

* 2 Menu, 172. † 9 Menu, 334.

‡ Servile attendance on *Bráhmans* learned in the *Veda*, chiefly on such as keep house, and are famed for virtue, is of itself the highest duty of a *Sudra*, and leads him to future beatitude—9 Menu, 334.

community. Of the other three classes, it is sufficient to say that they in some respects stand upon a common footing, since they have the common privilege or duty of studying the Vedas and also of reaching through a succession of elaborate ceremonies terminating in marriage, the distinction of being regenerate or twice-born.

Present position of Brahmins.

The Brahmins are said to have attained at the revolution, which was coeval with the first promulgation of the Institutes of Menu, that prominent rank which they have retained ever since, and which under all dynastic changes secured their authority in religion and legislation. They form the sacerdotal class and have the exclusive right of performing religious sacrifices and ceremonies and of administering the rules of caste. Strictly speaking they are prohibited from the pursuit of gain, and should devote themselves to the work of charity and religion, so that ultimately by penance and religious contemplation they may be absorbed into the divine essence. That, however, has long since become an exploded theory, inapplicable to the circumstances of the present age; apparently upon the principle enunciated by some Hindu law officers of the Sudder Court in 1825. They laid it down in a partnership suit between Brahmin wine merchants, that according to the shasters it is not proper for Brahmins to trade in wine. "If, however," they said, "two Brahmins* have acquired wealth by matters prohibited by the shasters, the share of each in the said wealth is equal." It was immediately held that the punishment of Brahmins for dealing in wine, and therefore in anything else, was not a matter for the consideration of a Civil Court; which

* Jyenarain Mookerjee *v.* Bulram Rai, Reports of Select Cases, Vol. IV (new edition), p. 107.

LECTURE I. accordingly deals with Brahmin traders precisely on the same footing as it deals with traders of any other caste. The functions of the Kshatriyas, or second class, belonged, from the first, more exclusively to this world; and originally they, as the warlike and manly caste, were the leaders and rulers of the community. The Vaisyas, or third class, included the industrious portion of the population,—the artificer, the husbandman, the tradesman, all whose common object was gain without the duty of service. With regard to the two lowest classes that existed in Menu's time, they are now re-placed by a considerable number of castes,* which to a great extent coincide with the different trades. In the neighbourhood of Poona, Mr. Elphinstone says, there are about 150 different castes, and in Bengal they are very numerous. They maintain their divisions, however obscurely derived, with great strictness.

Birth of Hindu law.

Although the Kshatriyas were originally possessed of the supreme power, and held in their hands the exclusive authority of Government, yet the birth of Hindu law is supposed to have taken place at a date subsequent to the transfer of the supremacy from them to the Brahmins. The revolution which effected this transfer took place under Parasurama, who appears to have combined the other three classes together in revolt against the arbitrary and oppressive measures of the ruling caste. He was grandson of Bhrigu, well known as the first promulgator of the Institutes of Menu. The power of the Kshatriyas was shattered in the struggle, and although they retained that which the Brahmins refused to exercise, *viz.*, the functions of the executive, the sacerdotal class assumed

* Elphinstone's History of India, p. 55.

the supremacy, which they thenceforward, although not always in the same degree, retained, both religion and the work of legislation being exclusively under their control. And as pointed out by Mr. Maine in his work on Ancient Law* "the religious oligarchies of Asia, either for their own guidance, or for the relief of their memory, or for the instruction of their disciples, seem in all cases to have ultimately embodied their legal learning in a code, but the opportunity of increasing and consolidating their influence was probably too tempting to be resisted. Their complete monopoly of legal knowledge appears to have enabled them to put off on the world collections not so much of rules actually observed as of the rules which the priestly order considered proper to be observed. The Hindu Code, called the law of Menu, which is certainly a Brahmin compilation, undoubtedly enshrines many genuine observances of the Hindu race, but the opinion of the best contemporary orientalists is that it does not, as a whole, represent a set of rules ever actually administered in Hindustan. It is in great part an ideal picture of that which in the view of Brahmins *ought* to be the law."

Its early character.

It must be remembered that Menu, like Moses, is the author of a revealed system of law rather than of a revealed religion. Inspired priests were the legislators for the people, and the religious, moral, and civil duties of men were mixed up together with little distinction. While the decalogue is based upon the indivisible unity of moral and religious duty, the Hindu legislators originally assumed the indissoluble connection of the civil and religious obligations of mankind. The total separation of

* Page 17.

LECTURE I. law from religion, however familiar to those who derive their law from Rome and feudal customs, and their religion from Palestine, was unknown, and would have been rejected by the religious oligarchs who, in framing minute rules of conduct and continual ceremonies for Hindus, were careful in all things to preserve their own collective supremacy and individual influence.

Hindu law was originally proclaimed as a direct emanation from the Deity. "That* Immutable Power," says the so-called Menu, "having enacted this Code of laws, himself taught it fully to me in the beginning; afterwards I taught Marichi and the nine other holy sages. . . ." Then Bhrigu, great and wise, having been appointed by Menu to promulgate his laws, addressed all the Rishis with an affectionate mind, saying: "Hear!"† Yajnavalkya also is described in the introduction to his own Institutes as delivering his precepts to an audience of ancient philosophers assembled in the province of Mithila. He gives the names of twenty sages who contributed to the work of legislation. The tenth century before the Christian era is the date which is approximately assigned to this re-constitution, as it were, of the Hindu community by the separation of the legislature from the executive, and the complete fusion of law and religion, both of which were thenceforth promulgated and administered by the same class. The law thus derived was of universal application to the entire Hindu community. But as centuries elapsed, the warlike and powerful caste of the Kshatriyas‡ regained their ascendency; and the

* 1 Menu, 58, 60.

† Colebrooke's Digest, Preface, p. xvi.

‡ Vivada Chintamoni, Preface, p. xix.

Brahmins, though possessed of the legislative and judicial functions, were reduced to a secondary position. The Rajpoot kings were supreme in their dominions, and the Brahmins, as nominal legislators, were compelled to obey a superior will. And under these circumstances it is conjectured that the various schools of law arose which prevailed in India before the Mahomedan conquest.

Its gradual growth.

The earlier Rishis delivered their precepts to the entire community. The later commentators addressed themselves to the inhabitants of particular localities, and in the gloss which they respectively put upon the ancient texts of which they treated, they may have been guided by the wishes of the reigning power, or by attention to the usages which had obtained in the particular districts during the lapse of ages. Thus the authority of the modern commentator, wherever his work was received, came to supersede the reverence due to the earlier sage. The most striking instance of this is afforded by the fate of Yajnavalkya. His Institutes, throughout India, are of the highest and most sacred authority, admitted and recognized everywhere. The Mitakshara is a commentary upon these Institutes less than 1000 years old, composed by a hermit named Vijnyaneswara; and is universally accepted by all the schools, even by that of Bengal, except so far as it is in that school controlled upon various points by what the followers of that school consider to be the superior authority of the work of Jimutavahana. The Mitakshara is perhape the most celebrated and the most widely authoritative treatise or commentary in existence on the work of the ancient sages. The Dayabhaga, on the other hand, acknowledges equally, with the Mitakshara, the authority of the Institutes of

LECTURE I.

Yajnavalkya; but at the same time its doctrines are upon several essential points in the law both of persons and of property widely different from those of the rival treatise. It is the work of Jimutavahana, who appears to have flourished later than Vijnyaneswara, but earlier than Raghunandana, and who therefore must have composed his work, according to Mr. Colebrooke,* at a date somewhat earlier than the beginning of the sixteenth century.

The rise of the schools.

The process by which the changes in Hindu law have been effected is primarily by the growth in particular districts of particular usages, which appear to have always been respected, unless plainly repugnant to law. Vrihaspati, early in the development of Hindu jurisprudence, laid down that "immemorial usage legalizes any practice," and "a decision must not be made solely by having recourse to the letter of written codes; since if no decision were made according to the reason of the law, or according to immemorial usage,† there might be a failure of justice;" and again, "a man should not neglect the approved customs of districts,‡ the equitable rules of his family, or the particular laws of his race;—in whatever country, whatever usage has passed through successive generations, let not a man there disregard it; such usage is law in that country." "Reason and justice are more to be regarded than mere texts, and wherever a good custom exists, it has the force of law."§

When commentaries so widely different in their character and in the principles which they enforce, as the Dayabhaga

* Preface to the Dayabhaga, p. xiv.

† Colebrooke's Digest, B. I., C. II., verse 78.

‡ Colebrooke's Digest, B. I., C. III., verses 98, 99.

§ Shamachurn's Vyavastha Darpana, 387, See Sir L. Peel's Judgment.

and the Mitakshara, nevertheless both assume that they accord with the ancient writ, and are each of them implicitly obeyed as the faithful expositors of the revealed or remembered wisdom of antiquity, it is obvious that Hindu law has proved capable of a certain variety in its development without departing from that which the orthodox followers of Menu will recognize as a faithful similitude to its earliest form. The commentary, as time goes on, finds its own commentators in its turn, who unite in the reverence which is due, but not in the meaning which they attach to the work which they expound. There are glosses and commentaries, for instance, on the Mitakshara, which are received by different schools, which nevertheless acknowledge the supreme authority of that work. "Hindu law," according to Mr. Colebrooke, in the paper written by him, and appended to the first volume of Sir Thomas Strange's work, "is to be sought primarily in the institutes or collections (sanhitas) attributed to holy sages; the true authors, whoever these were, having affixed to their compositions the names of sacred personages, such as Menu, Yajnavalkya, Vishnu, Parasurama, Gautama, &c. They are implicitly received by Hindus as authentic works of these personages." The rules of interpretation, he adds, are collected in the Mimansa, which is a disquisition on proof and authority of precepts, and is considered as a branch of philosophy, being properly the logic of the law. The Mimansa and the Vedas are chiefly studied in the south of India, while in Eastern India, *i. e.*, in Bengal and Behar, the dialectic philosophy or Nyáyá is more consulted, and is there relied on for rules of reasoning and interpretation upon questions of law as well as upon metaphysical topics. "Hence," Mr. Colebrooke proceeds, "have arisen

LECTURE I.

two principal schools, which, construing the same text variously, deduce, upon some important points of law, different inferences from the same legal maxims. They are sub-divided by further diversity of doctrine, into several more schools or sects of jurisprudence, which having adopted for their chief guide a favourite author have given currency to his doctrine in particular countries, or among distinct Hindu nations." The school of Benares is chiefly governed by the Mitakshara, whose authority is fortified by the works of Mitra Misser and Kamalakara, the Viramitrodaya being the most celebrated amongst them.

The five schools of the present day.

Five schools of Hindu law exist at the present day, *viz.*, the Bengal, Mithila, Benares, Maharatta and Dravida schools. The Dayabhaga, with its recognized commentaries the Dayatatwa and the Dayasangraha, are the peculiar authorities of the school of Bengal. In Mithila, the Vivada Chintamani and other works are especially followed. In the Madras Presidency, the Mitakshara and the Smriti Chandrica, and the Madhavya; and in the territories of Bombay, the Mayukha and the Kaustubha treatises are of leading importance. The Dattaka Mimansa and the Dattaka Chandrica are the standard authorities on the law of adoption, the latter being preferred in Bengal upon points in which they differ. Each school has, therefore, the authorities which it adopts as of peculiar and special weight. Books which are thus adopted by one school may be, and are, consulted by the other schools, when they do not contradict the special doctrine of the rival sect. Upon points of Hindu law, which are of general application, the authorities of any school may be indiscriminately cited, so long as they do not contravene the rules of law which have obtained exclusively in a particular province. We have, accordingly, for the sources of the Hindu law, as administered *in Hindu territories*, the old traditional authorities, the authoritative commentators, the approved customs of districts, and where all these fail, the exposition of law by learned Brahmins, who are the repositories of legal science and religious knowledge.

The influence on Hindu law of its English administration.

But when we have to enquire what is the Hindu law, as now administered by English Courts of Justice, and current at the present day in British territories, we must ascertain what has been the effect of English rule, and the changes effected in Hindu law by the enactments of the English Legislature, and by the doctrines which have grown up, from time to time, in the English Courts, and which, originally founded upon the opinions of pundits, have obtained the force of law. The action of the English Legislature and Courts for nearly a century has powerfully influenced the development of Hindu law, but it is none the less Hindu law, *i. e.*, law applicable exclusively to Hindus, because it has been from time to time moulded and fashioned to meet the changing circumstances in which the community has been placed. The difference between the Mahomedan and the English treatment of the subject race was simply that the Mahomedans, so far as we know, adopted their usual course of ignoring altogether the law, customs, and religion of those whom they conquered, while the English allowed to them the free exercise of their religion, and undertook to learn and administer, and subsequently to expound and develop their law. Its administration by an alien race would, no doubt, be a crisis in the history of the law of any people that ever existed. And with regard to Hindus, it has had this considerable result, which has not been without great influence, that it separated at once and widely the functions of the judge and of the priest; and terminated the influence or at least the ascendancy of the religious oligarchy which up to that time had monopolised the knowledge and administration of the law. The severance of the secular from the ecclesiastical authority, in the administration of justice, is an important epoch in the history of that administration. From that time the principles of religion enjoined upon religious grounds, and the rules of law enforced by temporal sanctions, as necessary to the well-being of the community, have a tendency to separate and grow apart; and that tendency has, no doubt, been encouraged and enforced by the action of the English Courts in respect to Hindus. They themselves cannot be said to have been entirely unconscious of the separable nature of religious, moral, and legal rules and prohibitions. The Bengal school, in this respect at least, in advance of the other schools, has given many proofs that it had begun to appreciate the distinction between what the jurists of modern Europe refer to as the *vinculum juris* and the *vinculum pudoris*. The doctrine of *factum valet* which has long obtained in that school, was grounded upon the distinction between the rule of morality and the rule of law. And a breach of positive prohibitions is often legalised by the doctrines of that school, on the ground, apparently, that though sinful, it has not involved the violation of any legal right. Every man, for example, is declared to have the full proprietary right in his own acquisitions. It follows that he has a legal right to deal with them as he pleases. But a precept is given that, in the distribution, a man should not show an undue preference to any individual member of his family. The legal right of the one to deal with his property as he pleases is paramount to the moral right of the other to be considered in the distribution. The moral precept may be infringed, but the law is not broken. "A fact," it is said in an apothegm, which in truth enunciates the later principle of a separation between moral and legal duties, in a manner which shews that the limits of its application had not been carefully considered, "cannot be altered by a hundred texts." This dictum has never been allowed to excuse the breach of any but purely moral obligations.

The doctrines of the Bengal school indicate a considerable advance in the development of Hindu jurisprudence. Without pretending to break away from, or ignore, the authority of the earlier sages, the founders of that school distinctly assert the superiority of legal to moral duties in the eye of the legislator, and begin the separation between religion and law. They further break in upon the old communal system of property, and insist upon the separate personal and proprietary rights of the individual in a manner which innovates upon the old theory and practice of joint family life. The authority of the old texts, and the reverence felt by the nation for its inspired lawgivers, were not sufficient to impede the influence of advancing civilization, or to prevent the introduction of these two important changes. They serve to indicate to us the direction in which Hindu law has manifested a natural tendency to develop itself.

The manner in which that influence is exercised.

It remains to consider what has been the effect upon that law, of its administration, improvement and extension within the last century. Besides the authorities to which I have already referred as the sources of that law, there have been established, during the last century, successive

LECTURE I. legislatures which have possessed the right and the authority to pass laws for the Hindu as well as the other communities existing in the British territories in India. And further there has been that virtual legislation which results from the working of the particular machinery which has been provided for the administration of justice. It must always be remembered that the English courts are not foreign courts administering Hindu law as a foreign law, taking in each case independent evidence as upon a question of fact, what that law is. They are the courts of the country, administering to Hindus, who are the natives of the territory in which their jurisdiction is established, their own rules of law,—the knowledge of which is as much supposed to reside in the breasts of the judges as is the knowledge of any other legal rules which they are empowered to enforce. The decisions which have been made, the doctrines which they establish, and the rules of property and conduct which have been acted upon for several generations, whether or not they can be shown to conflict with the ancient authorities, must be primarily attended to in order to ascertain what is now the law by which Hindus are governed, to which they are entitled and amenable, and which the courts are bound to administer. "I* have always understood," said Sir Henry Seaton, "that the law of a people was to be found not in the mere text of its code, which can never be more than the foundation of it, but in the practice which has prevailed under it, which may often be inconsistent with it, and even in some cases opposed to it." English judges have played an important part in extending and improving that law; for although the courts started

* See Shamachurn's Vyavastha Darpana, p. 387.

in their career with the theory recognized by the legislature that Hindu jurisprudence was a separate system, which was to be preserved to Hindus by virtue of what was tantamount to a solemn compact with them; yet that system was never dealt with as a foreign system, but as one which judges were bound to ascertain with such assistance from pundits, or otherwise as they could find, and administer as part of their own system. The result is, that the Hindu inhabitants of these territories are entitled to the same advantages, or exposed to the same disadvantages, which accrue to all the subjects of the Crown from the peculiar working of the judicial machinery provided by English Rule, and which is in operation throughout the country subject to that Rule. It is that, as years roll by, a substantive system of jurisprudence is established by cases, and extracted from law reports—capable of expansion—resting upon principles which are supposed to apply to all combinations of circumstances, and therefore growing with the growth of society.

Its earlier and later development compared.

The analogy between the case-law, which forms so large a portion of English jurisprudence, and the body of law which was known to the Romans under the name of "*responsa prudentum*," has already been pointed out.* The latter "consisted of explanatory glosses on authoritative written documents, and at first they were exclusively collections of opinions, interpretative of the Twelve Tables." The decemviral law remained in theory supreme, as much revered as the revealed scriptures of the Hindu. The *responsa prudentum* were supposed to be at any time subject to revision in so far as they departed from the letter

* See Maine's Ancient Law, p. 33.

of the ancient code; but practically they overruled the law, and guided it, as it were, through a process of self-development. Hindu law, long before the English had any thing to do with it, pursued, though in a slight degree, a similar career to that which awaited Roman and English jurisprudence. There was the ancient code, enshrined in the hearts of the people, revered as the word of the Most High, abounding with minute formalities, and prescribing the observance of various rites and ceremonies and of moral and social duties. Then came the doctrines of the commentators, and the formation of the various schools, all of which rested their authority upon an assumed conformity with the ancient text; which they nevertheless superseded to such a degree that it has become necessary in the words of the Privy Council, "not so much to enquire whether a disputed doctrine is fairly deducible from the ancient authorities, as to ascertain whether it has been received by the particular school which governs a particular district, and has there been sanctioned by usage."*

Thus far in the past, the process of development was that the later gloss of the practical lawyer of one period varied or abolished the rule of the earlier legislator. The next stage was at the time when the benefit and the burden of their own laws were secured to them by the English Government. From that time those laws must either be confined for ever within the limits of ancient texts and the subsequent commentators, or English legislation, whether actual or virtual, must be the source of changes. The actual legislation has hitherto proceeded with the consent

* Collector of Madura *v.* Mutu Ramalinga Sathupathy, 1 B. L. R., P. C., p. 12.

of Hindus, either by their recognizing the necessity of innovation, or by their convincing themselves that the change is but a return to their more ancient usages. In that way considerable improvements have been made: witness the position of the Hindu widow in Hindu society, which, under English rule, has been entirely altered not without proportionate results on the whole character of that society, and on the relative rights of individuals in it. Then with regard to the virtual legislation to which I have referred, it must, if it is to proceed with a due regard to the welfare of the community, be guided upon disputed points, quite as much by a consideration of what is consistent with the rules which it has itself enforced from time to time, and of what, having regard to the social changes either effected thereby or brought about by changing circumstances, is expedient and reasonable, as by attention to the exact words of the older doctrines. Those doctrines require consistent usage for their support, and when the usage is varied, the authority of the doctrine decays; for even, under the early Hindu system, clear proof of usage outweighed the written text of the law. At least one striking instance of a Hindu law, which is not derived from the shasters, has come down to us from Mahomedan times. I refer to the right of pre-emption which is recognized by Hindus in some parts of the country, on the ground of custom, and is considered by them to be governed in all respects by Mahomedan law.* Its origin and the rules and restrictions which affect its exercise are purely Mahomedan; but where the custom prevails, it is part of Hindu law as completely as the ruling of an

* See Fukeer Rawot *v.* Sheikh Emambuksh, 7 Suth. F. B., p. 143.

LECTURE I. English Court. And the longer a ruling or doctrine, however much it may differ from the written text, is enforced by the Courts, and conformed to by the community, the greater its authority becomes, whether by its force as a precedent under a purely English system, or as the parent of usage under the Hindu system.

The course pursued by the English.

In regard to the earlier sources of Hindu law, the efforts of translators have given us access to the Code of Menu, and to the leading treatises of such later authorities as Vijnyaneswara, Jimutavahana, Nanda Pandita, Devanda Bhatta, and others. Various digests were compiled by the most learned of the native lawyers by order of successive Governors-General, consisting of texts attributed to the ancient legislators; the last of which, that by Jagannatha, was, at the beginning of this century, translated by Mr. Colebrooke. Finally there are the celebrated treatises of Sir Thomas Strange and the two Macnaghtens, and the collection of the opinions, to which great weight has always been ascribed, of Mr. Sutherland, Mr. Colebrooke and Mr. Ellis. Forty years have elapsed since their united efforts placed a knowledge of the Hindu system within the reach of English Judges. During that time the superior Courts of Calcutta, Madras, and Bombay, and in the last resort, the Privy Council of the Sovereign, have been engaged, from time to time, in the work of extending, modifying, improving, and authoritatively declaring the rules of law, which at the present day bind Hindu society together in the British territories in India. Whether those decisions satisfy the minds of those who have engaged in what I may call antiquarian researches upon the subject, is a matter upon which it is unnecessary and useless to speculate. For the practical purposes of life, whether in regulating their conduct or dealing with their property, Hindus cannot escape from those rules. The law of their shasters has been administered to them by a power which is bound to treat them as free British subjects, and which advisedly endeavours to distinguish between their religion and their law.

The necessity for reviewing their administration.

In the course of the virtual legislation to which I have referred, numerous points have been warmly discussed, and many of them finally decided; but although decision has not always silenced controversy, I think I may take the law as I find it, when once it has been definitively laid down. But it is of the very nature of such a system that a body of law is, as it were, built up piecemeal, elucidated point by point, possibly without much method or consistent treatment. And a review of the various decisions, so far as I have had access to them, by the Courts of the three Presidencies and by the Privy Council, leads to the belief that the subject of Hindu law may, with advantage, be once more dealt with as a whole. It is impossible to reconcile all the decisions which have been made, but it is possible, nevertheless, to subject them to some method and arrangement and to deduce from them some guiding principles.

It is sometimes contended that Hindu law is still a matter of antiquarian research, and that any addition to our knowledge of the ancient authorities and any fresh construction of them which ingenuity can support, should make a corresponding change in the laws as they are now administered. But if the spirit of the compact which, under the auspices of Warren Hastings, was entered into between the English Government and the Hindu community be consulted, it will be found that although Hindus were to be, to a great extent, governed by a personal law of their own, yet they were incorporated on equal terms

Lecture I.

with other sects and classes into one vast community, with some portion of its law in common, and under a common government, legislative power and administration of justice. In securing to them the observance of their shasters as their right, it never could have been intended that their laws and usages should be for ever stereotyped and imposed upon them as an unalterable obligation, by a power which was to be incapable by its own compact of altering or modifying them as occasion might require. There must, in the ordinary course of things, be some room for their gradual growth and their constant adaptation to the changing circumstances of time and society.

The plan to this work.

The most equitable principle upon which to enforce their laws with reasonable immunity from such of them as may, from time to time, become unsuited to their condition, is to pursue the course which Hindus themselves had commenced, and which is consistent with our own, *viz.* to distinguish between legal and religious obligations, and to separate the legal and religious aspects of their institutions. Religion should be left as much as possible to rest upon opinion and to be modified by surrounding influences. It is within the spirit and meaning of the arrangement made, that the performance of the ceremonies and duties of religion should be free, neither prevented nor indirectly (as has been too often the case) enforced. It is in accordance with the tendency and the later teaching of Hindu legislators to consult their religious doctrines in order to ascertain the rights which spring out of, or are founded upon and limited by them, but not for the purpose of actively enforcing any obligation. The authority of religion and priests may be left to support itself without the indirect protection afforded by English Courts insisting upon the rigid celebration of sacrifices and ceremonies as essential to civil rights. It is not always easy to draw the line between securing on the one hand to Hindus their usages as their rights, and on the other hand continuing to impose them as burdens while they are or would be losing vitality and influence. And so too with rules of law and property, social convenience requires that they should be maintained with as much consistency as possible. A rule which has been observed for the last forty or fifty years is of infinitely higher authority for all social, political and practical purposes than obsolete laws which new researches may prove were in existence centuries ago. A decision by the Privy Council or by a Full Bench supersedes, if necessary, earlier authority; and therefore the results of legal decisions during the time that English Courts have administered Hindu law may be systematized with advantage in reference to several leading principles, and with a view to secure the consistent and intelligent application of them. Notably, the degree in which the legal and religious aspects of the various doctrines that obtain amongst Hindus are separate either in their nature or in their application, so far as it is the duty of English Courts to enforce that application, is of primary importance, and is the chief object which I shall keep in view in the course of these lectures. And another subject, of scarcely less importance, is the alteration which has been effected in Hindu law through the altered political position of Hindus. Hindus have been for a century free British subjects, possessed of the rights and duties which attach to that character. The public law to which they equally with the other members of the Indian community are subject, has gradually modified their social condition, and with it their

Lecture I. private law. Women, for example, whose family relationship is, according to the shasters, one of abject dependence, find that that state is inconsistent with their character of free citizens; and have gradually obtained freedom and rights of property far beyond those which ancient Hindu law would have sanctioned. There has been, in fact, a gradual dissolution of family dependency, and the growth of individual rights and obligations in its place. I shall endeavor to trace the growth of the different doctrines which are recognized at the present day, and to extract the rules of law from the authorities, modified by the virtual legislation of later years, as it has been effected in the Privy Council and in the Courts of the three Presidencies, in order to arrive at the existing rules of Hindu law, and to estimate the present position of Hindu jurisprudence.

LECTURE II.

THE POSITION OF THE HINDUS IN THE BRITISH EMPIRE.

International Conflict of Laws—Conflict of Laws in British India—Compared with that in early Europe—The Policy of the Sovereign Power to its different Classes of Subjects—Its Result—The British Government in relation to the Hindus—Crown Colonies and Settled Colonies—Position of the English before the Conquest—Principle on which they introduced their own Laws and imposed their own National Character before assuming the Sovereignty—Subsequent assumption of Sovereignty—Effect of it upon the Position of Hindus—Incorporated into a Community whose territory was governed by English Law—Their own Laws and Usages were reserved to them in certain civil matters—They were originally subject to the Mahomedan Criminal Law—Establishment of Courts of Justice—And of a Legislature—And of the Supreme Court—The Course pursued in the Presidencies of Madras and Bombay.

I HAVE already pointed out the limits within which a free choice is allowed to Hindus with regard to the law by which they are to be governed. Such freedom of choice is only permitted where there has been either a total change of religion amounting to a renunciation of the Hindu faith, or a change of religious usage within the scope of the religion, sufficient to indicate the adoption of the shasters of another school of interpretation. With regard to the general community of Hindus who retain their nationality and the faith peculiar to their race, it is necessary to point out what laws they are entitled to have applied to them, according to the terms on which the British Empire in India has been constituted, and the

LECTURE II.

principles which have been laid down for the government of dependent or conquered peoples.

International conflict of laws.

Modern jurisprudence, as it has grown up in Christendom, has always distinguished between a territorial and personal law—between those laws of any particular country which have no intrinsic force, *proprio vigore,* except within the territorial limits and jurisdiction of that country, and those laws which impress a particular character upon persons, and follow them until repudiated all over the world. It ascribes, moreover, to each individual at his birth, two distinct legal states or conditions:* one, by virtue of which he becomes the subject of some particular country binding him by the tie of natural allegiance, and which may be called his political *status;* another, by virtue of which he has ascribed to him the character of a citizen of some particular country, and, as such, is possessed of certain municipal rights, and subject to certain obligations, which latter character is the civil *status* or condition of the individual, and may be quite different from the political *status.* The civil *status* may be changed as often as a man pleases, and with it the personal law to which he is subject. The political *status,* on the other hand—the tie of natural allegiance—cannot be changed at the mere will of the party; the obligations resulting therefrom are attached to him whether he wishes it or not. The territorial law also imposes obligation on all who are within the territory, from which no one so resident can escape unless he is specially exempted from its operation.

The distinction so observed between personal and territorial law, and between that portion of personal law which

* *Udny* v. *Udny*, Law Reports, House of Lords' Scotch Appeals, *per* Lord Westbury, Vol. I., p. 457.

is separable and that which is inseparable from the individual, is founded upon considerations of international convenience. The effect of it is to secure to each community the enjoyment of its own distinctive laws and to prescribe the limits within which each individual may choose whether he will pass from one community to another, and adopt the law of the country of his selection.

Conflict of laws in British India.

The vast population which in India is gathered together under British Rule, is composed of races quite as distinct in manners and laws as those which inhabit the different countries of Europe; and the only reasonable manner in which it could be fused together and harmonized under a single Government was by proceeding upon a system analogous to that which regulates the relations of the separate and independent communities of the civilized world. The law which binds the Sovereign Power to all classes of its subjects, and determines their political *status*, and the territorial law so far as it could be made to apply, would form a common ground on which the aggregate community could rest. The personal law, wherever it was established and permitted, would be attached to a particular society to be renounced only with a renunciation, express or implied, of membership in that society. But from the commencement of British Rule to the present hour, neither the English Parliament, nor the Imperial Legislature, has declared what that territorial law shall be. Royal Commissioners at home and Supreme Court Judges here have differed as to the mode of introduction of English law and the extent to which it is in force. And an elaborate judgment* delivered in the High Court of Bengal, as late as the year 1868, was

* *Secretary of State* v. *Administrator General of Bengal*, *per* Markby, J., 1 B. L. R., O. C., p. 89.

LECTURE II.

occupied with a discussion of five different alternatives as to what is the territorial law which, it is obvious, must exist, but which no statute or proclamation has defined.

It seems to be almost incredible that, though it has been for generations a recognized principle of modern jurisprudence* that law is determined by the territory, yet the Indian Empire has been left for more than a century to doubts and conjectures as to the law by which it was governed, which a word from the Legislature could have removed and solved; and it has been so left, notwithstanding that for the last thirty years (owing to the large increase of classes who have no personal law) the subject has been one of paramount importance and frequent discussion.

Compared with that in early Europe.

The diversified society, which was formed when the Roman Empire was dissolved in the midst of barbarian conquest, was not in a similar difficulty. That was an age when the traditions of the forest and the *steppe* still clung to the nomad hordes, whose manners, customs and laws were determined by the community regardless of the territory. Their idea of law was that it applied to peoples, tribes, and classes—the notion of a law whose application

* Indian Law Commissioners' Report, No. VII., p. 449. "A country," say the Commissioners, "governed by one of the civilized nations of modern Europe, and yet having no *lex loci*, would be a phenomenon without example in jurisprudence." They quote the following passage from Savigny in reference to the barbarian conquest of the Roman Empire:— "Mixed together in the same territory, the two nations preserved distinct manners and laws, which engendered that sort of civil law called personal law in opposition to territorial law. In truth, it is a principle of modern times that law is determined by the territory, and that it governs the properties and contracts of all those who inhabit therein: under this arrangement citizens differ little from strangers, and national origin has no influence. But in the Middle Ages it was otherwise: in the same country, in the same town, the Lombard lived according to Lombard law, the Roman according to Roman law."

was determined by territorial limits, regardless of individuals, was foreign to their conception. And, therefore, it happens that the most striking instances of a variety of purely personal laws administered within the same territory, or by the same power, are to be found in that early period of European history when new communities were springing into life upon the ruins of the Empire. The Frank, Burgundian, and Goth lived together under the same administration, but, though residing in the same place, were subjected, each of them, to his own law, which clung to him irrespective of territory or locality. "It often happens," said Bishop Agobardus, in an epistle to Louis Le Debonnaire, "that five men, each under a different law, may be found walking or sitting together."* A curious diversity of personal laws resulted; but there was this contrast to the state of things in British India, *viz.*, that all were provided for by the laws which attached to their respective communities, and there was no necessity for a general law called the law of the country to reach those who would otherwise be subjected to no municipal rules whatever.

The policy of the Sovereign Power to its different classes of subjects.

Great Britain, in dealing with her Indian Empire, adopted the system of personal law, theoretically at least, with great reserve, confining its application to Hindus and Mahomedans. She omitted to secure to the remainder of her Indian subjects the right to the enjoyment of any personal law which they might originally have possessed; and, in consequence, left them subject to the law of the country, while she altogether omitted to declare what that

* Savigny's History of the Roman Law in the Middle Ages. Cathcart's Translation, Vol. I., c. 3, p. 100. See Story's Conflict of Laws, p. 5, note.

LECTURE II.

law should be. Yet it is difficult to conceive of a more heterogeneous population, and one of more varied wants, being gathered together under a common Government than that which inhabits the British territories in India; and which stands more in need of such a bond of union as a well digested system for the administration of justice would provide. Besides the two vast races which are respectively Hindu or Mahomedan by birth and religion, and the smaller community which is composed of the British-born subjects of Her Majesty, and the subjects of other European Sovereigns who retain their domicil of birth, there is the increasing class of mixed European and native blood called the East Indian; the class which is formed of those who belong to one race by blood, but have adopted the religion of another, as, for example Native Christians or Hindu converts to Mahomedanism; Buddhists; natives of India who are neither Hindu, Mahomedan, nor Buddhist; Europeans of whatever country domiciled in India; and Asiatics from the surrounding countries; besides Jews, Armenians and Parsees.

Its result.

The result has been that these different races or classes have been variously governed, the law applicable to any one of them not being the same in different parts of British India, but dependent upon treaties and enactments and charters which are, few of them, of general application. The extraordinary inequalities and difficulties, not to say confusion, which arose, were concealed, if not corrected, by the extensive jurisdiction of "justice, equity, and good conscience," which was far and wide conferred upon the Courts throughout the country; and which enabled them by a rough and ready method to supply the absence of law. In later times, however, it has been the policy of the

Imperial Government to endeavour to weld together, so far as possible, the heterogeneous society which it rules, by the creation of a body of law which shall be of general application; except where a personal law has been reserved as the right of a particular race, which, therefore, belongs to that race as fully as the law of his domicil belongs to an individual. It must be confessed, however, that that policy, notwithstanding the lateness of its inception, is being carried into effect with considerable caution and circumspection. A generation has passed away since the establishment of an Imperial Legislature in India and a Royal Commission in England, and except that a uniform Civil and Criminal Procedure has been prescribed, the Penal Code and the Indian Succession Act are the only measures which that policy has produced.

The British Government in relation to the Hindus.

We have, however, only to deal with Hindus; and I propose to describe the position assigned to them in the unnecessarily complicated system of the English Government of India; so far at least as the three Presidencies are concerned. In order to do so it is necessary to go back to the time of their conquest and to describe the manner in which the Empire was founded; and what legal position was assigned to Hindus in the new constitution. The relative position of conqueror and conquered as understood and acted upon by Great Britain is thus described by Chief Justice Cockburn, in his charge to the Grand Jury, in the case* of the *Queen* v. *Nelson and Brand*, which arose out of the proceedings in Jamaica during and subsequent to the insurrection of 1865:

* See Charge of the Lord Chief Justice of England to the Grand Jury at the Central Criminal Court, London, corrected by himself, pp. 10, 11.

LECTURE II.

Crown Colonies and Settled Colonies.

"From the time of the first acquisition of colonies by Great Britain, a distinction has been taken and established by legal authority between two classes of colonies, which are called by the technical names of Crown Colonies and Settled Colonies. A Crown Colony is one which has been acquired by conquest, or what is considered equivalent to conquest, by cession from some other State or Power. A Settled Colony is one which is established where land has been taken possession of in the name of the Crown of England, and, being unoccupied, has afterwards been colonised and settled upon by British subjects. With regard to such colonies as are acquired by conquest, except so far as rights may have been reserved by any terms of capitulation, the power of the Sovereign is absolute. The conquered are at the mercy of the conqueror. Such possessions keep, it is true, their own laws for the time, because it would be productive of the greatest inconvenience and confusion, if a body of people who had been governed by one law, should have that law, with which they are acquainted, suddenly changed for another of which not only they, but also the tribunals which are to administer justice among them, are totally ignorant. They, therefore, preserve their laws and institutions for the time, but subject to this, that they are under the absolute power of the Sovereign of these realms to alter those laws in any way that to the Sovereign in council may seem proper: in short, they may be dealt with legislatively and authoritatively as the Sovereign may please. Very different is the case of what is called a "Settled" Colony. In such a colony the inhabitants have all the rights of Englishmen. They take with them, in the first place, that which no Englishman can by expatriation put off, namely allegiance to the Crown, the duty of obedience to the lawful commands of the Sovereign, and obedience to the laws which Parliament may think proper to make with reference to such a colony. But, on the other hand, they take with them all the rights and liberties of British subjects—all the rights and liberties as against the prerogative of the Crown which they could enjoy in this country." LECTURE II.

Position of the English before the conquest.

There can be no doubt that the Indian possessions of the British Crown are not "settled colonies," and the *status*, both civil and political, of Hindus, as well as of the other native inhabitants, depends upon the history of the relation which existed in former times (from the first arrival of the English down to their assumption of sovereignty) between the rulers of the various territories, now called British territories in India and the British Crown. Take for example the Bengal Presidency. Originally the Mogul Emperor held the supreme sovereignty, and the English authority in the country was merely an authority over a factory established for purposes of trade. The nature of that authority, as exercised in Calcutta, cannot be given better than in the words of Lord Brougham in his celebrated judgment in the case of the *Mayor of Lyons* v. *East India Company*,* and quoted by Sir Barnes Peacock in his judgment in a much later case: "The district on which Calcutta is built was obtained by purchase from the Nawab of Bengal, the Emperor of Hindustan's lieutenant, at the very end of the seventeenth century. The Company had been struggling for nearly one hundred years to obtain a footing in Bengal, and until 1696 they never had more than a factory here and there, as the French, Danes, and Dutch

* 1 Moore's I. A., p. 272.

LECTURE II. also had. Till 1678 their whole object was to obtain the power of trading, and it was only then that they secured it by a firman from the Emperor. From that year to 1696, they in vain applied to the Native Government for leave to fortify their factory on the Hooghly, and it was only then that they made a fortification, acting upon a kind of half consent given in an equivocal answer of the Nawab. Encouraged by the protection which they thus were enabled to afford to the natives, many of them built houses as well as the English subjects; and when the Nawab, on this account, was about to send a Kaji, or Judge, to administer justice to those natives, the Company's servants bribed him to abstain from this proceeding. Some years afterwards, the Company obtained a grant of more land and villages from the Emperor, with renewed permission to fortify their factories. During all this period tribute was paid to the Emperor or his officer, the Nawab: first for leave to trade, afterwards as zemindars under the Emperor, and in the year 1757—the year memorable for the battle of Plassey—the treaty with Jaffer Ally was effected, indemnifying them for their losses, ceding the French possessions and securing their rights and binding them to pay their revenues like other zemindars. Eight years later they likewise received from the Native Government a grant of the Dewanny or receivership of Bengal, Behar, and Orissa; and of their subsequent progress in power it is unnecessary to speak. Enough has been said to show that the settlement of the Company in Bengal was effected by leave of a regularly established Government in possession of the country, invested with the rights of sovereignty and exercising its powers; that by the permission of that Government Calcutta was founded and the factory fortified in a

Lecture II.

district purchased from the owners of the soil by permission of that Government, and held under it by the Company as subjects owing obedience, as tenants rendering rent, and even as officers exercising by delegation a part of its administrative authority."

Principle on which they introduced their own laws and imposed their own national character before assuming the sovereignty.

Although the English thus settled in the country in a manner which, according to general or European international law, would have rendered them subject to the public and territorial laws there administered by its Mahomedan rulers, yet they did, in fact, retain within their factories their own laws for their own government. They did so from the necessity of the case having the power to secure to that extent their independence, which power they owed to the weakness or the indulgence of the Emperor. Such necessity would never have arisen in the case of the Christian subjects of one European state settling within the territories of another, where free access and intermixture were permitted. But the necessity did not arise solely from the immiscible character of the natives and from the fact that foreigners were not admitted to the general body* and mass of the society of the nation, but were obliged to continue strangers and sojourners. The necessity arose in this way, that the case was one for which no provision was made by any system of Asiatic jurisprudence.

For if the Europeans who settled in the Mogul dominion had been minded to submit to the territorial law of the country and to retain their own personal law, they would at once have discovered that there neither was, nor ever had been, a territorial law in existence of which they could have availed themselves. When the juridical systems of the East and West met, there was no point of con-

* See the *Indian Chief*, 3 Rob. Adm. Rep., p. 29.

LECTURE II.

tact. The Hindu and Mahomedan had each his personal law inseparable from his religion, inapplicable to others. The European brought with him the law which was inseparable from his domicil; but he found no *lex loci* to which he could submit or which could have been applied to him. Long discussions have often taken place as to what the *lex loci* of India was before the British took possession, and as to what it continued to be after that event. But the notion of a territorial law is European and modern. The laws which Hindus and Mahomedans obey do not recognize territorial limits. The Shasters and the Koran revealed religion and law to distinct peoples, each of whom recognized a common faith as the only bond of union, but were ignorant of the novel doctrine that law and sovereignty could be conterminous with territorial limits. The English, therefore, in India found themselves without a law of the place; * and unless they were to remain so, the necessity was imposed upon them of introducing their own law of the place as strongly as it would have been if the case had been one of a Settled Colony, and they were merely adopting as their own some waste space of the earth. And to such an extent was that necessity recognized, that in the case of the *Indian Chief*, which occurred while Calcutta was a mere factory in the dominion of the Mogul, it was held that a subject of the United States of America carrying on trade in Calcutta took his temporary national character not from the Mogul dominion but from the British factory.

* There was no law which could be enforced upon them where no interests but their own were concerned, unless they adopted the Koran. They would of course be subject to penal and revenue laws, which are imposed as a burden, and not as a benefit.

LECTURE II.

Subsequent assumption of sovereignty.

In course of time, however, the Mogul dominion vanished, and the sovereignty passed to the British Crown,—to a power which had already introduced its own law into the country, because it found no other law in existence which could apply to its subjects. So far as the Presidency of Bengal was concerned, that event occurred, as nearly as can be ascertained, in 1765.

In that year the Emperor conferred upon the East India Company the office of Dewan of those provinces (*i. e.* Bengal, Behar, and Orissa) from generation to generation, for ever and ever.* This grant of the Dewany was obtained by Lord Clive, and involved not merely the collection of revenue, but the administration of civil justice. In the following year the Nizamut, which comprised besides the right of arming and commanding troops and of commanding the police of the country the entire administration of criminal justice, passed practically into the hands of the English. The subordinate sovereignty so granted in perpetuity was developed into a real and independent sovereignty, and the supremacy of the Mogul Emperor silently vanished, having had from the first no real existence, and finally ceasing even in name. Whether provinces are formally ceded or are transferred by a process which is obviously the same thing as cession, the result is the same, *viz.*, that the inhabitants of the ceded provinces become British subjects, the sovereignty of the Company being necessarily subordinate to the Supreme Sovereignty of the British Crown.

With regard to the Port and Island of Bombay, it was not a factory originally, such as Calcutta, nor was the sovereignty over it acquired by the British in the same

* Aitchison's Treaties, p. 61.

LECTURE II.

gradual manner.* It never was held by the English of the Mogul, or indeed of any native power. By a treaty dated 23rd June 1661, Alphonso VI, King of Portugal, ceded to the British Crown the full sovereignty which he at that time possessed over the Port and Island of Bombay. In 1669 and 1674, by grants to the Company of the Islands of Bombay and St. Helena, of which Charles II had derived the sovereignty from the King of Portugal, they were empowered to make laws and constitutions for the good government of the Islands and their inhabitants. And, subsequently, by steps which it is unnecessary to trace, the sovereignty of the whole of the territories now known as the Presidencies of Madras and Bombay became vested in the British Crown.

Effect of it upon the position of Hindus.

Applying, therefore, the rule of law laid down by Chief Justice Cockburn, the Hindu inhabitants of the ceded territories "were, after the cession, placed under the absolute power of the Sovereign of England to alter their laws in any way that to the Sovereign in Council might seem proper: in short, they might be dealt with legislatively and authoritatively as the Sovereign might please." According to the doctrine of Lord Coke in *Calvin's case*,† their laws would have been *ipso facto* abrogated, "for that they be not only against Christianity, but against the law of God and of Nature contained in the decalogue." Such a theory does not, however, obtain sanction now. The rule is that such people retain their own law, whether a personal or a territorial law, until authoritatively altered. Hindus had a purely personal law; the extent to which

* See *Nàorji Beràmji* v. *Rogers*, *per* Westropp, J., 4 Bombay High Court Reports, p. 39.

† See Lord Coke's Reports, Part VII, p. 17.

they retained it, must be described, as also their legal position, in matters in respect of which their personal law did not apply.

It will be seen, therefore, that the date of the acquisition of sovereignty by Great Britain over each province of India is the dividing point of time at which the inhabitants of that province acquire a new political *status* and transfer the duties of allegiance. It is also the date at which it is important to ascertain the will of the new governing power, exhibited by its acts both prior and subsequent to its assuming the reins of administration as to the nature of the civil *status* and law which are thereafter to attach to its new subjects. An Empire, composed of races for the most part governed by laws which were inseparably blended with their religion, was subjected to a Power whose law was utterly inapplicable to them, but which, if and so far as it was introduced independently of charters, would necessarily, unless it were otherwise provided, be enforced throughout the entire country subject to its dominion. It is therefore the date at which it is important to ascertain how far English law had been introduced, and to what extent it was English policy to reserve to Hindus their personal law.

Incorporated into a community whose territory was governed by English law.

It must be recollected that the English brought with them, so far as they and their Sovereign were concerned, all the rights and liberties of British subjects, and, except so far as Parliament otherwise enacted, all the laws common and statute which were reasonably applicable to them. When the English Sovereign became the ruler of the Presidency of Bengal, the whole of his subjects, of whatever race or creed, were incorporated into one community under his government. That community, had there been no charters, or enactments applicable to any

LECTURE II.

portion of them, would have been thenceforth amenable to English law, subject, in the first place, to the right of the native inhabitants to retain their own laws until changed and afterwards subject to their right to retain them in such manner and to such extent as the Sovereign or Parliament should direct. The English law, in fact, became according to the most reasonable theory that can be framed, the public and the territorial law of the country.* And English law, public

* The following was the view expressed by the late Supreme Court as to the introduction of English law:

"I have no difficulty in saying upon the authorities that the law of England has been introduced generally *into Calcutta*, with such modifications as attend its introduction into any new settlement, and the particular modification imposed by the provisions of the 17th Section of 21 Geo. III, c. 70; and therefore that the descent of all real property in Calcutta from any person, other than a Hindu or Mahomedan, must be governed by the English law of inheritance as the *lex loci rei sitæ*." And upon a question of succession to the immoveable property of a Jew in the Mofussil, the Court proceeded: "I think that the Court is bound to decide this question by English law; but by English law understood in its widest sense; that is as a law which, to use Sir Lawrence Peel's words in Sibchunder Doss *v.* Sibkissen Bannerjee (1 Boulnois, 74), 'embraces all local laws and customs as to immoveable estate, which local customs and laws, where they prevail, vary, and so far control, the general law.' Therefore, if I could be satisfied that there really was a local law, or custom in the nature of one, differing from the English law of inheritance, which regulated the succession of immoveable property in the Mofussil, when held by others than Hindus, Mahomedans, or British subjects, I should be disposed to give effect to it; and should feel that in so doing I was acting, not in contravention of, but rather in accordance with, the principles of the law of England which, as it has been said elsewhere, we are bound to administer as *the general law of this Court*."—*Per* Colville, C. J., in Musleah *v.* Musleah, 1 Boulnois, p. 240.

The Commissioners, on the other hand, argue that English law is the territorial law of India, irrespective of Acts and Charters. They adopt the view of Master Stephen, in *Freeman* v. *Fairlie*, who after examining all the charters from 1726 downwards, says, "I find in none of them any express introduction of English law, but, on the contrary, they seem and private, therefore, so far as it had been introduced into the country, applied to Hindus* wherever its application was not intercepted by so much of their own law as was thereafter secured to them; and amongst other things their right to personal security to life and limb, and their right to personal liberty, were, undoubtedly, placed under the protection of English law.† LECTURE II.

To a certain extent.

The two questions which arise are in what manner and degree was English law introduced into the country; and to what extent was the enjoyment of their own laws secured to the Hindus. In regard to the first it must be recollected that the English had for some time contemplated the acquisition of sovereignty, and their legal position as described by Lord Brougham was not always kept in view; but, for reasons which I have already explained, they retained their own law for their own government within their factories and provided for its administration. In its earliest Charters the East India Company was invested with some legislative powers; and in 1622 James I granted them some judicial authority, and afterwards Acts of Parliament were passed and Charters granted by the Crown to provide

all to have proceeded on the assumption that English law was already in force in those settlements, and their provisions are directed chiefly to the establishing competent judicial authorities and rule of proceeding by which the existing law may be better administered." And they consider that they are entitled to cite Lord Stowell in support of the doctrine "that the English law must have come into our factories in India, as soon as they became our factories, and into our dominions in India as soon as they became our dominions."—Indian Law Commissioner's Report, No. VII, pp. 450, 451.

* But see Lord Kingsdown's judgment in Ranee Surnomoye's case, 9 Moore's I. A., 426. Sir Barnes Peacock's judgment in that case laid it down that the English law of forfeiture in the case of a *felo de se* was not introduced into India at all by the Charter of 1726.

† 1 Strange, p. 34.

LECTURE II.

for the administration of justice at least over British born subjects in places which still remained subject to a Mahomedan ruler. Those early Acts and Charters bear reference merely to the immediate wants of the English and other inhabitants of the limited portions of territory which were practically independent of the native Government. Thus, in 1661, Charles II, by Royal Charter, gave to the Governor and Council of the several places belonging to the Company in the East Indies power "to judge all persons, belonging to the said Governor and Company, or that should live under them, in all causes, civil or criminal, according to the laws of the kingdom." And in 1726 the East India Company were empowered by Royal Charter granted in 13 George I to establish at their Settlements Courts which were afterwards known as the Mayor's Courts "to try, hear, and determine all civil suits, actions and pleas between party and party." It was under this Charter that special provision was first made for the administration of all the common and statute law of England existing at that date. The jurisdiction under the Charter extended only to such causes as might arise within the town of Calcutta at Fort William in Bengal, or within any of the factories subject or subordinate thereunto; and if, as has been said,* and as seems to me the most reasonable conclusion from all the circumstances attending the establishment of English Rule, there exists in British India English law which is not due to the Charters which created the Mayor's Court or the Supreme Court of later date, and which is not personal law, the Charter of 1726 was at least the first well defined and well understood indication of an intention to introduce it, and may be

* See Secretary of State *v.* Administrator General of Bengal, *per* Markby, J., 1 B. L. R., O. C., p. 112.

regarded as the source, direct or indirect, of such English law (existing before that date) as now prevails in British India. LECTURE II.

Now with respect to the mode in which the enjoyment of their own laws and usages were secured to the Hindus, there is some recognition of their right to it in the Charter by which George II, in 1753, re-established the Mayor's Courts.* That Charter directed that suits and actions between Indian natives should be determined amongst themselves, unless both parties should submit themselves to the jurisdiction of the Mayor's Courts. Though the provision appeared to recognize the hardship of depriving the natives of their own laws, the Charter did not empower the Mayor's Courts to undertake their administration. And in Bombay they obtained no exemption from the jurisdiction of the English Courts. The English sovereignty was there established, and the natives, as British subjects, were amenable to such laws as the English chose to administer, and their own were not reserved to them. It is to the period subsequent to the assumption of sovereignty by the British Crown, acting through the Company, that we must look to ascertain the extent to which Hindus were thenceforth to be amenable to Hindu law.

Their own laws and usages were reserved to them in certain civil matters.

So far as the Bengal Presidency is concerned, the year 1765, as I have already pointed out, may be regarded as the approximate date at which, for all practical purposes, the English sovereignty began to be established over native populations. The course adopted appears to have been that, although English criminal law was introduced into the country by the Charter of 1726, the Mahomedan

They were originally subject to the Mahomedan criminal law.

* Morley's Administration of Justice in British India, p. 7.

Lecture II.

criminal law, which had been apparently, under the Mogul, of general application, was continued in force. The will of the conqueror to retain this Mahomedan law as the general criminal law of the country was made apparent by the steps which were immediately taken to provide for its administration. It was retained by force of Regulation IX of 1793, Hindus being subject to its administration, and European British born subjects being exempted from it. Criminal Courts were established, in which the Kazi or Mufti sat to expound the law, and determine the legal liability of all native prisoners including Hindus, subject to the supervision of the Company's officers, the late Sudder Nizamut Adawlut being the ultimate Court of Appeal. Subsequently, Statutes of the reign of George III and George IV affected the criminal law to which Hindus were subject; but finally the Penal Code superseded it, and one uniform administration of criminal law since 1862 has been the result.

Establishment of Courts of Justice.

On the other hand, with regard to civil law steps were immediately taken to secure to natives the observance of those rules which they held sacred, and by which they had been accustomed to regulate their conduct and engagements in civil life. A plan for the administration* of justice was drawn up by Warren Hastings, assisted by a Council, and it was subsequently adopted by the Government in 1772. The famous 23rd rule of that plan provided that Hindus should be governed by the laws of their Shasters with regard to inheritance, marriage, caste, and other religious usages or institutions. The cognizance of all disputes concerning civil rights was entrusted to certain provincial Courts which were presided over by Collectors on the

* See Morley's Administration of Justice in British India, p. 45.

part of the Company; who, in dealing with Hindus, were bound to consult the Brahmins who attended their Courts for the purpose of supplying them with information upon Hindu law and to assist them in passing the decrees. These Courts and the Criminal Courts were respectively subject to the Sudder Dewanny Adawlut, and the Sudder Nizamut Adawlut, which sat in the Presidency Town; and thus the judicial establishment of the country was completed.

And of a Legislature.

In the next year (1773) the Regulating Act was passed by the Imperial Parliament in England, which empowered the Governor-General and Council to make Rules and Regulations for the government of Bengal, and thus a legislative as well as a judicial authority was established in the province. The first Regulation was passed in the year 1780, and related to the administration of justice. The exact words of the 23rd Rule of Warren Hastings' plan were introduced into the 27th section, and then, as far as the Bengal Presidency was concerned, the administration of their own laws was secured to Hindus, and it was expressly declared "that in all suits regarding inheritance, marriage, and caste, and other religious usages or institutions, the laws of the Koran with respect to Mahomedans, and those of the Shasters with respect to the Gentoos, shall be invariably adhered to." In 1781, this section was re-enacted in the revised Code, with the addition of the word "succession."

And of the Supreme Court.

The Regulating Act, as it is called, which was passed by Parliament a year after the adoption of Warren Hastings' scheme, provided that it should be lawful "for His Majesty, by Charter or Letters Patent, under the great seal of Great Britain, to erect and establish a Supreme Court of

LECTURE II.

Judicature at Fort William in Bengal;" and, accordingly, in the next year (1774) that Court was called into existence. Thus two distinct judicial establishments existed in the country—the Supreme Court established by Act of Parliament and Royal Charter, the Adawlut system by the local Legislature and Government of Bengal. The essential difference which at first existed between them, so far as Hindus were concerned, was that, although the former provided, under certain circumstances, for the exercise of jurisdiction over natives, it did not secure to any of them the enjoyment of their own laws; while the authors of the Adawlut system, from the first conception of Warren Hastings' plan, down to the passing of the revised Code of 1781, consistently endeavoured to carry out that object, to which they attached pre-eminent importance. Finally, the home Legislature followed the example of the Indian statesmen, and in 1781, the declaratory Act, which was passed in consequence of disputes which had arisen between the Supreme Court and the Governor-General's Council, in order to explain and define the Court's powers and jurisdiction enacted by section 17, with regard to the native inhabitants of Calcutta, that "their inheritance and succession to lands, rents, and goods, and all matters of contract and dealing between party and party, shall be determined in the case of Mahomedans by the laws and usages of Mahomedans, and in the case of Gentoos by the laws and usages of Gentoos; and when only one of the parties shall be a Mahomedan or Gentoo, by the laws and usages of the defendant." The same Statute also enacted that regard should be had to the civil and religious usages of the natives, and that the rights and authorities of the fathers and masters of families should be preserved to them respectively within their said families; and that the Court in framing its process, and its rules and orders for execution thereof, in suits, civil or criminal, against the natives of Bengal, Behar, and Orissa, might accommodate the same to the religion and manners of such natives, so far as the same might consist with the due execution of the laws and attainment of justice. Thus, in the end, both the Supreme Court and the Adawlut systems for the administration of justice secured to the Hindus, within certain specified limits, and in a certain specified manner, the free use and exercise of their own laws and usages, so far as the Presidency of Bengal was concerned. The honor of initiating a policy, so obviously just, as that which secured the natives of India from the violation of their own usages, rests with the Bengal Government, and especially with Warren Hastings. They laid broad and deep the foundations of the British Empire in India on a basis of civil and religious liberty, and carried into execution a wise and liberal policy, far in advance of the sentiments and ideas which at that time prevailed in England, but consistent with justice, humanity, and prudence. They did so in an age which was conspicuous for the political and religious disabilities which prevailed, and which distinctly imperilled the cause of liberty in the West.

The result as regards Bengal.

The year 1781 is the important date at which, by the double action of the Imperial Parliament and the local Legislature, the use and enjoyment of their own laws and usages were first secured to the Hindus of the Bengal Presidency. Twelve years later, in the year 1793,* another

* By Regulation IV of that year, section 15, it was provided that in suits regarding succession, inheritance, marriage and caste, and all religious usages and institutions, the Mahomedan laws with respect

LECTURE II.

and an important epoch in the history of Hindu Legislation arrived. It was in that year that Lord Cornwallis established the system of judicature by which the collection of revenue and the administration of justice were confided to separate officers; and collected together the Regulations which had been passed in the thirteen years which had elapsed since the establishment of the Legislature into a Code which forms the basis of the existing Regulation Law throughout India.*

The course pursued in the Presidencies of Madras and Bombay.

Having thus deduced the title of Hindus to their own laws, and described the measures taken to administer them so far as the Bengal Presidency is concerned, I may refer to the other two Presidencies of Madras and Bombay. In both of them the same double system was observed. The Supreme Court at Madras was established in 1801, and that at Bombay in 1823; and they were eventually invested with the same powers and authorities, subject to the same limitations, restrictions, and control as the Supreme Court at Calcutta. But the Charters which established those Courts did not, like the Charter of the Bengal Supreme Court, precede the enactment of Parliament which secured to the natives the right to their own laws. The important Statute† in that behalf, so far as Madras and Bombay are concerned, was passed in 1797. It created the Recorders' Courts in those Presidencies, and contained the words which I have quoted above from the 17th section of the 21 Geo. III, c. 70. In addition

to Mahomedan, and the Hindu laws with regard to Hindus, are to be considered as the general rules by which the Judges are to form their decisions. In the respective cases, the Mahomedan and Hindu law officers of the Court are to attend to expound the law.

* 13 Geo. III, c. 63.

† 37 Geo. III, c. 142.

to these it gave the new Courts the power which the Supreme Courts also subsequently possessed in dealing with disputes between natives to determine them by such laws and usages as the same would have been determined by, if the suit had been brought, and the action commenced, in a native Court.

Upon this footing of Statute rests the right of natives, within the jurisdiction of the old Supreme Courts of Madras and Bombay, to the free use of their own laws and usages. With regard to the large population in those Presidencies, but not within the jurisdiction of those Courts, they attain the same end by a different road, by one which was first marked out for them by the Government of Bengal. For, in 1802, a judicial system was introduced into Madras, which was similar to that formed by Lord Cornwallis,*—Regulation III of that year being

* There are three systems of Regulation Law now current in India, all of them traceable to Lord Cornwallis. The power entrusted to the Governor-General in Council of making Laws and Regulations for the Presidency of Bengal, by the 13 Geo. III., was afterwards confirmed by the 37th Geo. III, c. 14; and in 1800 a further Act was passed by the Imperial Parliament which rendered the Province of Benares and all provinces or districts thereafter to be annexed or made subject to the Bengal Presidency, subject to such Regulations as the Governor-General and Council of Fort William had framed or might thereafter frame. The Governor of Madras and the Council of Fort St. George was empowered by the 39 & 40 Geo. III, c. 79, to make Regulations for the Provincial Courts and Councils at that Presidency, and in 1802 the Regulation was passed which ordered the formation of a regular code on the basis of the famous Bengal Regulation of 1793; and in the 47 Geo. III, an Act was passed which enabled them to make Regulations for the good order. and government of the town and its dependencies. This last mentioned Act conferred the same power on the Governor of Bombay and the Council of Fort St. David with reference to the affairs of that Presidency. Regulations were, however, passed from the year 1799, and the Code was taken with but little alterations from the Bengal Code. Those Regulations were passed in pursuance of a power inferred from the 11th Section of 37 Geo. III,

LECTURE II. almost in the same words in regard to the native laws as are contained in the Code of 1793. The same system was also adopted in Bombay in 1797,* and the native laws adopted in still more general terms. The words used are: "In suits regarding succession, inheritance, marriage, and caste, and all religious usages and institutions, the Mahomedan laws with respect to Mahomedans, and the Hindu laws with regard to Hindus, are to be considered as the general rule by which the Judges are to form their decisions." Besides, being adopted in Madras and Bombay the section itself was extended to Benares and the Upper Provinces by later enactments.† And in 1827, the date of establishment of the Bombay Supreme Court, the Bombay Regulations were rescinded in favor of Mr. Mount Stuart Elphinstone's Code, and the system so established endured with few alterations to the present time. The words used in that Code‡ were: "The law to be observed in the trial of suits shall be Acts of Parliament and Regulations of Government applicable to the case; in the absence of such Acts and Regulations, the usage of the country in which the suit arose; if none such appears, the law of the defendant; and in the absence of specific law and usage,—justice, equity, and good conscience alone."

c. 142. All these Regulations were rescinded and superseded by Mr. Elphinstone's Code of 1827.

Three systems of Regulation Law thus came into force in British territories in India, and still exist, except so far as they have been affected by the work of repeal:—that of Bengal, which extends from 1793 to 1834; that of Madras, which begins in 1802 and ends in 1834; and that of Bombay, which commenced in 1827, and comprises the results of only seven years of legislation.

* Reg. IV of 1799.

† Reg. V of 1799, sec. 36; Reg. III of 1800, sec. 6.

‡ Reg. VIII of 1795, sec. 3.

With regard to their criminal law, Hindus in the Madras Presidency, like those in Bengal, were subject to Mahomedan law. In the Bombay Presidency, however, they were to be tried by their own laws for criminal offences and not by Mahomedan law;* and in 1819, were granted the benefit of their own law in trials for state offences, having previously thereto been subject in that respect to Mahomedan law.† Since 1862, Hindus both in the Madras and Bombay Presidencies, as well as throughout India, have been subject to the Penal Code.

And the legislative authority to which they were rendered subject, was vested in Councils which were respectively established at Madras and Bombay by Acts of Parliament‡ at home. Since 1834 there has been one general legislative power for the whole of India which was vested in the Legislative Council of the Governor General by the 3 & 4 William IV., c. 85; the enactments of which apply to the whole of India unless otherwise specified. And finally the existing Legislatures were constituted by the Indian Councils' Act.

The origin and the limits, therefore, of the right of Hindus in the three Presidencies to their own laws and the measures taken to secure to them the enjoyment of that right are to be found in the Regulations and Acts of Parliament which I have quoted. As respects the large portion of British territories not included in those Presidencies, but known as the Non-Regulation Provinces, the legal position in civil matters of Hindus must be ascertained by reference to the rules and orders and other proceedings of

* Reg. X of 1819.

† Reg. IV of 1827, sec. 26.

‡ 24 & 25 Vict., c. 67.

LECTURE II. Government which have been taken in each district for the purpose of administering justice, and which were recognized as having the force of law by the Indian Councils' Act.* Since the passing of that Act those provinces have been placed under the legislative authority of the Imperial Legislative Council, which has established Courts of Justice both in British Burmah and the Punjab.

* 24 & 25 Vict., c. 67.

LECTURE III.

THE HINDU FAMILY.—THE JOINT WORSHIP.

The Hindu Family—Importance of Religious Observances—They are not enforced by Law—Gurus—Purohits—Office of Purohits formerly hereditary—Such doctrine overruled—Their Services are now the subject of contract—No legal obligation to contribute to the expenses of the Joint Worship—Dewutter—Who can endow—The Endower's interest ceases—Superintendence of Endowed Property—It cannot be partitioned—Muths or Temples—Mohunts—The Rites of the Shraddha—Description of them—The motive for their performance—Ekodishta Shraddha—Parvana Shraddha—Sapindakarana—Description of Sapindakarana—General Observations.

The Hindu family.

THE family joint in food, worship, and estate and the village community are the two institutions which complete the frame of Hindu society. Co-proprietorship, bringing with it a community in rights and duties, was originally, and still to a great extent remains, the leading feature of that society when in its normal and natural condition. The right to the joint enjoyment of property, and the duty of jointly performing many acts of secular and religious interest, are derived to Hindus from their birth, continue until relinquished by the act of partition, which is one of the most important of their lives, and constantly tend to revive as the separated member of one family forms new ties around himself.

So far as a *gotra*, or family, is concerned, its members are connected by blood relationship, marriage, or adoption ;

H

LECTURE III.

but the village community, though similar in its constitution, is more comprehensive, and includes within its brotherhood all to whom either tradition or an obvious fiction, in spite of different *castes*, assigns a common parentage. It is an organized society, which is bound together upon the same principle of community in property and in personal rights and duties as the family is bound together; but with machinery for government, police, and the general administration of its affairs.

Importance of religious observances.

It is, however, with a joint family, and not with the village community, that we have to do. Commensality belongs to the subject of customs and manners, and not to law, and needs no description here. But with respect to worship, the personal *status* and proprietary right of a Hindu, and even the school of law to which he is amenable, turn upon, or at least are connected with, the observance of religious ceremonies. Some of these ceremonies, therefore, cannot be disregarded in dealing with Hindu law; and with regard to the family, one of the first subjects to be attended to, is its relative position to the ministers of religion.

Although Courts of Law do not, as a general rule, discuss the disabilities which arise from the non-performance by a Hindu of religious ceremonies, leaving those ceremonies to the cognizance of the authorities or spiritual guide of his family or *caste*, yet in respect of some of them, they affect, or have been long held to affect, the legal *status*,—as for example, the capacity to be adopted. The law of adoption has never been free from the influence and effect of the religious observances which mark the progress of a Hindu in the three upper castes to a state of regeneration. The law of succession to the estate of a deceased is distinctly based at least according to the school of Bengal upon the religious system, which provides for the performance of various rites and ceremonies in honor not merely of the deceased, but of his ancestors; one of the main objects in view, in regulating the order of succession, being to provide for the due celebration of those religious observances.

They are not enforced by law.

Although the non-performance, or the incapacity to perform some of the religious observances enjoined by the shasters, may impose disabilities on the individual who thus fails in his religious obligations, yet it does not appear that there is any recognized legal duty to perform them such as the Courts would interfere to enforce directly or indirectly. "The duty," said Sir Colley Scotland,* "of individuals to submit to and perform certain religious observances in accordance with the ritual or conventional practice of their race or sect, is, in the absence of express legal recognition and provision, of imperfect obligation of a moral, not a civil, nature. Of such obligations the present Civil Courts cannot take cognizance. And it is of great importance, I think, in this country, that the Courts exercising their civil jurisdiction, as now provided, should carefully guard against entertaining suits in respect of mere ritual observances and the conduct of the various kinds of native religious worship and ceremonies, and of what, as incident thereto, may be due to the sacred character or the religious rank and position of individuals. With such matters the Courts cannot properly deal, and if their jurisdiction extended to interference in them, the law would, I fear,

* Striman Sadogopa *v.* Kristna Tatachariyar, 1 Madras High Court Reports, p. 301.

LECTURE III. be made instrumental in upholding and continuing the ceremonials and superstitious observances of idol-worship, for the benefit merely of the few who profit by them." Although the suit, in which these observations were made, was one for the enforcement of a right to certain honors and emoluments said to belong to the plaintiff in his capacity of spiritual guide and teacher, yet they are of general application even to the most sacred rites which Hindus, in the course of their lives, ought to perform. The obligation to do so is a moral, or religious one, but one not enforced by any legal sanction. But although the Courts cannot, or do not, enforce the performance of rites,—say for example of tonsure, or the *upanayana*, they sometimes, to a limited extent, take cognizance of them as affecting the *status* of the individual. They do not compel a man to perform the *shraddha* of his ancestors, but they have regard to his right or duty to do so, as it affects the devolution of property, or creates a necessity for the disbursement of ancestral funds. And it is impossible to present a complete view of the Hindu family, without discussing some of the questions which arise from the joint-worship of the family; and I think it necessary, therefore, to refer to the duties of priests and the position which they occupy, the law relating to endowment of idols, and also the nature of the most important of the religious observances which influence so largely the condition of the law.

Gurus. I will first refer to the *Guru*, or spiritual guide of the family, and the *Purohit*, or the priest who officiates at and presides over the performance of the religious ceremony. The word "*guru*" properly means master, and serves to denote the position of authority which the religious adviser occupies: kings are *gurus* of their kingdoms, and masters are *gurus* of their servants. But it is chiefly applied to persons who wield both a temporal and spiritual authority, which they are supposed to derive from the superior sanctity of their lives. It extends to give them a superintendence over the different castes, and to control and compel the observance of customs and ceremonies. They could expel a man from his *caste;* or on sufficient expiation of his offences restore him; their benediction is equivalent to the remission of sins, and their curse is the source of all evil. They are generally, but not always, Brahmins, and their dignity descends from father to son. They sometimes conduct religious ceremonies.

Purohits.

The functions of the *Purohits* are to conduct worship and all ceremonies; to assign names to new-born infants, and calculate their nativity; to bless new houses, walls, and tanks; purify and consecrate temples, and conduct marriages and funeral obsequies. One of the privileges claimed by a lower order amongst them is the right of making horoscopes and of publishing the Hindu Almanac, which is compiled upon the approximation and agreement of tables and formulæ which are of great antiquity, and extremely numerous. From the Almanac so formed are learned the good and evil days, and the lucky moments so important in the eyes of a Hindu in determining when ceremonies should be held.*

* I derive this account of *Gurus* and *Purohits*, from the work of the Abbé Dubois, a missionary in Southern India, who, having escaped from the massacres of the French Revolution, devoted himself to acquire, by long and personal intercourse, an intimate acquaintance with Hindu customs and manners.—*Abbé Dubois's Customs and Manners of the Hindus* (1817), pp. 64-74. I am also informed by Baboo Shamachurn Sircar, the learned author of the *Vyavastha Darpana*, that such is a correct description of their duties in Bengal, and at the present day.

LECTURE III.

The relations of the *Purohits* to their *Jujmans** were not, at any time, of an exclusively spiritual nature, but were complicated by considerations arising from the pecuniary claims which the former had for the services which they rendered. This brought the character of the office under the discussion of the Courts, the nature of the issue between them being whether both parties were perfectly free to form or continue such relations, or whether the office of *Purohit* to any Hindu family was hereditary in its tenure, with certain emoluments attached to it, as of right, which the *Jujmans* were bound to pay. Officiating priests, it is said in Mr. Colebrooke's Digest,† are of three sorts: (1) hereditary priests honored by former generations with employment; (2) priests appointed by the party or *Jujman* himself, either for a long time or for a particular purpose; (3) those who officiate on account of previous friendship. In the outset of this contest, the *Purohits* succeeded in establishing the hereditary claims, which, according to ancient custom, attached to their office; and they carried their triumph so far as to have it judicially recognized that they might, by agreement, distribute their *Jujmans* amongst themselves, in whatever manner they pleased, without the slightest reference to the feelings and wishes of those to whom they looked for their reward.

Office of Purohit formerly hereditary.

A remarkable instance of this occurred at Tipperah, where it appeared that, from time immemorial, certain Brahmins had held the office of *Purohits* to the Sahoos of that place,

* Literally, sacrificers, used in reference to *Purohits* in the same sense as parishioners, or spiritual pupils.

† Colebrooke's Digest, B. II, C. III, Section II, sl. 43.

some families who belonged to the Bunniah caste of Hindus. Those Brahmins had long been accustomed to share the fees arising from the performance of religious ceremonies, but their numbers having increased, they consented amongst themselves to partition their *Jujmans* into two lots, one a four-anna share of the whole, and the other a twelve-anna, assigning to each lot those who should thenceforth be their particular *Purohits.* After a time, the *Purohits* who obtained the larger share of clients encroached upon the smaller body, and deprived them of some of the fees which, according to the partition, were exclusively due to them. These latter, accordingly, instituted proceedings against their rivals, and also against the *Jujmans* who had deserted them, to enforce against both of them an exclusive right of ministration. The Zillah Judge ruled* that the plaintiffs had a right to officiate as priests to the defendant *Jujmans,* by virtue of the partition referred to, and whether the *Jujmans* would or not; and as he considered that the *Jujmans* had contumaciously refused to employ them, he threatened to punish them by the imposition of a heavy fine if they persisted in their refusal. All of the defendants contended that the *Jujman* was at liberty to employ whatever Brahmin he pleased, and the rejection of the plaintiffs was explained by the statement that they were in the habit of demanding such exorbitant fees for the performance of sacrifices and other ceremonies as rendered it impossible to have them performed properly. The plaintiffs simply denied the right of a *Jujman* to dismiss his *Purohit,* and alleged that the right

* Radhakishen and others *v.* Sham Serma and others, Reports of Select Cases, Vol. II (new edition), p. 332.

LECTURE III.

of performing the duty of a *Purohit* was frequently bought and sold like other property. The provincial Court at first confirmed the decree of the Zillah Judge, and after some vacillation, owing to the conflicting *vyavasthas* of the pundits, ruled in effect that a *Jujman* could, on paying a fine, discard a qualified *Purohit.* The Sudder Court, in appeal, after taking elaborate opinions from their pundits, finally ruled that a *Jujman* could not discard a faultless *Purohit,* and that the plaintiffs were qualified to perform the duties of *Purohits.* It was finally decreed that the plaintiffs should be put in possession of their right to officiate, as *Purohits,* in the houses of the defendant *Jujmans,* in the way in which they claimed, without the slightest reference to the wishes or feelings of their employers.

Such doctrine overruled.

The effect of this decision was to secure to *Purohits* hereditary legal offices of considerable value, some supervision of their charges being reserved, since oppression in that respect might amount to a fault which would justify removal. So stringent a rule, however, could not be adhered to, and in 1850,* the doctrine was established that *Purohits'* fees were partly voluntary, and partly payment for work and labor done; they were no longer the subject of partition on the ground of hereditary right, but might be the subject of a partnership account. And in a later year,† the Sudder Court of Bengal ruled that, although, under the Hindu law, there was no doubt that the office of a *Purohit* was, to a certain extent, an hereditary office,

* Hurgobind Surma *v.* Bhowaneepershad Shah (13th June 1850), S. D. Decisions, Vol. VI, p. 296; and Ramakant Surma and others *v.* Gobindchunder Surma (13th May 1852), S. D. Decisions, Vol. VIII, p. 398.

† Jowahur Misser *v.* Bhagoo Misser, 13 S. D. Decisions, p. 362.

and although it had been ruled that a *Jujman* could not dismiss a faultless *Purohit,* yet the Courts would refuse to try the question of his faultlessness, and refer it to the conscience of the *Jujman.* The practical result, of course, is that *Jujmans* are at liberty to dismiss and select their own *Purohits,* and have also the power of determining to whom their offerings should be paid; and thus the hereditary office of *Purohits,* with the right annexed to it of officiating in certain families, whether with or without their consent, has been practically abolished; and Hindus, under the present system, are at liberty to select their own priests, according to their own wishes.

Their services are now the subject of contract.

In addition to the freedom which Hindus are now enabled, by the action of the English Courts, to exercise in forming or dissolving their relations with their *Purohits,* they are not compellable in law to perform the moral obligation which custom and usage impose of supporting the worship of the family idols, even though they are in possession of the family estate. Co-sharers in ancestral estate cannot be compelled to contribute to expenses so incurred against their will.*

No legal obligation to contribute to expenses of the joint worship.

The ordinary method of providing for the support of idols, priests, and worship is by endowment, by the dedication of certain property to an idol, or to a temple, or to the maintenance of Brahmins, or to other religious purposes, which property is thenceforth known by the name of *dewutter* property. Such endowments are recognized, so long as they appear to have been *bonâ fide* made, and are, undoubtedly, encouraged by Hindu law. They must, however, be real and not nominal endowments;† the crite-

Dewutter.

* Shamloll Sett *v.* Hurrosoonderee Gooptu, 5 S. W. R., p. 29.

† Mahatabchand and others *v.* Mirdad Ali and others, 5 S. D. R., p. 268.

LECTURE III.

rion being the publicity of the dedication or grant, and the appropriation of the rents, issues, and profits to the purposes for which the grant purported to have been made. As a general rule,* written evidence of an endowment will be required. Its absence however is not necessarily fatal, provided all the circumstances of the case place the fact of endowment beyond a doubt. Amongst those circumstances the fact that the proceeds of the property have been applied to the support of an idol, is strong, but not always conclusive, evidence that the idol has been endowed with such property.

In the case of lands so dedicated before the grant of the dewanny in 1765, they cannot be subjected to the payment of Government revenue.†

Who can endow.

As long ago as 1830,‡ the doctrine was approved that a father, even under Mitakshara law, can, without the assent of his son, aliene a small portion of the ancestral property for pious purposes, which were specified to be the performance of ancestral rites, and the support of Brahmins and priests. On the other hand, in Bengal, a case§ was decided in the Supreme Court in 1814, which recognized the right of a Hindu to apply the whole of his property to the support and worship of his family idol. That, however, is by virtue of his absolute ownership. It would appear that although Hindu law approves the devotion of the proceeds of property to specified religious or pious purposes, and places those purposes on the same footing with the

* Muddun Lall v. Sreemutty Komul Bibee, 8 S. W. R., p. 43.

† Reg. XIX of 1793, Sec. 2; Collector of Moorshedabad v. Bishennath Rai and others, Select Reports (new edition), Vol. I, p. 231.

‡ Gopalchunder Pande v. Bala Kunwar Singh, 5 S. D. A., p. 28.

§ Sir F. Macnaghten's Considerations of Hindu Law, p. 335.

maintenance of dependents, yet it does not favor endowment to the extent of enabling an owner to dispense with any fetters on his power of alienation. A widow, for example, cannot endow, without the consent of the reversioners, however beneficial such dedication may be deemed to be to her deceased husband's soul. "Great benefit is done to a departed soul," it is said, "by paying his debts, by bestowing his daughter in marriage, and supporting his family; indeed, if these duties be neglected, he is doomed to hell." Nothing is said of such a duty as endowing an idol; and accordingly it has been held* that that is beyond the competence of a Hindu widow.

The endower's interest ceases.

As soon as land or other property has been validly dedicated and assigned to the support of religion the donor ceases to have any right in it;† it is no longer heritable by his heirs, and he cannot aliene it. Lands, which are held by a zemindar for a religious appropriation, even though he retains the superintendence, are not considered to form part of his zemindaree, nor to be the subject of his ownership. The management of such land passes to the Sebait of the idol, or the mohunt of the temple, as the case may be, who can neither aliene it, nor grant a pottah‡ of it, except for the term of his own life.

Subject to any usage to the contrary, the right to such management passes by inheritance. In Bengal, however, the succession to the superintendence of *muths*, or temples, is generally elective.§

* Kartick Chunder Chuckerbutty *v.* Gourmohun Roy, 1 S. W. R., p. 48.

† 2 Macnaghten's Hindu law, 305, Case xiii.

‡ Radha Bullubh Chund *v.* Juggutchunder Chowdry, Select Reports (new edition), Vol. IV, p. 192.

§ 1 Strange's Hindu Law, p. 151.

LECTURE III.

Superintendence of endowed property.

The general superintendence of endowments was vested in the Board of Revenue, by Regulation XIX of 1810, which recited that there was reason to suppose that the produce of endowed lands was, in many instances, appropriated, contrary to the intention of the donors, to the personal use of the individuals in possession. The Regulation further provided that "it shall be the duty of the Board of Revenue and Board of Commissioners to take care that all endowments made for the maintenance of establishments of the above description be duly appropriated to the purpose for which they were destined by the Government or individual by whom such endowments were granted. In like manner, it shall be the duty of those Boards to provide, with the sanction of Government, for the due repair and maintenance of all public edifices which have been erected, either at the expense of the former or present Government, or of individuals, and which either at present are or can conveniently be rendered conducive to the convenience of the community."

When the donor reserves to himself and family the direction and superintendence of the religious establishment, it is necessary to show, before the lands can be claimed as dewutter, that the proceeds* have been *bonâ fide* appropriated to religious purposes; and so long as that is done, there is no objection to the donor retaining to himself and his family the management, receiving the rents and appointing the various officers who perform the worship. He then holds not in his character of owner, but as Sebait; and in that capacity his power of alienation is gone.† His

* Collector of Moorshedabad *v.* Bishennath Rai and others, Select Reports (new edition), Vol. I, p. 231.

† Bhowanipersad Chowdree *v.* Ranee Jugudumbha, Select Reports (new edition), Vol. I, p. 437.

competency extends no further than to the superintendence of the worship of the idols and to the payment of revenue to Government; and perhaps to granting a pottah for the term of his own life.

LECTURE III.

It cannot be partitioned.

Although dewutter lands cannot be either partitioned or aliened the heirs of the grantor for whose benefit the worship is conducted, can, by consent, form separate religious establishments, and separately perform the services, each one taking a separate share of the rents* for that purpose, or taking the whole for his proportionate part of the year, or of any other space of time which may be divided between the parties for their *pallas*, or turns of worship. Obstruction† to the use and worship of an idol by one joint worshipper is ground for the other insisting upon a separation and a removal of the idol to his house.

Muths, or temples.

With regard to *muths*, or temples, they appear to be of three descriptions,‡ *viz.*, *mouroosi*, *punchaiti*, and *hakimi*. In the first, the office of chief mohunt is hereditary, and devolves upon the chief disciple of the existing mohunt, who, moreover, usually nominates his chief disciple as his successor. In the second, the office is elective, the presiding mohunt being selected by an assembly of mohunts. In the third, the appointment of presiding mohunt is vested in the ruling power, or in the party who endowed the temple. The law of the shasters in regard to the appointment of a presiding mohunt of a *muth*, or temple, called "mouroosi," was declared by the pundits, in an early case, to be that the principal *chela*, or pupil, is entitled to succeed; but

* Elder widow of Rajah Chutter Sein *v.* Younger widow of ditto, Select Reports (new edition), Vol. I, p. 239.

† Dwarkanath Roy *v.* J. Chowdrain, 4 S. W. R., p. 79.

‡ Mohunt Rama Nooj Doss *v.* Mohunt Debraj Doss, 6 S. D. R., p. 262.

LECTURE III.

that if he be personally unfit or disqualified by any sufficient cause,* then the presiding mohunt should, during his life-time, select one personally qualified from amongst his pupils, who will thereupon be entitled to succeed.

The rule as to the succession to the office of mohunt must depend upon the usage of each mohuntee. "If a person,"† said Sir Barnes Peacock, "endows a college or religious institution, the endower has a right to lay down the rule of succession. But when no such rule has been laid down, it must be proved by evidence what is the usage, in order to carry out the intention of the original endower. Each case must be governed by the usage of the particular mohuntee."

Mohunts.

Instances are frequent* of the office of mohunt being purely elective, the assembly of electors being composed of the neighbouring mohunts. The nominee, however, of the late incumbent is usually preferred.

In the case of hereditary *muths*, a successor is usually nominated by a mohunt during his life-time; otherwise, after his death, the *chelas* and *guru bhaees* assemble and select the eldest *chela*, if properly qualified, or they may select a successor from the *chela* of another *muth*. If they cannot agree‡ in their choice, the ruling power is applied to, who commands an assembly of mohunts to select a proper person, whom he confirms in the *guddee* or superintendency. In the case‡ of a *muth* at Juggernath, the former mohunt appointed no successor; several claimants started up, complaints were preferred to the Register, the

* Narain Doss *v.* Bindrabun Doss, Select Reports (new edition), Vol. II, p. 192; Ramrutton Doss *v.* Bonmalee Doss, Select Reports (new edition), Vol. I, p. 226.

† Greedharee Doss *v.* Nundkishore Dutt Mohunt, Marshall's Reports, p. 573.

‡ Ramchurn Doss *v.* Chutter Bhoje, 7 S. D. R., p. 205.

head civil authority in the district, and he, after consulting the brethren of the *muth*, appointed the *chela* of the last mohunt. The Commissioner of the province, who was vested with the full powers of the Sudder Adawlut, cancelled the whole of the Register's proceedings as illegal, and referred the case to the Local Agent, under Regulation XIX of 1810, who directed another assembly to appoint a proper successor to the late mohunt. The assembly elected a *guru bhaee*, who was, therefore, appointed to the *guddee* by the Local Agents, and the appointment was confirmed by the Commissioner, and upheld by the Sudder Court, who ruled that all was done according to established usage.

Passing from the position occupied by the ministers of religion, the next subject is the ceremonial which they preside over, so far as it is relevant to the law as now administered.

The rites of the Shraddha.

Of the common rites which serve to bind the Hindu family together, the *shraddha*, or funeral obsequies, rendered to deceased ancestors is unquestionably the most important. It fills so large a space in the daily life and thought of the Hindu, it influences so deeply the whole character of Hindu civilization, binding together at least seven successive generations of men in bonds of mutual dependence, which are consecrated by the strongest religious sentiment, and strengthened by the traditions of more than three thousand years; it underlies, moreover, in Bengal, so completely the whole of the Hindu law of inheritance, that I think it useful, with a view to the clear understanding of the legal, as well as the social, organization of Hindus, to give a somewhat detailed account of it. These obsequies consist of oblations of food and libations of water, which it is the

LECTURE III. first and most indispensable duty of a Hindu to offer to the manes of his ancestors, without which those ancestors will be tormented with hunger and thirst, and will be repulsed from a region of bliss, while the sonless man will sink into *put*, or the region of everlasting torment. The presence of a son, natural or adopted, to perform the ceremony, is indispensable to its complete spiritual efficacy, and occasions the anxiety which pervades the community for the possession of male offspring. In the Dattaka Mimansa, the well-known treatise of Nanda Pandita on the subject of adoption, it is cited from the Vedas, or revealed scriptures, that a Brahmana, immediately on being born, is produced a debtor in three obligations: to the holy saints, for the practice of religious duties; to the gods, for the performance of sacrifice; to his forefathers, for offspring. "By a son," says Menu, "a man obtains victory over all people; by a son's son, he enjoys immortality; and afterwards by the son of that grandson, he reaches the solar abode."* Here, therefore, the instrumentality of the son in obtaining immortality for his father, and in absolving him from his three-fold debt, is declared; and is in practice, as well as theory, the governing principle of family life. The reason is emphatically added, that, without him the obsequies would fail;† the most significant rites of the *shrad-*

* 9 Menu, p. 137.

† See Colebrooke's Digest, B. V, C. IX, Sec. II, sl. 514. "The first rites must be performed; but the last rites shall only be celebrated by sons and the rest." And in a note it is added "The first funeral ceremony is the cremation of the corpse; the middle rites consist in gathering the ashes and performing the obsequies for a person recently deceased,—these extend to the first annual *shraddha*; the last rites are the monthly, annual, and other obsequies for ancestors long since deceased."

dha,* *i. e.*, the *parvana shraddha*, performed by those who succeed in the direct line, it is said, would fail; and unaided by the *puttra* (son), the soul of the Hindu must sink into that *put* from which it is the province of the son to deliver him.

Description of them.

I derive the following account of the ceremony, from a paper contributed to the 7th volume of the Asiatic Researches, by Mr. Colebrooke. It commences with the preparation by the sons of a funeral pile, on a spot which is duly consecrated. Then follows the cremation,† or burning, which is so managed that some of the bones remain for the subsequent ceremony of burning the ashes. Libations of water are offered to the deceased after the burning. Ten days of mourning‡ ensue, and then his son, or nearest kinsman, gather his ashes and offer a *shraddha*, singly, for him. Food is then distributed to the assembled *Brahmanas*. Then spreading *kusà* grass near the fragments of the repast, and taking some rice with *tila* and clarified butter, he must distribute it on the grass while the *Purohitas* recite for him these prayers: "May those in my family who have been burnt by fire, who are alive, and yet unburnt, be satisfied with this food presented on the ground, and proceed contented towards the supreme path of eternal

* Shamachurn's Vyavastha Darpana, p. 740. The substitute for a son is necessary, notwithstanding a widow's capacity to present the oblations of food and libations of water to the manes of her husband; for the son is required chiefly to perform the *parvana shraddha* to deliver the father from the hell called '*put*,' and to prolong his lienage, which are beyond the capacity of a widow.

† Described from a paper in Asiatic Researches, Vol. VII, p. 232-262. The body of a child under two years old must be buried, not burnt.

‡ That is in the case of Brahmins, twelve in the case of Kshatryas, fifteen in the case of Vaisyas, and one month in the case of Sudras.

Lecture III.

bliss." Then taking in his left hand another vessel containing *tila,* blossoms, and water, and in his right hand a brush made of *kusà* grass, he sprinkles water over the grass which is spread on the consecrated ground, naming the deceased, and saying "may this oblation be acceptable to thee." He afterwards takes a cake or ball (*pinda*) of food, mixed with clarified butter, and presents it saying, "may this cake be acceptable to thee;" and deals out the food with this prayer: "Ancestors, rejoice; take your respective shares, and be strong as bulls;" and again sprinkles the water on the ground to wash their oblations. He next offers a thread on the funeral cake saying, "may this raiment be acceptable to thee," the priest repeating his texts. He then strews perfume and leaves on the funeral cake, and places a lighted lamp upon it. Afterwards he sprinkles water on it, and offers rice, and the priests offer salutations to the gods.

Object of their performance.

In these, the first funeral obsequies, the object in view is to effect, by means of oblations, the re-embodying the soul of the deceased, after burning his corpse. The houses and persons of the mourners must then be purified; and after that, the second obsequies begin, the object of which is to raise the shade of the deceased from this world (where else it would continue to roam amongst demons and evil spirits) up to heaven, and there beatify him, as it were, amongst the manes of his departed ancestors.

Ekodishta Shraddhas.

These ceremonies, in honor of a single ancestor, are denominated the *ekodishta shraddha.* They are offered, according to a note to Colebrooke's Digest, monthly, during the first year: two extra *shraddhas* being performed before the end of the 6th and 12th month respectively, making, with the ceremony of cremation and the final ceremony, sixteen *shraddhas* in all.*

Parvana Shraddha.

The *shraddha* in honor of progenitors is termed *parvana shraddha.* It is the offering of a double set of oblations at the *parva, viz.*, three cakes to the father, paternal grandfather, and great grandfather, and three to the maternal grandfather, his father, and grandfather, and the remnants to each set of the three remoter ancestors of each line.† It is in abeyance, and cannot be performed, after the death of their next male descendant, until the *sapindakarana* in his honor have been performed, that is until the last deceased has been associated with his forefathers, and the first in the line of those who received offerings from him has received the last oblations of food to which he is entitled. Numerous occasions for performing the *parvana shraddha* are prescribed to the rigid Hindu; but general custom is content with observing them on the last night of the moon preceding the Doorgah Poojah, and on the occasion of visiting places of pilgrimage. At this *shraddha* three funeral cakes are offered to three paternal ancestors in male line, and three more to three maternal

* See Colebrooke's Digest., B. V, C. VIII, Section 1, sl. 399. "Sixteen *shraddhas* must be performed for a *Brahmana* recently deceased. The first on the day immediately following the period of mourning; twelve monthly oblations; one additional *shraddha* before the expiration of the sixth month; another before the expiration of the year; and lastly the *sapindakarana*, or first annual obsequies, performed on the anniversary of his death. Thenceforward, obsequies should be annually celebrated for an ancestor on the date of his death, besides monthly *shraddhas* and other ceremonies directed by Menu in the third chapter of his Institutes (See 3 Menu, 247). In Mithila and some other provinces, the obsequies for a *Brahmana* recently deceased are abridged, and by a fiction completed on the second day after mourning."

† Shamachurn's Vyavastha Darpana, p. 20.

LECTURE III.

Sapinda-karana.

ancestors in the male line, and two to the *Vyswadevas* of assembled gods.

The final ceremony marks the complete emancipation of the great-grandfather of the deceased from dependence on the filial attentions of his descendants, and is denominated the *sapindikarana.* It is the rite of associating the deceased with the manes of the departed ancestors by admixture of the *pindas* before described, and in strictness it should take place on the anniversary of the day of the death.* But according to Mr. Colebrooke, in his paper, to which I have before referred, in the Asiatic Researches, in most provinces, in case of there being only one son, the periods for these sixteen ceremonies, and for the concluding obsequies of *sapindakarana,* are anticipated, and the whole is completed on the second or third day after the death; after which they are again performed at the proper seasons in honor of all the progenitors, and not of the deceased singly. The ceremony of *sapindakarana,* which takes place on the anniversary of death, combines the last *ekodishta shraddha,* or obsequies performed singly for the deceased, with the *parvana shraddha,* or obsequies which the deceased was in the habit of offering in his life-time to his three immediate ancestors in the male line—his father, grandfather, and great-grandfather. Thenceforth the deceased is associated with his three ancestors, and the last obsequies have been paid to the great-grandfather; and

* Shamachurn's Vyavastha Darpana, p. 898. *Sapindakarana* is the rite of associating the deceased with the manes of the departed ancestors by admixture of *pindas* (oblation balls or cakes of rice, &c.) It should strictly take place on the anniversary of the day of death; but in the case of the deceased leaving an only son, or no son, it may also be performed at any time within one year from the deceased's death after the performance of the fourteen monthly *shraddhas* called *masiks.*

the next *parvana shraddha* will be in honor of the deceased, his father and grandfather. Previous to the performance of the *sapindakarana*, the deceased is not denominated a '*pitri*,' or departed ancestor.

LECTURE III.

Description of Sapindakarana.

This ceremony, which is the dividing point of time at which the deceased is associated with his ancestors, at which his great-grandfather finally enters the abodes which are prepared for him, and ceases any longer to be dependent on the efforts of his descendants, and at which the son of the deceased finally assumes the same relationship to his ancestors, which his father held before him, may be described as follows.* Four vessels are prepared and filled with water for the feet, scented wood, flowers, sesamum seed, and consecrated severally to the deceased and his three ancestors. From that consecrated to the deceased, three equal portions are poured into the other three, a small quantity only being retained, and two prayers are recited. Then four funeral cakes are offered to the deceased and his three ancestors, that consecrated to the deceased being divided into three portions and mixed with the other three cakes. That portion of the '*pitri*' consecrated to the deceased, which was retained, is then offered to him, and the whole ceremonies of *ekodishta* and *parvana shraddhas* are completed.

General observations.

I have gone fully into the details of these ceremonies, because they serve to exhibit the spirit which has been infused by Hindu religion into Hindu life, and the mode in which successive generations depend upon one another, and by which families are bound together. The *shraddha* fills as large a space in the life of the Hindu as the festival of the Passover did in that of the Jews. The frequency

* Dattaka Mimansa, p. 99, section VI, note.

LECTURE III.

with which it is, or used to be, performed, the minuteness of the details which are prescribed, and the long duration of its hold on the national mind, and the extent to which it has influenced the condition of their law, show the depth of the importance which, throughout Hindu history, has been attached to it in the minds both of priests and people. It is the great primeval institution of Hindu civilization, and has not merely expressed, but has powerfully influenced, the character and spirit of the people who have for ages clung to its impressive and prolonged observances as a consecration of that deep religious and domestic sentiment which distinguishes them amongst mankind. The spirit displayed in them is unfavorable to the creation of individual will and independence; and largely influences the personal relations or rights and duties of the members of the family. It would be impossible that a Hindu father who enters upon his position as head of the joint family, by offering these indispensable obsequies to his helpless ancestors, knowing that he too in his turn will be equally dependent in the future on his descendants, could imbibe any very resolute sense of dominion such as the old principle of the *patria potestas* gave to the Roman. Obligation, instead of power, is the chief characteristic of his position, from the first to the last.

These funeral obsequies and the rules concerning them are often referred to as the keystone of the Hindu law according to the Bengal school of inheritance and succession. It would, perhaps, be more correct to say that they are evidence of the principle upon which kinship, or the scale of proximity of relations to each other, was established in early Hindu society and preserved to the present times. When a society is composed of an aggregate of families rather than of individuals, it is essential to draw the line sharply and distinctly, so that all may understand it, at the points where old family ties cease, and new ones are formed. Such ties must necessarily be artificial, and vary according to the circumstances of the community. Consanguinity is the natural tie which binds mankind together, but it is more comprehensive and indefinite than is suited to the purposes of society. Municipal or artificial rules must be resorted to in order to ascertain how many of those who are connected by blood shall be regarded as composing a single family. The family tie, moreover, includes those who are not connected by blood, and loses sometimes those who are so connected. Marriage and adoption are the two modes by which an individual passes from one family to another; they are both of them regulated by civil law, and that law may be based upon a different principle in different societies. Then as children and descendants increase and multiply, inasmuch as every child is connected by birth with two families, there must be a further artificial rule to determine the limits of each family, and that rule proceeds upon a different principle in different societies. The great institution of the *patria potestas*, which was as permanent amongst the Romans as the *shraddha* is amongst Hindus, owed perhaps something of its vitality to the fact that it determined the principle upon which families in theory and in practice were separated and constructed.

The rules which regulate the performance of Hindu obsequies, that is of the sacred rites which are observed at each break in the continuity of the family, by pointing out who had the right to perform them, disclose the principle*

* See Lecture V.

LECTURE III. upon which the limits of the family were ascertained, and also the extent to which it was permissible to retain a membership in two families; and further the principle upon which proximity of relationship is calculated. These are purely artificial principles. They differ in different societies, and they considerably affect the character and constitution of any community. In Hindu society they are disclosed to us in the rules which have been observed in the immemorial usages of the *shraddha* ceremonial.

LECTURE IV.

THE HINDU FAMILY—THE JOINT ESTATE.

THE MITAKSHARA AND THE DAYABHAGA.

Classes of Property—Ownership—Three Classes of Ownership—The Joint Estate according to the Mitakshara—Title to it accrues by birth—Son's interest in the father's Estate under the Mitakshara Law—Mother and Grandmother—Father's power under the Mitakshara Law over his self-acquired Immoveables—Son's interest in the father's Estate under Mithila Law—Opinion of the High Court of Bengal concerning it—The Son can set aside a sale, by the father, of the Joint Estate—Sons have no interest in their father's Estate according to the Dayabhaga—The Joint Estate according to the Dayabhaga—Power of alienation --History of the Doctrine of the father's absolute power in Bengal over the Joint Estate—General Observations—The Dayabhaga and Mitakshara—Hindu Coparceners, English Joint Tenants, and Tenants in Common compared—Hindu Coparceners' power to alienate their own shares of Joint Property.

IN treating of the subject of the Hindu family, joint in food, worship, and estate, the next branch of it which invites discussion is the subject of proprietary right. It is not intended in the present course of lectures to go fully into the question of the Hindu laws of property. The legal rules of inheritance, succession, and alienation will be amply sufficient to form the subject of a separate course of lectures.

Classes of property.

With regard to the term property, using it in its sense of dominion over things, it must be treated in reference to the character of the things which are the subject of property, and also with reference to the nature of the dominion which may be exercised. As regards the subject of property, it is divisible amongst Hindus, as also

LECTURE IV. amongst the English, into things personal and real, or using the phraseology, which is ordinarily used in Hindu law, things moveable and immoveable. The distinction between things moveable and immoveable amongst Hindus is very similar to that which exists between things real and things personal amongst the English. But the law which regulates succession amongst Hindus is the same with regard to both classes of property. There is some difference, however, between those two classes of property with respect to the power of alienation which may be exercised over them.

Further, the thing itself, whether moveable or immoveable, which is the subject of property, is capable of division into its component parts; whether by division of the thing itself, or of the mode of its enjoyment. The various holdings of immoveable property, or in other words tenures in land, are instances of it, and every tenure is as distinct a subject of property as is the land itself.

Ownership. Then, with regard to the right of the family or individual, that is the dominion over the thing which is the subject of ownership or property,—the term involves the ideas of possession, enjoyment, and power of disposition. The rights thus indicated are in their nature separable, whether they exist in things moveable or immoveable. Together they complete the full right of ownership, and when separated, the separation is always traceable either to the act of the party or to an express provision of law.

Besides the classification of the different subjects of property, we must also classify the different kinds of dominion which may be exercised over them, *i. e.*, the different kinds of ownership. In English law, division of ownership gives rise amongst other things to *estates*, whether in fee, or in tail, for years, for life, in remainder, or in reversion, which estates may be held in different modes, *viz.*, in severalty, in joint tenancy, in tenancy in common, or in coparcenery. An estate is the condition or circumstance in which an owner stands in reference to his property; it denotes the extent of his ownership. The estate is measured by its length of duration, and is the same whether a man holds in severalty, in joint tenancy, or in tenancy in common. . Conventional estates, which are created by act of the parties, depend upon the law of contract, and may be the same in all countries. But estates which are created by operation and construction of law, *i. e.*, whose duration and incidents are defined by legislative provisions or custom having the force of law, however numerous in English law, are or were unknown to Hindus.

Three classes of ownership.

Amongst Hindus, in early times, there was the joint family fund (whether consisting of things moveable or immoveable), separately acquired property, and *stridhun*; and we may easily suppose that Hindu law originally had no other notion of ownership, but that of full ownership, whether by a family or individual. There has been added to them, what is now known as the Hindu widow's estate, the duration of which is for life, and whose incidents have been recently annexed to it.

The mode of acquisition may be referred to, as constituting the primary and principal source of difference between the three classes of ownership according to Hindu law. There is self-acquired property, which is separate property acquired by a man's own exertions, which he takes, using English phraseology, by purchase. It has been held*

* Mudden Gopaul Thakoor *v.* Ram Buksh Panday, 6 S. W. R., p. 71.

LECTURE IV.

that property received at a partition is not self-acquired property in the ordinary sense of the term, and is not to be dealt with as such. To form self-acquired property, there must be consideration moving from the acquirer, not simply valuable, for the mere personal regard of a stranger inducing him to make a gift would be sufficient. Then there is ancestral property, which he takes by inheritance. Property acquired by inheritance is always joint family property, for when the acquirer is dead, his heirs are jointly entitled; and it at once assumes the character of joint property, and so also do its accretions, whether derived by a process of accumulation, or by the employment by one or more of the members of the joint family of its joint funds. Thirdly, there is *stridhun*, or the separate property of a woman, which includes what was given to her by her father, mother, husband, or brother, and what was received by her at her marriage, or at her husband's marriage to another wife, and any other separate acquisition.* It has been held not to include property which has devolved upon her by inheritance.† According to Menu, Katyana, and Nareda, there are six sorts of a woman's separate property. And in the Dayabhaga it is laid down that the husband has power over the earnings of his wife, and over any presents which she may receive from any other but kindred. Over other classes of her separate property, that is over *stridhun* generally, the wife has sole power, except that she may not aliene her immoveable estate, which has been given to her

* Dayabhaga, Chap. IV., Sect. I., verse 4.

† Vengamalathammal *v.* Valayuda Mudali, 3 Madras High Court Reports, p. 312.

by her husband.* His distress will confer upon him the right to use her separate property.

LECTURE IV.

The joint estate according to the Mitakshara.

The rival treatises of the Mitakshara and the Dayabhaga are mainly at issue upon the true character of the joint estate, and the true effect of partition thereof as the source of proprietary right. According to the former, heritage (*dâya*) signifies that wealth to which a man becomes entitled by reason of relationship to its owner; such relationship being the means whereby the ownership of the whole may reside in several persons jointly; and partition (*vibhaga*) is the adjustment of rights of ownership regarding the whole by distributing them over particular portions of the aggregate. "According to the true notion of an undivided family," said Lord Westbury, delivering the judgment of the Privy Council in a case † which was governed by the Mitakshara law, "no individual member of that family, whilst it remains undivided, can predicate of the joint undivided property, that he, that particular member, has a certain definite share. The proceeds of undivided property must be brought according to the theory of an undivided family to the common chest or purse, and then dealt with according to the modes of enjoyment of the members of an undivided family. But when the members of an undivided family agree among themselves with regard to particular property that it shall thenceforth be the subject of ownership in certain definite shares, then the character of undivided property and joint enjoyment is taken away from the subject-matter so agreed to be dealt with, and in the estate each member has thenceforth a definite and certain share which he may claim a right

* Doe *v.* Kupper Pillai, 1 Madras High Court Reports, p. 85.

† Appoovier *v.* Ramasubba Hirjan, 8 S. W. R., P. C., p. 1.

LECTURE IV.

to receive and to enjoy in severalty, although the property itself has not been actually severed and divided."

Title to it accrues by birth.

The result of the discussion by the author of the Mitakshara of the texts which relate to joint property is that he declares that the title to it of each joint owner accrues by birth, although the father retains independent power in the disposal of moveables for indispensable acts of duty, and for purposes prescribed by texts of law, as, for example, gifts through affection, support of the family, relief from distress, and so forth. "It seems clear," said the High Court of Bengal,* "that proprietary right is created by birth, and not by conception. A child in the womb takes no estate. In cases where, when the succession opens out, a female member of the family has conceived, the inheritance remains in abeyance until the result of the conception can be ascertained." The Mitakshara further declares, with regard to immoveable estate, whether ancestral or self-acquired, that the father is subject to the control of his sons and the rest. Such control is effective in the case of ancestral immoveable estate, but not in the case of its being acquired by the father's own exertions. There is, however, this exception, that while the sons and grandsons and unseparated kinsmen are minors, and incapable of giving their consent to a gift and the like, then a single individual may give mortgage or sell immoveable property during a season of distress, for the sake of the family, and especially for pious purposes. The authority, therefore, of the individual over the joint property is exceptional, and only arises under circumstances of unavoidable neces-

* Mussamut Goura Chowdrain *v.* Chummun Chowdry and others, *per* Kemp, J., S. W. R. (1864), p. 342.

sity, or under such circumstances as may, in construction and intendment of law, render the individual the agent of the family.

Son's interest in the father's estate under the Mitakshara law.

Sons, grandsons, and great-grandsons, therefore, have all of them a right by birth in the grandfather's estate, but it must be understood that as respects the grandson there is this qualification that, according to the text of Yajnavalkya, "the ownership of father and son is the same in land and chattels which belong to the grandfather;" and that whatever limits or terminates the father's right in the grandfather's property, as, for example, a separation, also limits or terminates the right of the grandson; the grandson's right in the ancestral property, though it arises from birth, being nevertheless solely derived through the father. "A son* or grandson," however, "has a right of prohibition if his unseparated father is making a gift, donation, or sale of effects inherited from his grandfather; but it is nowhere stated in the Mitakshara that such right of prohibition can be exercised by any one in favor of an unborn son." It is the primitive notion of the joint family and of joint property, where individual title is lost sight of in the collective rights of all the members, which the Mitakshara law preserves. The joint property is the joint fund from which all must be maintained, and over which whatever power is exercised is exercised by all or on behalf of all the owners. The acquisition of separate title by the individual in the joint property, depends upon partition which may take place either at the option of the father, or of the son after his father's death, or at the option of the

* See Juddonath Tewarree *v.* Bissonath Tewaree, *per* Mitter, J., S. W. R., p. 61.

LECTURE IV.

son in the father's life-time and against his wish, if there be no prospect of further issue either on account of the father's age and character, or on account of the age of both parents.

Mother and grand-mother.

Either the mother or the grandmother is entitled to a share when sons or grandsons divide the joint estate between them, but she cannot be recognized as the owner of such share until the division is actually made; she has no pre-existing right in the estate except a right to maintenance. She may acquire property by partition, for partition is one of the recognized modes of acquiring property under the Hindu law. But partition is in her case the sole cause of her right to the property.*

Father's power under the Mitakshara law over his self-acquired immoveables.

With regard to the right of the father under the Mitakshara law to make a valid sale, without the consent of his sons, of immoveable property acquired by himself, some obscurity formerly existed. On the one side there is the text of the Mitakshara;† "the father is subject to the control of his sons and the rest, in regard to the immoveable estate, whether acquired by himself or inherited from his father or other predecessor;" and also the text of Yajnavalkya "land or other immoveable property, a man shall neither give away nor sell, even though he acquired them himself, unless he convene all his sons." On the other hand, there is another passage in the Mitakshara.‡ "So likewise the grandson has a right of prohibition, if his unseparated father is making a donation or a sale, of effects inherited from the grandfather; but he has no right of interference, if the effects were acquired by the father. On the contrary, he must acquiesce, because he is dependent." In

* Mitakshara, Chap. I., Sect. I., verse 27.

† Colebrooke's Digest, B. II., C. IV., Sec. I., sl. 14.

‡ Mitakshara, Chap. I., S. V., verse 9.

the next verse the difference is thus explained: "Although a son have a right by birth in his father's and in his grandfather's property, still, since he is dependent on his father in regard to the paternal estate, and since his father has a predominant interest, as it was acquired by himself, the son must acquiesce in the father's disposal of his own acquired property; but since both have indiscriminately a right in the grandfather's estate, the son has a power of interdiction if the father be dissipating the property."

The apparent conflict between these passages was the subject of discussion by the High Court of Bengal in the case of *Mudden Gopaul Thakoor* v. *Ram Buxsh Pandey and others*;* and was considered to be reconciled by treating the right which sons have in their father's self-acquired property as an imperfect right incapable of being enforced at law. The right of suit, it was said, is nowhere mentioned as extending to the case of a father alienating his own self-acquired immoveable property; and the Court held on those grounds, and on the ground of general convenience, that a father, under Mitakshara law, is not incompetent to sell immoveable property acquired by himself.

Therefore, under the Mitakshara, the right to aliene self-acquired property is absolute; and whatever right the son or grandson may have in it, the law compels him to acquiesce in the exercise of a full power of disposition by the acquirer. Such property is exempt from partition if it be acquired without detriment to, or use of, the joint estate.

* 6 S. W. R., p. 71. See also Bawa Misser *v.* Rajah Bishen Prokash Narain Singh, 10 S. W. R., p. 287.

LECTURE IV.

The son* cannot exercise any control over his father's self-acquired property, even though the father be an outcast.

Son's interest in the father's estate under Mithila law.

With regard to the right of the son in the father's ancestral immoveable property under Mithila law, it has been held† by the Bengal High Court to be the same as under the Mitakshara. The Vivada Chintamani does not, in express terms, define the rule upon the subject; but it states with regard to the father's self-acquired property that the sons have no ownership, which appears to imply that they have ownership in the ancestral estate. The Mitakshara rule, in the silence of the Vivada Chintamani, must prevail amongst the followers of the Mithila school; and therefore amongst them, as amongst those of the Benares school, the son's ownership in his father's ancestral estate accrues on his birth. The son and father are joint owners of it, and the son can compel his father to divide it with him whenever he pleases.

Opinion of the High Court of Bengal concerning it.

The result is that, except in Bengal, an alienation of the the ancestral joint estate made by the father without consent of all the heirs, or made without proof of legal necessity, or of its being made for the benefit of minors, or under such circumstances as to render the father the agent of the family for that purpose, is void.‡

The true nature and character of the son's interest under Mitakshara law in ancestral estate, during the father's lifetime, was discussed by the Full Bench of the Bengal High Court, in a case§ which was before them respecting the vali-

* Ojoodhya Persad Sing v. Ramsarun, 6 S. W. R., p. 77.

† Kantoo Lall v. Gridharee, 9 S. W. R., p. 469.

‡ Sheo Pershad Jha v. Gungaram Jha, 5 S. W. R., p. 221.

§ Rajah Ram Tewarree v. Luchman Persad, 8 S. W. R., p. 15.

dity of an alienation of joint estate by the father, which was not questioned by the sons till fifteen years after the sale. The question was whether the sons' cause of action against the purchaser to set aside the alienation as invalid arose at the date of the sale to and taking possession by the purchaser, or at the death of the father. One of the sons had attained his majority at the time of the alienation, and the father lived on till about six years before the suit; and if the sons' cause of action arose at the father's death, the suit could have been maintained. But the Full Bench ruled otherwise, and it was held that the suit was barred for that, according to the true principles of Mitakshara law, the right in the ancestral property, which a son takes during his father's life-time, is of such a nature as to enable him to prohibit alienation, or if the alienation has been made, at once to question it. "By birth alone, he acquires that right, and he can compel a partition of such property during his father's life-time. The father cannot, without the consent of the son, alienate it except for sufficient cause, and the son may prohibit the father from so doing. If the sale was valid as to the father's share, it must have operated as a severance of the joint interest in the property included in the conveyance. If so, the son might have sued the purchaser for a partition of the property, or to recover his own share of it. The father's death, in that case, would not alter his rights. If the sale was invalid as regards the father's share, the son might have sued in the father's life-time for a partition, or to recover the whole estate, to be held as joint family estate. Whether the conveyance was operative or not as regards the father's share, the son's cause of action arose from the date of the purchaser's taking possession."

LECTURE IV.

The Full Bench also ruled that even if the son took the father's share at his death by survivorship that would not give him a new cause of action; for his cause of action was complete in his father's life-time. The Full Bench further decided that no new cause of action accrued upon the birth of the minor plaintiff, although he was not born until nine years after the sale. The Court reasoned in this way: that, before his birth, his father and his brother might have made a partition of the estate, and if they had done so, he would have had no interest in the share allotted to his brother;* and before his birth his father might have sold the share allotted to him; and also the father and his elder brother, or the father with the assent of the elder brother, might, before his birth, have sold the estate, and the sale would have been binding upon him. If the father and elder brother had been dispossessed by a wrong-doer, the cause of action would have accrued at the time of the dispossession, and a new cause of action would not have accrued at the birth of the younger son, whose right accrued at his birth to the estate as it stood at the moment of his birth.

There is, however, a limit to the son's right to prohibit alienation of the ancestral estate by the father.† Though the latter may not dissipate, or waste, the estate, he can always aliene where any legal necessity is shown to exist, such as the payment of joint family debts, and the maintenance of the joint family, and the performance of his father's *shraddha*.

The son can set aside a sale, by the father, of the joint estate.

In the case of a sale of joint property by a father, without the consent of the son, under no pressure of

* Mitakshara, Chap. I., Sec. 6.

† Bissumbhur Naik *v.* S. Mohapathar, 1 S. W. R., p. 96.

necessity, it seems that the son's right to set it aside and recover the estate is absolute. The purchaser cannot compel the son to refund* the purchase-money, unless he can show (and the burden of proof lies on him) that the purchase-money was carried to the assets of the joint estate, and that the son had the benefit of his share in it; in short, that the money had been so dealt with as to render him, the purchaser, an incumbrancer upon the estate in respect of the whole or any part of it. Whether a son can recover from his father's purchaser the whole, or only his own share, of the estate, has not been finally decided.

It should be remembered that, under Mitakshara law, each member of an undivided family has, before partition, a joint interest in the whole of it, but not a separate title to a share. The rules of inheritance are framed with a view to his ultimately possessing a share, and some of the cases, with respect to his power to alienate, also assume that he will or may become possessed of a share. If the Mitakshara joint estate is dealt with on the theory that what can be done is done, and assumes that the title is divided by anticipation, the essential difference between it and the Bengal joint estate would vanish. But it seems that the tendency of the decided cases, as far as the High Courts are concerned, points in that direction; and the result is, that a considerable change is being effected in the doctrines and rules of property and family relation of the Mitakshara school.

Sons have no interest in their fathers' estate according to the Dayabhaga.

It is that control of the son over his father's property, or rather the co-existent rights of father and son in the joint estate, which provoked the hostility of Jimutavahana

* Modhoo Dyal Singh *v.* Gobin Sing, 9 S. W. R., p. 511.

LECTURE IV.

and the school of Bengal. They quote* Menu and Devala to show that the son has no ownership in the ancestral estate in his father's life-time, and they deny that birth is a means of acquisition. "Besides," they proceed, "if sons have property in their father's wealth, partition would be demandable even against his consent; and there is no proof that property is vested by birth alone, nor is birth stated in the law as a means of acquisition." It is the survival of a brother, or any distant relation, which, at the demise of the owner, must constitute the acquisition of the collateral; and the same principle should also be sufficient to account for the succession of a son or a grandson to rights which did not accrue to him till relinquished by the death of his ancestors.

The joint estate according to the Dayabhaga

According to the Dayabhaga, heritage (*daya, da,* to give) involves the idea of succession to the previous, and not to the co-existing, right of another. The ownership of one man being extinct, heritage is that property, which, dependent on relation to him, arises upon his death, natural or civil. Such a theory is consistent with the maxim of English law, *nemo est hæres viventis,* and is widely different from the Mitakshara law, which is based upon the theory of the co-existent rights of the ancestor and his future heir. Partition, according to the Dayabhaga, is not the severance of joint rights to the whole into separate rights to shares, but is a division of the subject of property amongst those who are already separately entitled to it, but who jointly enjoy it; whose right is already divided into distinct shares in property which has not however been distributed and made in portions the subject of exclusive appropriation.

* 8 Menu, 410.

Under the Mitakshara system, the associated brethren take the share of their deceased brother who was joint with them by survivorship, to the exclusion of the widow; but Jimutavahana denies this right of survivorship, and says that the property of co-sharers is referred severally to unascertained *portions* of the aggregate, each co-parcener having no proprietary right to the whole.

Power of alienation.

Consistently with this view, the power of the sons to partition the joint property is denied, except upon the extinction of the father's ownership; and, then, since any one parcener is proprietor of his own wealth he can singly demand partition. While the father is owner, he can distribute either his self-acquired or his ancestral estate at his discretion, so far as his moveables and his own acquisitions are concerned; while the alienation of the ancestral estate is only fettered by a moral prohibition, which is not considered to be of sufficient weight to cut down or limit the power of alienation, which is involved in the notion of full proprietary right. If the father be, as the true construction of the Dayabhaga and the spirit of the Bengal system lead us to believe, the absolute individual owner of the ancestral as well as other estate, it would be inconsistent and contradictory to limit the power of alienation.

History of the doctrine of the father's absolute power in Bengal over the joint estate.

The fetter upon alienation imposed by Mitakshara law, in obedience to the text of Vyasa, "they who are born, they who are yet unbegotten, and they who are actually in the womb, all acquire the means of support, and the dissipation of their hereditary maintenance is censured," was disregarded by Jimutavahana, who observed that Vyasa's texts "are intended to show a moral offence: since the family is distressed by a sale, gift, or other transfer, which

LECTURE IV.

argues a disposition in the person to make an ill use of his power as owner." They are not meant to invalidate the sale or other transfer. So, likewise, other texts, like this, "though immoveables or bipeds have been acquired by a man himself, a gift or sale of them should not be made by him, unless convening all the sons," must be interpreted in the same manner. For here the words "should be made" must necessarily be understood. Therefore since it is denied that a gift or sale should be made, the precept is infringed by making one. But the gift or transfer is not null: for "a fact cannot be altered by a hundred texts." Acting upon this doctrine, the absolute power of alienation by a father even of ancestral immoveable estate was upheld as consistent with the principles of the Bengal school.

Four leading cases on the subject are cited by Mr. Macnaghten.* First,† a father by will disinherited his two elder sons in favor of the two younger, and it was decided, in 1789, that the will was operative. In the second case‡ he settled his whole ancestral zemindaree on the eldest son, subject to a pecuniary provision for the others; and it was decided in 1792, that the settlement was valid on the ground of the father's power of alienation and not merely of the impartibility of the subject. Thirdly,§ a father gave his whole ancestral estate to one son to the exclusion of the rest; and the gift was upheld in 1812. Fourthly,‖ such a gift

* Principles of Hindu Law, p. 6.

† Rushiklall Dutt and another v. Choytun Churn Dutt, cited by Sir Thomas Strange in his Elements of Hindu Law, p. 262.

‡ Eshanchund Rai v. Eshorchund Rai, Select Reports (new edition), Vol. I., p. 2.

§ Ramkoomar Neace Bachesputtee v. Kishenkinker Nieh Bhoosun, Select Reports (new edition), Vol. II., p. 52.

‖ Sham Singh v. Mussamut Umraotee, Select Reports (new edition), Vol. II., p. 92.

was declared invalid in 1813, solely because, after dispute, it was decided that the Mithila, and not the Bengal, law applied to the case. There are several cases cited by Sir Francis Macnaghten in his Considerations of Hindu Law, in which wills and deeds of gift of ancestral immoveable estate, as well as other kinds of property, were upheld. The result is that the rule of law was long ago declared to be that a Hindu in Bengal, or rather according to the doctrines of the Bengal school, may leave by will, or aliene in his life-time, his possessions, whether inherited or acquired; and the gift or legacy, whether to a son or stranger, will hold good, however reprehensible it may be as a breach of an injunction and precept.

It was, however, in the fifth case (*e*)* cited by Mr. Mac-

* Bhowannychurn Bunhoojea *v.* Heirs of Ramkant Bunhoojea, Select Reports (new edition), Vol. II., p. 259.

There was considerable perplexity at that time, *viz.*, in the early part of this century, with regard to the father's power over ancestral estate according to the school of Bengal. The fifth case referred to in the text, which temporarily overruled the previous doctrine on the subject, was of this nature.

The plaintiff sued in the Court of the 24-Pergunnahs, his father, two brothers, and the widows of a deceased brother. A short time previously, the father had partitioned, in *unequal* shares, all his estates amongst his three sons. The deed of partition was executed by the father, but not carried into effect during his life-time. He died pending the suit. The pundits declared that a father could not legally make an unequal distribution of ancestral property among his sons. With respect to acquired property, he might do so. It was also declared that possession under the deed of partition not having been obtained the deed was no evidence of right. Vyasa says that, to support a claim resulting from occupancy, five things are requisite; that it should be accompanied by a title, and that it should be long unobstructed, unimpeached, and in sight of an adverse party. The text of *Vishnu* was referred to by another pundit:—" When a father separates his sons from himself, his will regulates the division of his own acquired wealth; but in the estate inherited from the grandfather, the ownership of

LECTURE IV.

naghten, decided in 1816, that an unequal distribution made by a father amongst his sons of ancestral immoveable property

father and son is equal." Another pundit stated that the deed of partition sufficiently demonstrated the relinquishment of right on the part of the father, which, accordingly, became vested in those in whose favor the deed was executed. The deed was binding, he said, without possession; the want of possession not having proceeded from the neglect of the parties interested. Another pundit stated the deed was invalid as respects the ancestral immoveable property, but valid as respects the moveable and acquired property.

From the above it appeared that the pundits differed upon two points, whether a title under which there had not been occupancy was of no avail, unless there had been wilful neglect of the party entitled; secondly, whether an unequal distribution made by a father of his own acquired property among his sons is binding on them, unless the father, in making such unequal distribution, has been influenced by some of the motives which the law enumerates as sufficient to authorize it.

The Court decided that the deed of partition never having been carried into effect was invalid, and not binding on the parties mentioned in it.

The result of the case was a concurrence of opinion on the part of the Sudder Dewanny pundits, that a father, in the partition of ancestral immoveable property amongst his sons, is not authorized according to the Bengal school to make any unequal distribution of such property beyond one-twentieth part in favor of the eldest son.

In the case of *Essen Chund Rai* v. *Eshor Chand Rai*, no opinion had been taken from the law officers of the Sudder Court; while in the case of *Ramkoomar Naee Bachusputtee* v. *Kishenchunder Tark Bhoosun*, there was a difference of opinion amongst them, and six years after its decision, the two pundits of the Supreme Court, the pundit of the Calcutta Provincial Courts, and a pundit attached to the College of Fort William, were consulted. The following question was put:—A person, whose eldest son was alive, makes a gift to his younger of all his property, moveable and immoveable, ancestral and acquired. Is such a gift valid according to the authorities current in Bengal or not? and if it be invaild, is to be set aside or not? Their answer was: "If a father, whose eldest son is alive, make a gift to his younger of all his acquired property, moveable and immoveable, and of all the ancestral moveable property, the gift is valid, but the donor acts sinfully. If, during the life-time of an elder son, he make a gift to a younger son of all the ancestral immoveable property, such gift is not valid. Hence, if it have been made, it must be set aside. The learned have agreed that it must be set aside, because such is illegal and invalid, four pundits of distinction having declared that such was the law, and that the power of alienation only extended to moveables and self-acquired immoveables, and that even in those cases the exercise of the power was sinful. Concurring with the opinion expressed by the pundits in this last case, and combatting the reasons on which the judgments in the first three proceeded, Mr. Macnaghten came to the conclusion that the Dayabhaga could only he held to have conferred a legal power of alienating property, when such power is not expressly taken away by some other text. He argued that although a man may disregard a moral precept, yet he must be shewn to possess legal capacity to perform an act, before that act can be held to be a valid one. It was not a question whether the prohibition was moral or legal, but whether the power existed. A man had been declared to be master of his moveables and his acquisitions, and, unless prohibited, could alienate them ; but he was not master of his ancestral estate, and therefore could not alienate, even though there were no prohibition at all.

In consequence of Mr. Macnaghten's approval of the doctrine laid down in this fifth case, and disapproval of the doctrine that a Bengal father had absolute power over his ancestral immoveables, the late Supreme Court consulted

a gift is *a fortiori* invalid, inasmuch as a father cannot even make an unequal distribution among his sons of ancestral immoveable property, as he is not master of all ; as he is required by law even against his own will to make a distribution among his sons of ancestral property not recovered by himself ; as he is incompetent to distribute such property among his sons, until the mother is past child-bearing, lest a son subsequently born should be deprived of his share ; and as while he has children living, he has no authority over the ancestral property."

LECTURE IV.

the Judges of the late Sudder Dewanny Adawlut,* who, after mature consideration, declared in 1831 "that a Hindu who has sons can sell, give or pledge, without their consent, immoveable ancestral property situate in the province of Bengal; and that, without their consent, he can, by will, prevent, alter, or affect their succession to such property." They rested this opinion upon the decisions of the Court and the customs and usages of the people, one of them appealing to the authority of Mr. Colebrooke and his knowledge of the law, and of the practice and observance of the Court, in which he was for so many years the chief Judge. The Supreme Court adopted this view, also supporting it by reference to the established doctrines of the Court and the usage of Bengal.

It is now † clearly settled, beyond all further question, that the Hindu law, according to the school of Bengal, makes no distinction between ancestral and self-acquired property as respects the right of alienation by sale, gift, will or otherwise. In *Nagaluchma Ummal* v. *Gopoo Nadaraya Chetty*,‡ it was said by Lord Kingsdown,—"Throughout Bengal, a man who is the absolute owner of property may now dispose of it by will as he pleases, whether it be ancestral or not."

General observations.

Whether or not this doctrine of unlimited power of alienation is to be supported by any express texts, it seems to be consistent with the scope and object of Jimutavahana's teaching. Although he prescribes rules for distribution amongst sons, should a father choose to partition, he express-

* Shamachurn's Vyavastha Darpana, p. 568.

† See the judgment of Peacock, C. J., in Ganendra Mohan Tagore v. Upendra Mohan Tagore, 4 Bengal Law Report, O. C., p. 159.

‡ 6 Moore's I. A., p. 344.

ly lays it down that the sons have no proprietary right while the father lives, and that their right accrues at his death. Moreover, the spirit of the Dayabhaga system of property is, that the rights and responsibilities of the individual should not be lost or merged in those of the joint family. Though the sons are joint with the father, the latter has the sole proprietary right in and power over the estate, ancestral or otherwise, while he lives; and even in the case of brothers succeeding to the inheritance, as a joint and undivided family, it is not the joint title of all of them, but the separate title of each to an unascertained share that the Dayabhaga enforces and protects. The whole system of Jimutavahana is an innovation upon the communistic theories of the Mitakshara; and if the doctrines of the late Supreme or Sudder Courts, were (which is at least open to doubt) a still greater innovation, they pursued the path which the great authority of the Bengal school had already pointed out, and took another step in the direction which he had pursued.

The rules for partition cannot be insisted upon as limiting proprietary rights which are otherwise absolute. The absolute right and title of the father to the whole estate, and of each son after his death to his share, is paramount to all other considerations; and annexed to that absolute title is an unlimited power of disposition which the obligations imposed by the joint family system, whether temporal or spiritual, for the maintenance of the living or for the benefit of the dead, are unable to restrict.

The Dayabhaga and Mitakshara.

The two systems are widely opposed to one another, both in respect of the nature of the joint estate, the source of proprietary right, and also with respect to the rules of succession and the power of alienation which prevail under each

LECTURE IV.

of them. While the author of the Mitakshara insists that property vests by birth alone, Jimuṭavahana denies the correctness of that theory, and refers to the death of the relative as the means of acquisition. In the Dayabhaga, partition is denied to be a cause of property: it is ownership of a share which gives the right to call for a division and ascertain the extent of that share, and secure its separate enjoyment. According to the Mitakshara, this is not so. It is not the son's ownership of a share, but his proprietary right in the whole ancestral estate, merged in the co-equal rights of other members of the family, which gives him a right to partition. From partition there accrues to him a right to a share of the estate, in lieu of his right to the whole; and separate enjoyment .and possession result from the newly acquired individual ownership.

Hindu co-parceners, English joint tenants, andtenants-in-common compared.

The rights of the members of a joint family, in a Hindu joint property, whether under the Mitakshara or the Dayabhaga system, are essentially different from the rights which joint tenants or tenants in common possess under English law in estates which they respectively held. In fact, the Mitakshara joint property scarcely presents any points upon which a comparison between it and the English system of joint tenancy could be instituted. The inchoate rights vested in the sons by birth, indefinable as estates in the land, but which include a right to maintenance, a right to call for a partition under certain circumstances, and a right to defeat any alienation made without their concurrence, are peculiar to the Hindu system.

The tenants in common of English law may to some extent be compared with the holders of a joint estate according to the Bengal school; in that there is no entirety of interest amongst the tenants under either system, and no right of survivorship amongst them. The shares in both cases are distinct, though undivided; that is to say, there is a division of title but not of enjoyment, or of the subject of property. But in Bengal the joint holders of an estate may, and generally do, all derive their title by descent, while English tenants in common do not; a tenancy in common arising sometimes from the destruction of a previous joint tenancy, and often when two or more persons hold an estate either with interests which accrue under different titles, or under the same title (other than descent) which has accrued at different periods.

Hindu co-parceners' power to alienate their own shares of joint property.

But although there is this entirety of interest, to use an expression of English law, in each joint owner in the Mitakshara joint family, a parallel in that respect cannot be drawn between the English system of joint tenancy and the joint proprietorship of a Hindu family according to that school of law. For amongst Hindus the right of survivorship is not absolute. Though it prevails as against the widow according to the Benares doctrine, it does not prevail against the son and the grandson, who succeed to the father's share to the exclusion of the rest of the family.

The recognition of succession *per stirpes* and not *per capita* in this manner shews that, to the mind of a disciple of the Mitakshara school, some notion, though an obscure one, of a division of title was present. The extent to which this separation of title may be attended to, in respect of a joint owner's power to alienate his interest in the joint estate, tends in some degree to assimilate, in practice, the Mitakshara joint estate with that which is known in Bengal. According to the law, as it prevails in Bengal, a member of an undivided family may un-

LECTURE IV.

doubtedly aliene his share of the family property, and the only remedy of the rest of the co-sharers as against the purchaser would be to insist upon a partition. By the Benares school the title of the member of a joint family is to the whole estate, and his power to aliene that joint estate has already been discussed. According to the Mitakshara he has no title to a share until partition. But however that may be in theory, in practice he has, to some extent, for purposes of inheritance, and also, as it has sometimes been held, of alienation. It has been held* that the interest which a son takes in the father's ancestral estate under Mitakshara law is from the first a vested interest and saleable at any time.

Mr. Colebrooke too has laid it down that "a mortgage, sale or gift by one of several joint owners, without the consent of the rest, is invalid for others' shares. In Bengal law, it is clear that it is good for his own share, and for his only. In the other provinces it is as clear that the act is invalid as it concerns others' shares; and the only doubt which the subtelty of Hindu reasoning might raise, was whether it be maintainable even for his own share of undivided property." And further, his opinion appears to be in favour of the validity of an alienation by one of the sharers of his own share, for he uses the expression "the consent of the sharers, express or implied, is indispensable to an alienation of joint property beyond the share of the actual alienor, and that an unauthorized alienation by one of the sharers is invalid beyond the alienor's share as against the alienees."† And, according to the course of decisions in the

* Gourmaun Dass v. Ramsarun Dass, 5 S. W. R., p. 15.

† See 2 Strange's Hindu Law, p. 344.

Madras Supreme Court, it is said that an alienation of his share by a member of an undivided family is valid. Following those decisions, the Madras High Court has ruled to the same effect.* On the other hand, in Bombay, it has been held that, in Western India, a member of an undivided family cannot, without the consent of his co-parceners, make a gift of his share in the undivided property, or dispose of it by will.† LECTURE IV.

A Full Bench‡ of the High Court of Bengal not long ago discussed the question whether a member of a joint Hindu family, governed by the Mitakshara law, could mortgage his undivided share in a portion of the joint family property, in order to raise money on his own account, and not for the benefit of the family. There had been conflicting decisions on the subject, but the Full Bench ruled that, although one member of a joint family under that law can compel a partition against the will of his co-parceners,§ yet he had no authority to mortgage his undivided share in a portion of the joint family property, in order to raise money on his own account, and not for the benefit of the family. Authorities, both ancient and recent, were cited in favor of the view thus put forward.

And upon general principles of Hindu law, it was argued that such power of alienation could not exist. Although, it was said, according to the law of England, if there be two joint tenants, a severance is effected by one of them conveying his share to a stranger, as well as

* Virasvami Gramini *v.* Ayyavsami Gramini, 1 Madras, 471.

† See Gangubai *v.* Ramanin, 3 Bombay A. C. J., 66, and the authorities cited in a note to the report.

‡ Sadabart Prosad Sahu *v.* Foolbart Koer, 3 Bengal Law Reports, F. B., p. 39.

§ See Mitakshara, Chapter I., Section V, verse 8.

LECTURE IV.

by partition; yet joint tenants, under the English law, are in a very different position from members of a joint Hindu family under the Mitakshara law. "For instance, if a Hindu family consist of a father and three sons, any one of the sons has a right to compel a partition of the joint ancestral property; but upon partition during the life of the father, his wives are entitled to shares; and if partition is made after the death of his father, his widows are entitled to shares, and daughters are entitled to participate.* If partition is made during the life of the father, and another brother is afterwards born, that† brother alone will be entitled to succeed to the share allotted to the father upon partition; but so long as the family remains joint, and separation has not been effected, either by partition or by agreement, every son who is born becomes, upon his birth, entitled to an interest in the undivided ancestral property. In such a case, neither the father, nor any of the sons, can, at any particular moment, say what share he will be entitled to when partition takes place.

"The shares to which the members of a joint family would be entitled on partition are constantly varying by births, deaths, marriages, &c., and the principle of the Mitakshara law seems to be that no sharer, before partition, can, without the assent of all the co-sharers, determine the joint character of the property by conveying away his share. If he could do so, he would have the power by his own will, without resorting to partition, the only means known to the law for the purpose, to exclude from participation in the portion conveyed away those who, by subsequent birth, would become members of the joint family, and entitled to shares upon partition."

* See Mitakshara, Chapter VII.

† See Mitakshara, Chapter I., Section VI.

LECTURE V.

THE HINDU FAMILY.—ITS MANAGEMENT, AND LIMITS.

The Family as a Corporate Body—Its early Character—Decay of the Communal System—Position of the Manager—Liability of the Manager to the Family—Partition is the remedy for a disatisfied Member—Liability of the Manager to account—Power of each Member over the whole Joint Estate—According to the Bengal School—According to the Mitakshara—Exercise of such authority where an Infant is interested—Liability of Surviving Members for the Debts of a Deceased—The Limits of the Family Relation—The Roman Family included all who were under the same *patria potestas*—The Hindu Family includes all who give, receive and share the Pinda—Sapindas—Lineal limits of the Sapinda connection—Its Collateral Branches—Sapindaship of Women—Bandhus—Saculyas—Samánodakas.

I ENDEAVOURED, in my third lecture, to exhibit the nature of the religious usage which bind together the joint family, and also the important ceremonies which, from time immemorial, have been performed whenever a break occurs in its continuity, that is when the death of some member of it leads to a step being taken in the order of succession. Connected with this religious feeling, several topics presented themselves, including the relation of the family to its priests, the nature of the establishments for the purpose of maintaining religious services, and the law relating to *dewuttur* property, *viz.*, that portion of the estate which family or individual devotion has consecrated to the maintenance of worship, priests, and idols.

The next question to be discussed is the true character of the legal position of the joint family as a corporate body. The family as a corporate body.

LECTURE V.

The family was, and to a great extent is now, the unit of Hindu society, just as in Western nations, the individual is the unit which law regards. The shasters, however, by no means placed the family under the despotic power of its chief. The *kurta* did not possess his family and his property. He rather possessed his property through his family. His obligations outweighed his authority. The relative position in the eye of the early Hindu law of these independent corporate bodies, acting through one or more of their members, is probably now somewhat obscured. Their law has been administered by those to whom society, as an aggregation of families instead of individuals, is a thing unknown in practical experience; and besides, the social condition of Hindus themselves in that respect has, in recent history, undergone considerable transformation. When, therefore, we come to define the relation of each member, especially of the managing member, to the joint family and the joint estate, we are brought into contact with a relationship which has no counterpart in English law. Neither the term partner, nor principal, nor agent, nor even coparcener, will strictly apply. He is in fact a sort of representative owner, his independent rights being limited on all sides by the correlative rights of others, and burdened with a liability, co-extensive with his ownership, to provide for the maintenance of the family.

The notion of joint rights and duties which underlay this representative ownership, and which pervaded the communal system, is so widely different from the experience of Western nations, where the individual alone is regarded, that it is almost impossible to understand how the system can operate consistently with justice to individuals. Under such a system the family was, to use

Mr. Maine's expression, "a corporation, and its head was its representative, or we might almost say, its public officer. He enjoyed rights and stood under duties; but the rights and duties were, in the contemplation of his fellow citizens and in the eye of the law, quite as much those of the collective body as his own." There can be little doubt, I think, that under the English administration of law, the personal relations of Hindus and the nature of their rights in property have been somewhat modified; the tendency of Hindu law being to sink the individual in the family, and the tendency of the English administration of it being to insist upon individual rights and responsibilities as much as possible. The early notion of a Hindu family was probably that of a corporate body, the power of each individual member to bind the corporation or affect its position never having been very clearly defined; being chiefly controlled by the members themselves, and when that control failed, being in that case probably of a most extensive description, if we may judge from the rule which even now prevails to some extent, that the sons and grandsons of a man are bound to pay his debts whether he left assets or not. The acts of each member probably bound the corporation; and every member of it was liable since responsibility pervaded the whole family. However this may have been as matter of theory, it is only now of importance to consider to what extent in the present state of the law the members of a joint family are held to be legally responsible for the acts of any of their number.

LECTURE V.

Its early character.

At the present day the members of a Hindu family may be joint in food, worship, and estate, and at the same time each of them may acquire and possess separate estates, enjoy

Decay of the communal system.

LECTURE V.

rights, and incur obligations with which the other members have nothing to do. The separate acquisition of property by such persons is now of daily occurrence. The joint relationship may exist with regard to property, which is of infinitesimal value compared with that which belongs to each or any of the members separately. According to a text of Nareda,* before partition, brothers might not become witnesses or sureties for each other, and might not reciprocally give and receive presents or make contracts with each other, except with regard to property separately acquired. But although originally reciprocal gifts† and mutual contracts amongst them were considered to be inconsistent with their relations to one another, and although they were as coparceners debarred from‡ becoming sureties for one another, and from making mutual loans, yet such rules can hardly be considered to be law at the present day. Whatever may have been the case in the earliest times, a Hindu does not now lose his separate rights and liabilities by being a member of a joint family. The separate responsibility of any one member of an undivided family upon a contract which he has entered into in such a way, and for such purposes as do not bind his co-heirs, will be enforced, if necessary, by a partition. The principle upon which the Courts, following the suggestion of Sir T. Strange and Mr. Colebrooke, decree the satisfaction of a debt so incurred out of the share which would have come to the debtor on partition is that, as the coparcener has contracted, he ought to fulfil his contract; that it is in his power to enforce partition for his own purposes, and therefore

* Colebrooke's Digest, B. V., Chap. VI., sl. 387.

† 1 Strange's Hindu Law, p. 228.

‡ *Ibid*, p. 229.

that he should be compelled to give to his creditor the same remedies that he is entitled to himself.*

Position of the manager

The management of a joint family "regards the dealings and transactions† that are carried on under it, professedly on behalf of the family; the obligatory force of which becomes of importance alike to the members in general and to creditors. In his capacity as manager, all his acts and disbursements to be of validity, must be for the general good, if not for the immediate and indispensable maintenance of the whole; for objects chargeable on the common stock, including works of piety, which it concerns all, should not go unperformed; with this difference that when his acts have been for the support of the family, the charge is, *in its nature,* binding upon the joint property, though the remedy may eventually be against him only by whom it was incurred, so acting: whereas, if in the course of trade, or for charitable purposes, in order to its being so binding, it must have had the consent of the rest, expressed or implied. Accordingly, it imports creditors to take notice, whether the family with which they are about to deal or contract be divided or undivided; and if the latter, at their peril to see that the transaction be one by which the rest of the co-heirs will be concluded; since otherwise he only with whom it has been entered into will be answerable for it, and not the common stock."

Debts for necessaries, or for the nuptials of any of the family, are chargeable on the common fund so long as the expenses attending them have been reasonable according to

* Palanivelappa Kaundan *v.* Mannaru Naikan and another, 2 Madras High Court Reports, p. 416.

† 1 Strange's Hindu Law, p. 199.

LECTURE V.

the usage and means of the family.* Contracted fairly for the use of the family, by whatsoever member of it, it binds the whole; but if unreasonably or extravagantly contracted, it binds him alone who incurred it,† unless adopted by the rest. In short, as soon as any limit is set at all, to the joint liability for the acts of one, the obvious principle to apply is, that those acts should be *bonâ fide* performed, and should be reasonably within the scope of the authority of the member so acting, to be implied from the circumstance that he has acted for the advancement of the common good.

Liability of the manager to the family.

Such being the limit to the powers which are conferred upon the managing member of a joint Hindu family by virtue of his position, there is the further question of the extent to which he incurs a legal liability to the rest of the family for the manner in which he exercises them. It has been suggested that he is not, by reason of his occupying that position, bound to render any accounts whatever to the members of the family. "There is no analogy whatever," it is said, "in this respect between the members of a joint Hindu family and the members of a partnership. Each partner is the agent of the other, bound by his contract to protect and further the interests of his co-partners, unless

* 1 Strange's Hindu Law, p. 167.

† See Jagannatha's Digest, Book I., sl. 207, 208, 209. *Yajnavalkya.*—Neither shall a wife or mother be in general compelled to pay a debt contracted by her husband or son, nor a father to pay a debt contracted by his son, unless it were for the behoof of the family: nor a husband to pay a debt contracted by his wife. *Vishnu.*—Neither shall a wife or mother be in general compelled to pay the debt of her husband or son, nor the husband or son to pay the debt of his wife or mother. *Nareda.*—A debt contracted by the wife shall by no means bind the husband, unless it were for necessaries at a time of great distress; a man is indispensably bound to support his family. A wife or mother shall not in general pay the debt of her husband or son.

relieved from that responsibility by special arrangement; and each partner is entitled to consume, on his own account, no more of the partnership property than the share of the profits. If he exceeds this, he becomes immediately a debtor to the concern. But in a Hindu family, it is wholly different. No obligation exists on any one member to stir a finger, if he does not feel so disposed, either for his own benefit or for that of the family: if he does do so, he gains thereby no advantage; if he does not do so, he incurs no responsibility, nor is any member restricted to the amount of the share which he is to enjoy prior to the division. A member of the joint family has only a right to demand, that a share of the existing family property should be separated and given to him: and so long as the family union remains unmodified, the enjoyment of the family property is in the strictest sense common; as against each other, the members of the family have no rights whatever, except that I have mentioned, and the only remedy for a dissatisfied member is by partition. But this relation is purely a voluntary one. Like many other relations which are of frequent occurrence, the law has ascertained and defined, or attempted to ascertain and define, what it is in its unmodified form; but it has not imposed on any family the necessity of adopting that relation, or of adopting it in its modified form only: it is therefore capable of being modified in every way, and is frequently modified either by the concurrent will of the family or by the will of the ancestor from whom the property is derived."*

Partition is the remedy for a dissatisfied member.

Partition therefore is asserted to be the only remedy for a dissatisfied member of a joint family, that is, one who is

* S. M. Runganmani Dasi *v.* Kasinath Dutt, *per* Markby, J., 3 B. L. R., O. C., 4.

LECTURE V.

dissatisfied with the mode in which the family resources are *in good faith* jointly applied and enjoyed. Partners have a right to enjoy the fruits of their adventure in certain definite shares; and hence they are accountable to one another in respect of those shares. But joint family property, according to the true theory of Hindu law, is one and undivided, both in title and in fact. The title, possession, and enjoyment were originally all common, and remain so now under the Mitakshara system; and where the practice of the family accords with the theory of its constitution, there will be no right to an account, at least for the purpose of rectifying any inequality there may have been in the previous enjoyment by the parties of their joint property. But law is daily penetrating within the family, and assuming to regulate the relative rights of its members. According to the Bengal school, the members are entitled to separate shares before partition, that is, they have each a separate title to a share of which the possession and enjoyment are common. Though, as a rule, the right to the particular account described above as between themselves does not accrue to each member from the family relationship, yet that family relationship is in practice often modified, especially where the family is employed in the joint acquisition of property, as well as in its joint enjoyment. The circumstances of each case must be examined; and if the intention was that there should be partnership rights and accountability, such intention would govern the relationship between them.

Liability of the manager to account.

But although the Courts will not interfere to rectify what I may term past inequality of enjoyment of the common stock as between the coparceners, yet there is in several cases a right to an account between them, and the *kurta* or any other member who interferes therewith is not without his responsibility.* "He is entitled to obtain credit from his coparceners for all sums of money *bonâ fide* spent by him for the benefit of the joint family, and he is certainly liable to make good to them their shares of all sums which he has actually misappropriated, or which he has spent for purposes other than those in which the joint family was interested. Of course, no member of a joint family is liable to his coparceners for anything which might have been actually consumed by him, in consequence of his having a larger family to support, or of his being subject to greater expenses than others; but this is simply because all such expenses are justly considered to be the legitimate expenses of the whole family. Thus, for instance, one member of a joint Hindu family may have a larger number of daughters to marry than the others. The marriage of each of those daughters to a suitable bridegroom is an obligation incumbent upon the whole family so long as it continues to be joint, and the expenses incurred on account of such marriage must necessarily be borne by all the members, without any reference whatever to their respective interests in the family estate." A reference was made in the case in which the above remarks were delivered to a Full Bench of the High Court at Calcutta whether the managing member of a joint Hindu family can be sued by the other members for an account. They ruled that he could, and the Chief Justice in his judgment made the following remarks:—"The members of a joint Hindu family are entitled to the family property, subject to such dispositions of it as the managing

* Obhoy Chunder Roy Chowdry *v.* Pearee Mohun Goho, *per* Mitter, J., 13 S. W. R., F. B., p. 75.

LECTURE V.

member is entitled to make either by virtue of the power which is given to him by law as manager, or of the power that may be given to him by consent of the other members of the family. Subject to the exercise of these powers and to any disposition of any portion of the family property which may have been made by virtue of them, the other members of the family are clearly interested in that property. It appears to me that the principle upon which the right to call for an account rests is not the existence of a direct agency or of a partnership where the managing partner may be considered as agent for his co-partners. It depends upon the right which the members of a Hindu family have to a share of the property; and where there is a joint interest in the property, and one party receives all the profits, he is bound to account to the other parties who have an interest in it for the profits of their respective shares, after making such deductions as he may have the right to make. That appears to me to be the right principle, and it is the principle upon which the English Courts of Equity act in the case of joint tenants and tenants-in-common, and not merely in cases of partners."

Power of each member over the whole joint estate, according to the Bengal school.

With regard to the power of each member of an undivided family to aliene the joint estate, a passage of Vyasa declares that "even one sharer may make a gift, mortgage, or sale of immoveables, in a time of distress, for the benefit of the family, and especially for religious purposes." It was held,* on the authority of this text, that according to the Bengal school a conveyance of the whole undivided property executed by the managing co-sharer, without the

* Prannath Dass v. Calishunker Ghosal, Select Reports (Bengal), new edition, Vol. I., p. 60.

consent of co-sharers, while he was in confinement on account of his inability to pay a balance of revenue due to the zemindar, was valid. It is to be observed,* however, that Jagannatha, in his Digest, considers that a sale or transfer by one sharer is valid, so far as concerns the seller's own share, but not so for the shares of his co-heirs who do not consent.† Jimutavahana also denies that one person has the power to make sale or other transfer of property held in coparcenary. He allows to the father an absolute power of alienation independent of his sons, and to a co-heir an absolute power to aliene his share without the consent of his co-heirs. According to the Bengal school, as a general rule, a coparcener‡ can only aliene his own share; if ever his authority extends to aliene the whole estate, without the consent of other sharers who were capable of consenting, it only arises under very exceptional circumstances; as for example when he is in entire possession of the patrimony, and conducts the affairs of a family like a father. In such a case he would be regarded as the agent and representative of the co-heirs, and his alienation of the estate for the benefit of the family would bind them, on the ground of their implied consent. But inasmuch as, according to the Bengal school, the right of a coparcener is a separate right to an unascertained share, and not a joint right to the whole as under the Mitakshara, the authority of one member of an undivided family to dispose of the shares of the others can only arise under most exceptional circumstances.

* See note to above case.

† See the Dayabhaga, C. II., s. 27.

‡ See opinion of Mr. Colebrooke, in 2 Strange's Hindu Law, p. 344.

LECTURE V.

According to the Mitakshara.

The power of a joint owner to make a valid alienation of joint property beyond his own interest in it, arises more readily under the Mitakshara. The consent of the other joint owners, expressed or implied, is equally indispensable; but it will be presumed under a variety of circumstances, especially[*] where the management of the joint property entrusted to the part owner who disposes of it, implies a power of disposal; or where he was the only ostensible or avowed owner; and generally, when the acts or even the silence of the other sharers have given him a credit, and the alienee had not had notice. It has been held by the Madras High Court that, in the absence of evidence to the contrary, it will be presumed that where the manager of a joint family mortgages the joint estate, he does so for a debt contracted for family purposes and the mortgage will bind all the adult members of the family. In fact, when all the members of the family have attained majority, they become bound, if a knowledge or reasonable means of knowledge by them of the transaction appears, or an acceptance by them of any benefit under it.

Exercise of such authority where an infant is interested.

The existence of an infant member of the joint family, at the time of the alienation, makes the Court watch more carefully the exercise of authority over the estate. In that case it must be proved that the debt was contracted *bonâ fide* for the benefit of the family. In estimating the power of the managing member to aliene under such circumstances, it is necessary to attend to the rule laid down by the Privy Council,[*] *viz.*, " the power of a manager for an

* Tandavaráya Mudali *v.* Valli Ammal, 1 Madras High Court Reports, p. 398.

† Hunoomanpersad Panday *v.* Mussumat Babooee Munraj Koonwar, 6 Moore's I. A., p. 393; and Weekly Reporter (1864), p. 285.

infant heir, to charge an estate not his own, is, under the Hindu law, a limited and qualified power. It can only be exercised rightly in a case of need or for the benefit of the estate. But where, in the particular instance, the charge is one that a prudent owner would make in order to benefit the estate, the *bonâ fide* lender is not affected by the precedent mismanagement of the estate. The actual pressure on the estate, the danger to be averted, or the benefit to be conferred upon it, in the particular instance, is the thing to be regarded."

LECTURE V.

Liability of surviving members for the debts of a deceased.

Lastly, with regard to the liability of survivors for the debts of the deceased, the debt of the ancestor imposes an obligation on his descendants, which in Bengal, however, is only binding in a moral sense, having no legal force independent of assets.* Jagannatha in his Commentary thus discusses the question of the son's liability for his father's debts. "Suppose a man whose son is an infant, and whose wife has contracted a debt jointly with her husband, but he dies, and the son inherits his property; in that case, by whom should the debt be paid? By the son alone, for he is under a double obligation to discharge the debt; *under a civil obligation,* because he holds assets; *under a moral obligation,* because he is son of the deceased. But if the debtor leave no assets, what should follow? It is replied that the son ought nevertheless to pay the debt; for redemption from debt is stated as the benefit arising from male offspring alone."

It is fully established that the assets of a deceased Hindu may be followed by creditors into the hands both of heirs and of strangers, the obligation to pay

* See Colebrooke's Dgiest, B. I., C. V., verse 211.

LECTURE V.

attaching not upon the death only of the ancestor, but on his becoming an anchoret, or having been so long absent from home as to let in a presumption of death.‡ But it was ruled by the High Court of Bombay § that, according to the doctrine of the Maharashtra school, which in this respect supports the doctrine of the Mitakshara, the grandson of a Hindu is bound to pay the debts of his grandfather, whether he had assets or not, but without interest. The text of Brihaspati was referred to, that the sons must pay the debt of their father when proved, as if it were their own, that is with interest; the son's son must pay the debt of the grandfather, but without interest, and his son, that is the great-grandson, shall not be compelled to discharge it unless he be heir and have assets. The rule of law according to the Mayukha‖ is that the debts of the ancestor are not to be paid by the great-grandson, the wife, or the others, if they have not taken the estate. To this slight extent, therefore, a limit is assigned to the collective responsibility of the family for the debt of one; but it is added that this receipt of ever so small a portion of the estate imposes the liability of liquidating the debt to whatever amount. For there is no such law as that payment shall follow only on receipt of property equal or more than equal to the debts to be paid.

The limits of the family relation.

In concluding this sketch of the constitution of a Hindu family, and before I proceed to define the legal position of its individual members, it remains to ascertain the limits to which the family relation extends. In a state of society in which the family is a corporate body of so much importance,

* 1 Strange's Hindu Law, p. 166.

† 2 Bombay High Court Reports, p. 64; 1 Strange, 167.

‡ See the Vyavahara Mayukha, Chap. V., Sec. IV., verses 12, 16, & 17.

its boundaries must be ascertained in some artificial manner, and the line drawn which separates the family from the kindred. The principle on which this separation is made, and on which proximity of relationship within and without the family is calculated, is the very basis of the system which binds the society together. In the earlier periods of Roman history, their system was more highly artificial than anything to which I shall have to call your attention as existing amongst Hindus. It is the tendency of the artificial system to give way as the ties of the strictly family relationship weaken; but the tie of *agnatio*, founded upon the ancient principle of the *patria potestas*, survived through the whole period of Roman history, and bound the *familia* together. So, amongst the Hindus, the tie of the *pinda*, or funeral cake, has been from the earliest times of which we have any record, and is at the present moment the bond of union between the members of the family, sanctioned alike by law and religion. To ascertain the nature of this tie and the manner in which it connects together those whom it reaches, is essential for the purpose of understanding the Hindu law of inheritance and system of society.

The Roman family included all who were under the same *patria potestas*.

Nature imposes the single tie of blood relationship, and every civilized nation adds that of marriage. Matrimony is the basis on which an English family rests, and the relative rights of husband and wife and parent and child are the only subjects which in dealing with private rights it affords for consideration. The Roman *familia* extended over a wider area, and the tie of *agnatio* comprehended all who were or might have been included under the sway of the same father. All such were agnates of each other. They included wife, sons, and daughters, and grandchildren in the male line of both sexes, and also the children, if any,

LECTURE V.

in the male line in the succeeding generations; but originally it excluded the married daughters and married granddaughters, for they had passed by marriage beneath another *patria potestas*, and were therefore no longer the agnates of the *familia* in which they were born. So also a son, who was emancipated, or who had been adopted into another family, lost his relationship of agnation. In the time of Justinian, the tie of *agnatio* came to be regarded as more indissoluble, and then the agnates included all who were related to one another through males. The married females and the sons who had been adopted into other families remained the agnates of the family of their birth; though, of course, their descendants were excluded.

Now the principle upon which a limitation is artificially set to the tie of blood, and a certain number of kindred selected to form a *familia*, is simple enough to understand. All the descendants of any married pair, however distant may be the pair from which we commence our calculation, are connected by blood relationship, that is, are the cognates of one another without regard to the circumstance of the descent being traceable through a male or a female line. Practically, and for ordinary purposes, such for example as the ascertaining the prohibited degrees within which marriage may be contracted, we do not go many generations back, in order to find a married pair from whom to trace the descent of cognates. But having done so, by merely laying down the principle that *mulier est finis familiæ*, and that her children belong to the family of her husband, the tie of *agnatio* binds only those who trace a descent through the male line, and are or have been or may have been governed by the same *patria potestas*. The daughter, or other female descendant in the male line, who has married, or the son or other male descendant in the male line who has been adopted by a stranger, may, according to the later Roman legislation, remain agnates, but their descendants belong exclusively to the family which has been obtained by either marriage or adoption.

LECTURE V.

The Hindu family includes all who give, receive, and share the *pinda*.

In Hindu law the family is selected from the kindred on an entirely different principle, but with, of course, a somewhat similar result. As the *patria potestas* was the bond of union in the Roman family, the limits to which the family extended being exactly conterminous with the boundaries which confined the authority of the father; so, amongst Hindus, the *pinda*, or funeral cake, is the connecting link which binds the family together. The difference is between an alliance by subjection, whether past or present, to the same *patria potestas;* or an alliance by reason of offering funeral oblations to a common ancestor. We must enquire, therefore, into the nature and extent of that alliance, and how far the obvious expedient of excluding the female who has been transferred to another family by marriage, and the son who has been transferred by adoption, has been resorted to in finding a limit to the family.

The kindred from whom the family is selected are of course ascertained in precisely the same way, whatever people we refer to for the sake of illustration. Cognation denotes a natural tie; and it is a relative term. The degree of relationship which is signified depends upon the nearness or remoteness in the scale of ascent of the particular married pair with whom we commence our calculations; but it includes all who can trace a common descent. For the purpose of ascertaining the degrees of kinship or affinity within which a Hindu marriage is prohibited, we go back to the seventh degree, and all who trace a common descent come within the degrees which are affected by the prohibition.

The primary idea of a Hindu *gotra,* or family, is that it includes all who are *sapinda* to each other. To understand this relationship thoroughly is important, for it underlies all the rules of law which regulate at least in Bengal the succession to the estate of a deceased Hindu.

The relation of *sapinda* is of two descriptions,—through consanguinity and connection by funeral oblations. The former means connection by containing a portion of the same body. And according to the Mitakshara, *Achara kánda* "whenever the word *sapinda* is used, there consanguinity must be known to exist directly or indirectly."* But although the lawyers of the Benares school occasionally use the word in the sense of denoting mere consanguinity, yet amongst them, as also amongst those of the Bengal school, the word *sapinda,* in its ordinary meaning, denotes connection through the *pinda* or funeral cake.

Sapindas.

The definition of *sapinda* may be taken from the words of Mr. Justice Dwarkanath Mitter in his judgment delivered in the case of *Amrita Kumari Debi* v. *Lakhinarayan Chuckerbutty,*† in which the position of sister's son, as a *bandhu,* and therefore as an heir, was declared. He says: "It is a well known principle of Hindu law, recognized in all the schools current in the country, that the relation of *sapinda* exists not only between the immediate giver and the immediate recipient of funeral oblations, but also between those who

* See Shamachurn's Vyavastha Darpana, p. 889.

† 2 Bengal Law Reports, F. B., p. 33.

are bound to offer them to a common ancestor or ancestors. This principle is based upon the theory according to which a Hindu is supposed to participate after his death in the funeral oblations that are offered by any one of his surviving relations to some common ancestor, to whom he himself was bound to offer them while living; and hence it is that the man who gives the oblations and the man who receives them, and the man who participates in them, are all recognized as *sapindas* of each other. Thus, for example, brothers are not required to perform the obsequies of each other, but they are nevertheless *sapindas*, being connected with each other through the medium of the oblation which they are respectively bound to offer to their common ancestors. The same rule holds good in the case of the brother's son, and in fact of every *sapinda* who does not stand in a direct line of ascent or descent with the deceased proprietor himself."

Connection through the *pinda*, therefore, denotes relationship through giving, receiving or participating in funeral oblations offered to a deceased ancestor. The common root of *sapindas*, that is the degree in the scale of ascent from which a family of *sapindas* starts, is the third from the living proprietor. From the earliest period of Hindu history the obligation to present funeral offerings extended to the ancestor in three degrees.* "To three," says Menu, "must libations of water be made, to three must oblations of food be presented; the fourth in descent is the giver of those offerings, but the fifth has no concern with them." A Hindu, therefore, is bound to offer funeral oblations to his father, grandfather, and great-grandfather; and also in

* 1 Menu, p. 186.

LECTURE V.

right of his mother, and in the fulfilments of duties of *sapindaship* which she is disqualified from discharging, but which she owes to her ancestors, he must also offer funeral oblations to her father, grandfather, and great-grandfather in the male line.

In his turn he is entitled to receive those oblations from his son, his grandson, and his great-grandson in the male line, and also from his daughter's son, who offers them in right of his mother.

Lineal limits of the Sapinda connection.

So far with regard to the direct line, the limits of the relationship include seven degrees, three in ascent and three in descent from the living proprietor in the male line. It differs from the agnatic relationship in at least two important particulars, namely, that there is a limit imposed both in the scale of ascent and descent beyond which you cannot trace this connection; and, secondly, the principle of *mulier est finis familiœ* is not observed, but the woman's duties of *sapindaship* devolve upon her son, and he is for those purposes included in his maternal family. But her sons are her only descendants who derive from her the connection through the *pinda* with her family; her daughters and her son's sons and daughters are all excluded.

Its collateral branches.

Then as respects collateral branches, connection by the *pinda* depends upon the same principle, and we have to ascertain who amongst them are bound to offer oblations to the same ancestor. For example, the proprietor's brothers and their sons and grandsons all offer oblation to the father of the proprietor, and therefore, they are included amongst his *sapindas*. His paternal uncles, again, and their sons and grandsons offer to his grandfather and great-grandfather; so also the brothers of his grandfather and their sons and grandsons offer to his great-grandfather. There is a limit, therefore, in all directions, lineally and collaterally, to the connection between kindred by means of the funeral cake. The nearness or remoteness of that connection is measured by the nearness or remoteness of the common ancestor whose obsequies such kindred are bound to perform.

Sapindaship. of women.

The place which women occupy in reference to *sapindaship* is, perhaps, somewhat singular. They are the *sapindas* of all with whom their brothers are *sapindas*. But their duties devolve upon their sons, who stand in their place, and are bound to offer funeral cakes to their fathers, grandfathers, and great-grandfathers. Such sons, in consequence, include as their *sapindas* all with whom their mothers' brothers are *sapindas*, but they do not transmit to their descendants the duties or the connection, which terminate with them.

Bandhus.

Sapindas thus connected through a female are an exception to the otherwise exclusively agnatic character of the *sapinda* relationship. They are called *bandhus*, *i. e.*, kinsmen sprung from a different family but allied by funeral oblations.* These, according to the Mitakshara, are of three kinds: *i. e.*, *bandhus* to the person himself, to his father; or to his mother. The author of the Commentary then cites a text, either of Baudhyána or of Vriddha Satapa, which contains the following enumeration: "The sons of his own father's sister, the sons of his own mother's sister, and the sons of his own maternal uncle, must be considered as his own cognate kindred. The sons of his father's paternal aunt, the sons of his father's maternal aunt, and the sons of the father's mater-

* Mitakshara, Chap. II., Sec. VI.

LECTURE V. nal uncle, must be deemed his father's cognate kindred. The sons of his mother's paternal aunt, the sons of his mother's maternal aunt, and the sons of his mother's maternal uncles must be reckoned his mother's cognate kindred." Such enumeration, if exhaustive, would confine the *sapinda* relationship through a female to those only who belong to the same degree or generation, limiting it simply to cousinship in the same degree. It is impossible, however, to believe that the relationship can have been intended to be so restricted, or that those in a man's own degree or generation should be regarded as *bandhus* to him, but that those in the degree above or below him, should be regarded as strangers to him, though *bandhu* respectively to his father or son. The Privy Council, in the case of *Gridhari Lal Roy* v. *Government of Bengal,** has treated this restriction as arbitrary and inconsistent with the definition as given in the Mitakshara. They ruled that the maternal uncle was *bandhu* to the deceased, and the Full Bench of the High Court, by the judgment of Mr. Justice Mitter above referred to, and delivered before the arrival of the Privy Council decision, ruled that the sister's son of the deceased stood in the same relationship of *bandhu.* The Privy Council referred to the Viramitrodya as a treatise of high authority at Benares, and properly receivable as an exposition of what may have been left doubtful by the Mitakshara, and declaratory of the law of the Benares school. With regard to the law of Bengal upon the subject,† there never was any doubt.

Bandhus, therefore, even under Mitakshara law, are not

* 1 Bengal Law Reports, P. C., p. 51.

† See the Dayabhaga, Chap. XI., Sect. VI., verses 13, 14.

Lecture V.

merely to be sought amongst* those who are in the same degree of relationship but also in the one above or below it. The specific enumeration should be taken as affording examples of the class. In general, all *sapindas* who trace their connection through a female are *bandhus* to one another. They are necessarily a limited class, for the *pinda* relationship through a female terminates with her son.

Saculyas.

The cognates above the fourth degree in ascent, *i. e.,* above the great-grandfather of the living proprietor, and also below his great-grandson, are not included in the list of his *sapindas.* But the great-grandfather was himself, when alive, the centre of a circle of *sapindas* which upwards included three generations of such ancestors, and extended downwards to include the living proprietor. Those three male ancestors in the degrees above the great-grandfather are not, however, *sapindas* of the living proprietor, but stand towards him in a relationship denominated *saculyas.* They were *sapindas* to the same person in a line of ascent or descent, *i. e.,* the *sapindas* of grandfather and are therefore *saculyas* of each other. *Saculyas,* or distant kinsmen,§ are those who share the divided oblation, *i. e.,* who share the remains of the oblation wiped off with *kusá* grass. They include, therefore, the three generations above and below those whom I have previously described as the *sapindas* of the living proprietor. They are the cognates upon the same principles as are applied to determine,

* Colebrooke's Digest, B. V., C. VIII., Sec. I., verse 435. "The fourth person and the rest share the remains of the oblation wiped off with *kusa* grass; the father and the rest share the funeral cakes; the seventh person is the giver of oblations; the relation of *sapindas,* or men connected by the funeral cake, extends therefore to the seventh person, or sixth degree of ascent or descent."

LECTURE V. selected within those limits the relationship of *sapinda.* Such *saculyas* are also termed his *sapindas* for purpose of mourning, and in case of impurity by reason of a kinsman's death;* but not in respect of the funeral cakes.

Samanodakas.

Last in order come the class of *samanodakas,* or kindred connected by a common libation of water, and they must be understood to reach to seven degrees beyond the kindred connected by funeral oblation of food; or else, as far as the limits of knowledge as to birth and name extend. According to the text of the Mitakshara,† "if there be none such" (alluding kindred of the same family connected by funeral oblations) "the succession devolves on kindred connected by libations of water; and they must be understood to reach to seven degrees beyond the kindred connected by funeral oblations of food; or else, as far as the limits of knowledge as to birth and name extend. Accordingly, Vrihat Menu says, the relation of the *sapindas,* or kindred connected by the funeral oblation, ceases with the seventh person; and that of *samanodakas,* or those connected by a common libations of water, extends to the fourteenth degree, or, as some affirm, it reaches as far as the meaning of birth and name extends, this is signified by *gotra* or the relation of family name."

* See Mitakshara, Chap. II., Sec. VI., verse 6.

† See Shamachurn's Vyavastha Darpana, p. 305.

LECTURE VI.

THE MEMBERS OF THE FAMILY--MAINTENANCE AND GUARDIANSHIP.

Position of the Kurta—Right to Maintenance—Power to aliene the Family Estate to provide Maintenance—The Joint Right to Maintenance—The various Rights of Maintenance—The Widow's Right—Amount of Maintenance assigned to a Widow—Widow's Right to live in the Family-house—The Wife, Sons, and Grandsons—The Daughter-in-law—The Stepmother—General Observations—Guardianship—Position of Women—Paternal Male Kindred preferred as Guardians—The Mother's Claim recognized at the present time—Paternal Grandmother preferred to the Stepmother—Recent Legislation.

THE object of the last three lectures has been to explain the character of the institution known as the Hindu joint family, and the nature of the tie, social and religious, by which it is bound together, and also the view which the law, as at present administered, takes of it in determining the relations of each member to the whole family, in respect of what may be termed his representative ownership of the family estates. The relative rights and duties of the members of the family must form the next subject of attention.

So long as the family retained in its full force the corporate character which was originally assigned to it in the Hindu system, law did not readily penetrate within its precincts. The relative duties imposed by the shasters were numerous, and regarded all the affairs of life. The rules so prescribed could not have been originally intended

LECTURE VI.

to be minutely observed. They were probably such as the priestly order considered proper to be observed. The distinction between moral and religious obligations on the one hand, and those enforced by definite legal sanctions on the other, belongs to a later period of national life than that in which the early Rishis flourished; but it must, nevertheless, be considered that many of the precepts of the shasters were addressed to the conscience of the individual rather than dictated as laws to the community.

Position of the kurta.

In the description of the celebrated ceremonial which Hindu devotion has created in honor of ancestors and for the fulfilment of filial obligations, in performing which the father of the family enters upon his new position, and assumes the place of *kurta,* we see the character of his obligations to those who have gone before him and of his dependence upon those who may come after him. Whilst he lives, he alone, in respect of his sonship, that is to the exclusion of his own sons and grandsons, can perform the obsequies. His brothers, and failing them, their sons or grandsons, have an equal right with himself, and are under an equal obligation with himself, whether joint or separate, to perform those obsequies.* But so long as he lives, the offerings of either his son or his grandson would have no efficacy, and the same rule applies to his brother. It is the son, or *puttra,*† says Vrihaspati, who delivers his father from the hell called *put,* even by the sight of his countenance.

* See 2 Strange's Hindu Law, p. 285. The correct rule, according to the opinion of Mr. Colebrooke, is that all the brothers, whether by the same or different mothers, should meet and perform together the funeral rites and ceremonies of their deceased father, from his burning till the sixteenth day from his death; the expense to be borne in common. All future ones should be performed by each separately.

† Colebrooke's Digest, B. V., C. IV., Sec. XV., verse 304.

On him, say Menu and Vrihaspati, he devolves the burden of debt, by him he procures immortality, through him he joyfully becomes exonerated from every debt to living progenitors. "Heaven is not for him who leaves no male progeny," but the son who goes as a pilgrim to Gaya conveys his father beyond the region of horror.

If the deceased left several sons, the eldest takes entire possession, as the new *kurta* of the joint family. The others may live under him, with their families, as they lived under their father, unless they choose to be separated. The title of the eldest prevails, because it is through him that the father discharged his debt to his ancestors. Whilst* the elder lives, the rest are not independent; but seniority, say the shasters, is founded both on virtue and age.

Right to maintenance.

With regard to the right to be maintained, the general principle is, as laid down by Mr. Ellis, that as long as† the family continues undivided, all the parceners, their wives and families, are entitled to a joint maintenance: on division, widows, wives, and children can claim only on the portion of their respective husbands and fathers. The necessity of providing for that joint maintenance extends to confer on an adult parcener a power of sale over all or a sufficient portion of the joint estate. The performance of obsequies and the maintenance of the dependent members of the family are the two primary duties of a Hindu. It is declared that the approved means of reaching heaven is to support those who should be maintained, and that hell is the portion of that man whose family is afflicted with pain by his neglect; there-

* Colebrooke's Digest, B. II., C. IV., S. I., verse 15.

† 2 Strange's Hindu Law, p. 291.

LECTURE VI.

fore, it is added, let him maintain his family with the utmost care. They who are born, says Nareda, or yet unborn, and they who exist in the womb require funds for subsistence; the deprivation of the means of subsistence is reprehended.*

Power to aliene the family estate to provide maintenance.

This obligation to provide for the maintenance of the joint family is the foundation of the father's authority over the joint estate. By the law of the Mitakshara,† which prevails over all of India, except so far as it is in Bengal superseded on various points by the doctrines of the Dayabhaga, his sons have rights co-equal with his own in the ancestral property of the family, whatever be its nature, whether moveable or immoveable; and also in any immoveable property acquired by himself. It is in the power of the son, equally with the father, to compel partition or the delivery up of a divided share in the joint estate, even though the birth of more sons is still a possibility. But the necessity of providing for the maintenance of the dependent members of the family will operate to confer upon the father a power of disposition commensurate with that necessity.

But in Bengal, the doctrine of Jimutavahana prevails, who argues from the text of Nareda‡ "let sons regularly divide the wealth when the father is dead;" and of Menu,‡ "after the death of father and mother, the assembled brethren must divide§ equally the paternal estate; for they have not power

* 1 Colebrooke's Digest, B. II., C. IV., S. I., verses 11, 12.

† See the Mitakshara., Chap. I., Sec. V.; and also Chap. I., Sec. I., verse 27, and see verse 28. Even a single individual may conclude a donation, mortgage, or sale of immoveable property, during a season of distress, for the sake of the family, and especially for pious purposes.

‡ See the Dayabhaga, Chap. I.

§ 9 Menu, 104.

over it, while their parents live," and of Devala, "when the the father is deceased, let the sons divide the father's wealth, for sons have not ownership while the father is alive and free from defects;" that the sons have no vested interest in the joint estate during the life-time of their father, but upon his decease. Therefore, amongst the followers of the Bengal school, the proprietary rights of the father, both over his ancestral, as well as his acquired estate, are not restricted or impeded in their exercise by the rival interests of his sons. But, at the same time, there is this limitation to the father's power, morally, though not legally, over his estate. Vrihaspati says that a man may give away, *i. e.*, has an absolute power of disposition over what remains after his family are clothed and fed: the giver of more, who leaves his family naked and unfed, may taste honey at first, but shall afterwards find it poison. The validity of such gift, if made, is recognized in Bengal, "for a fact cannot be altered by a hundred texts," but it would be at the expense of the moral, and in some cases of the legal, duty of maintaining the members of the family, which is the first temporal obligation of the Hindu.

The joint right to maintenance.

Under the Mitakshara system, sons, grandsons, and great-grandsons must all of them be maintained out of the joint estate, for all have an interest in it. It would appear that this right to be so maintained extends to every member of the joint family, and the dependents of each member. The adulterous wife, the man excluded from inheritance, the illegitimate offspring in whatever caste must all be maintained.* The Privy Council has de-

* Colebrooke's Digest, B. II., C. IV., S. II., verse 18.

LECTURE VI. cided* that the illegitimate son, even of a man of the three regenerate tribes, is entitled to maintenance. No other claims take precedence; even sacrifice is mockery, if to the injury of the dependent members of the family; for he "who leaves his family naked and unfed, may taste honey at first, but shall afterwards find it poison." The moral duty is thus referred to in a text: "As the suspended water-pot," says Devala,† "matures the *pippala* tree, so a father, grandfather, and great-grandfather cherish a son from the moment of his birth with honey, flesh-meat, pot-herbs, milk, and milky food, reflecting he will give us the annual *shraddha*."

So also when partition has been effected, the right to be maintained still exists. When the parceners separate, each parcener becomes, under ordinary circumstances, the head of a new joint family, consisting of his wife or wives, his children and their wives, and they are all entitled to a joint maintenance, out of what, by reason of the separation, has become the joint fund exclusively appropriated to them. Such right to maintenance by each member, out of the joint estate, springs directly from the nature of a joint family with its incidents of a community in food, worship, and estate. So long as the family live together in possession of joint estate, the dependent members cannot be excluded.

But, on the other hand, when disputes arise, when dependent members leave the joint dwelling, or when there remains no joint estate, the right to be maintained and the means of enforcing it, under such circumstances, is a subject not yet clearly defined. The right may be

* Mutuswamy Jagavera Yettappa Naiken v. Venkataswara Yettappa, 2 Bengal Law Reports, P. C., p. 15.

† Murdun Singh v. Purhalad Singh, 7 Moore's I. A., p. 18.

only a moral one, incapable of being enforced; or it may be a legal one, and in that case either limited by the existence of joint estate or enforceable by action independently of there being any joint estate; and further the joint fund may either be indicated as the source of payment, or a right to maintenance out of it may be a charge upon it which may follow it into the hands of a purchaser.

The various rights of maintenance.

To distinguish the various classes of rights to maintenance is a task which has not yet been accomplished by judicial decision. Probably the only persons in whose hands the estate would be actually subject to a charge for maintenance, which would follow it into the hands of a purchaser, would be those who take as substituted heirs in respect of the maintenance of those whom they exclude. The brother or brother's son, and sons under Mitakshara law, and the son and son's son and so on, under all the schools of law, take in substitution for the widow, who is nevertheless "half the body of her husband," but excluded by sex from her position as next heir. So also the sons or brothers of an excluded person—excluded I mean by any disability to inherit—take as substituted heirs. It is reasonable that he who takes an estate, in substitution for another, should take it distinctly charged with the other's right to be maintained out of it. The brother's widow, therefore, under the Mitakshara system, stands in a much more favorable position, with regard to her right to claim maintenance from her husband's brother. He excludes her from the inheritance, if her husband was joint with him at the time of his death. It has been held by the Bombay High Court that, whether he was joint or separate, his widow must be maintained by his brother.

LECTURE VI.

The widow's right.

It has been ruled, under Mitakshara law, that a Hindu widow's maintenance* is a charge upon the whole estate in which her husband had a share, and therefore upon every part thereof. It is superior to the right of partition and also of alienation. If her husband's brothers divide the estate, she can enforce her whole claim if she chooses against the share of each. If she obtains a decree against one of them, the remedy of that one is by a suit against the other two for contribution. The widow's right to be maintained is paramount to the title of her husband's brother to his divided share; and *a fortiori*, it is so where sons, or grandsons or great-grandsons take her husband's estate. The widow's maintenance is also, according to the Bengal school, a charge upon the estate of her husband. He cannot, by disposing of it by will,† deprive her by implication of it. It is however a personal right. It cannot be aliened by her. She has no saleable right, title, or interest in the lands which are charged with her maintenance.‡

With regard to the obligation of a widow to reside in the family dwelling-house or with her husband's relations, it has been held§ that she does not forfeit her right to maintenance, if when less than a proper amount is afforded to her she seeks shelter under the roof of her own parents. In another case the childless widow of a Hindu, who had predeceased his father, and therefore inherited none of the ancestral estate, and who moreover had left no property of any kind from which his widow could be maintained, went and lived with her own father. After a time she sued the heirs of her husband's

* Ramchundra *v.* Sabitribai, 4 Bombay H. C. R., p. 273.

† Comulmoney Dassee *v.* Rommanath Bysack, 1 Fulton, p. 189.

‡ Bhyrub Chunder Ghose *v.* Nubo Chunder Ghose, 5 S. W. R., p. 111.

brother for maintenance. The Court held,* that though the members of her husband's family were her legal guardians, and therefore bound to maintain her, yet she forfeited her claim by withdrawing herself from their protection.† In Bombay‡ it has been held that a widow, if destitute of the means of living, is entitled to maintenance from her husband's relations, although she may have shared her husband's estate, and supported herself for a long time by trading.

The widow's right to maintenance is therefore a primary charge on the estate, while it remains joint, and extends in Bengal to secure to her, on partition by her sons of her husband's estate, a share equal to that of her son. This share, in the case of there being more than one widow, has been declared by a decision of the High Court which followed, without approving them, the decisions of the Supreme Court, to be not a share equally with each one of the sons of her husband by both of his wives; but that her maintenance attaches on the shares of her own sons, irrespective of those of her co-widows, and in case of her desiring a separation, she takes a share equal to that of one of her own sons.

Amount of maintenance assigned to a widow.

According to the shasters, cited in Macnaghten, widows should receive as maintenance "each evening one prastha, $1\frac{1}{4}$ seer of rice, and a new cloth every three months, and afterwards mere food and old garments which are not tattered."

* And see Shurno Moye Dossee *v.* Gopal Loll Doss, Marshall's Reports, p. 497; Hursoondory Goopta *v.* Nubogobind Sein, 6. S. D. Dec., p. 423.

† Oojulmonee Dossee *v.* Joygopal Chunder, 4 S. D. Dec., p. 491.

‡ Bai Lakshmi *v.* Lakundas Gopaldas, 1 Bombay High Court Rep., p. 13.

LECTURE VI.

Such a rule was consistent with the state of ideas and feelings which led to the practice of *suttee.* Widows who declined to be burnt were treated as persons who had failed in an important religious duty, and a bare subsistence embittered by contempt and neglect was all that was assigned to them. But when the rite of *suttee* was declared a criminal act, the ill-treatment of widows was no longer to be defended as conducive to its performance; and, therefore, in fixing the amount of maintenance, the Court reverted to the old rule prescribed by the shasters, *viz.*, that she should pass her days in purity and retirement, and with that object in view, fixed the amount of her maintenance proportioned to her husband's property and station in life.

The notion, therefore, that a Hindu widow, even a childless one, is entitled to demand for maintenance only so much as will provide her in food and raiment, with sufficient for her husband's *shraddha,* has long ceased to prevail. The Pundits were inclined to uphold the practice by which the males of the family seized all the property of it, and reduced the females to a state little short of slavery.* But the correct doctrine under Mitakshara law appears to be that a sonless widow succeeds to the entire share of her husband immediately if partition have taken place; eventually if it have not. Before partition, she is entitled to maintenance to the extent which is equivalent to the use of the joint property in the same way as her husband was entitled to it, remembering always that as a female she is under the protection of her natural guardian.

The amount† allowed for the maintenance of a widow

* See 2 Strange, p. 298. Mr. Ellis.

† 2 Strange's Hindu Law, p. 301.

should be in proportion to her wants, that is, sufficient for her own support and that of those immediately dependent on her. The means of the estate should be considered, and the general circumstances of the particular case, the guide for settling the amount of maintenance, there being no fixed rate or proportion laiddown. According to Mr. Ellis,* she is entitled to a maintenance, the measure of which is equal to a share of the estate, with the rest of the coparceners. If, he says, she have property of her own, not consisting merely in jewels, clothes and ornaments, and the like, but from which an income is derivable, in that case it is to be made up equal to a share. And if she have sons, the measure of her maintenance should be equal to share of her husband's estate with her sons.

LECTURE VI.

Widow's right to live in the family house.

According to the Bengal school, which confers upon the heir who succeeds to the estate so much more authority over it than he has under the Mitakshara, the ancestor's widow can follow the estate so inherited, with her claim for maintenance out of it. And further, in reference to the remedy which the widow has for enforcing her right to maintenance,† there is the text of Katyayana :—" Except his whole estate and dwelling-house, what remains after the food and clothing of his family, a man may give away, whatever it be, whether fixed or moveable, otherwise it may not be given." From this it would seem that a son cannot turn his father's widow and the other females of the family who are entitled to maintenance out of the dwelling selected by the father for his own residence, and in which he left the female of his family at the time of

* 2 Strange's Hindu Law, p. 305.

† Colebrooke's Digest, B. II., Chap. IV., Sec. II., sl. 19.

LECTURE VI.

his death. It is laid down that the passage above cited from Katyayana, which says that a dwelling-house may not be given, is not a mere moral precept; and that the son and heir of the father has not such a right in the dwelling of the father, that he can at once, of his own pleasure, turn out all the females of the family, or sell it and give the purchaser a right to turn them out.*

It would appear, therefore, that a Hindu widow, and those entitled to maintenance, can insist upon remaining in the family dwelling-house, and can also insist upon being maintained out of the joint estate, into whosesoever hands that dwelling-house and estate may pass; unless when they are sold expressly to provide the widow and other persons with the maintenance to which they are entitled.

The wife.

The wife, of course, is entitled to maintenance, and if she be denied,† or if an inadequate maintenance be assigned to her, she may sue to have a proper amount ascertained and secured.

It has been held,‡ however, that a wife leaving her husband's house without sufficient cause, and especially if she be an adulteress, cannot claim maintenance. The daughter‡ is not entitled to a separate subsistence, but she, like the grandmother and the stepmother, is entitled to be maintained while the family live together.

A wife does not by a single act of disobedience, or even by leaving her husband's house, and carrying on an independent calling, forfeit for ever her rights to maintenance.

* Mangala Debi v. Dinanath Bose, 4 B. L. R., O. C., p. 81.

† Ranee Echamoye Dossee v. Rajah Opoorbokristo Deb Bahadoor. See Shamachurn's Vyavastha Darpana, p. 393.

‡ Ilata Shavatri v. Ilata Narayanan Nambri Divri, 1 Madras, p. 372.

If* she be ready to return to him, he is bound to maintain her. While,† however, she is unwilling to return and remain apart from him, she is not entitled to be maintained by him, assuming, of course, that such desertion is without sufficient cause.

Sons and Grandsons.

As respects sons and grandsons under the Bengal school, and under the Mitakshara system where there is no joint estate, they do not appear to have any legal claim to maintenance after they have attained majority. An attempt was recently made by an adopted son, to enforce a claim of that nature against his adoptive father in the Court of Moorshedabad. The High Court‡ of Bengal said:—"We find no authority, either in the Hindu law or in the Jain shastras, to support the position that the father is obliged to support a grown up son."

The daughter-in-law.

The moral right of a daughter-in-law, whether as wife or widow, to be maintained whilst living in the joint family, is undoubted; but the extent of her legal right is not very clear. As a wife she can sue her husband, if he does not maintain her, and as a widow she could probably make good her claim as against the joint estate so long as it remains in the family, and she herself continues to reside with them. But if her husband was separated at the time of his death and left no estate, she has no legal right, according to a ruling of the Full Bench,§ which she can

* Nitye Laha *v.* Soondaree Dossee, 9. S. W. R., p. 475.

† Kallyanemonee Debee *v.* Dwarkanath Surmah Chatterjee, 6 S. W. R., p. 116; Ilata Shavatri *v.* Ilata Narayanan Nambudiri, 1 Madras High Court Reports, p. 372.

‡ Premchand Peparah *v.* Hulaschund Peparah, 4 Bengal Law Reports, App., p. 23.

§ Kasheenath Doss *v.* Khettermonee Dossee, 9 S. W. R., p. 413; and see for final ruling of seven Judges, 2 B. L. R., A. C., p. 17.

LECTURE VI. enforce by suit against her father-in-law or his heirs. Of course, if one of those heirs was her own son, her right to maintenance as mother out of her son's share would immediately arise. In the case referred to the Full Bench, the widow had left her father-in-law's house, alleging ill-usage as the reason. But the Chief Justice said: † "The obligation of an heir to provide, out of the estate which descends to him, maintenance for certain persons whom the ancestor was morally or legally bound to maintain, is a legal as well as a moral obligation, for the estate is inherited subject to the obligation of providing such maintenance. A son who takes his father's estate by inheritance is bound to provide maintenance for his father's widow, the obligation is a charge upon the estate which continues as long as the widow remains chaste, whether she continue to live in the family of the heirs or not." It was also pointed out that as between the father's widow and the son, the son was the preferential heir; but as between the son's widow and father, the widow was the preferential heir. The father-in-law therefore does not take the husband's estate, as substituted heir for the widow, and the son's widow cannot stand in any higher position than any other dependent member of the family. So long as there is joint estate, she cannot be excluded from maintenance while living joint with her husband's family; when separate, her claim is only a moral one, and she has no greater right to sue her father-in-law for maintenance after her husband's death, than she would have had during his life-time, if her husband had been unable to maintain her.

It was only necessary in the case referred to, to hold that the daughter-in-law had no right to sue for maintenance

† 9 S. W. R., p. 413.

when the father-in-law had no ancestral property. The rule seems clear that the ancestor's estate is liable while in the hands of his heir, to answer all the legal obligations for maintenance which were imposed upon the ancestor. With regard to moral obligations, the Chief Justice observed that it was only reasonable that the heir should be held legally liable to do what the ancestor was morally liable to do, and which it was to be presumed he would have done out of the estate if he had lived; but he said "I am not sure that even in such cases the legal liability is carried to that extent;" and further on he observed, "we must not convert all the moral obligations enjoined by the Hindoo law into legal liabilities, we should do much mischief by want of care in this respect."

The actual ruling in the case before the Full Bench and in appeal from it, having regard to the facts of it, was that when a son dies in his father's life-time, the widow has not such a right to maintenance by her father-in-law as can be enforced at law irrespectively of his possession of ancestral property. The question is still open whether she has such a right as she can enforce against him when ancestral property remains in his hands. Her moral claim in that case seems to be obvious, according to the doctrines of Hindu law; and so long as there is ancestral property, and she chooses to live with her husband's relations with the other dependent members of the family, she could not legally be refused maintenance. Under the Mitakshara law, she could probably enforce her claim by reason of her husband's right in the ancestral property.

The stepmother.

With regard to the stepmother's right to maintenance, the Bengal Sudder Court, in 1821, approved and acted upon the following opinion delivered by their Pundits:

LECTURE VI.

"Srikrishna Tarkalankara, in his commentary on the Dayabhaga, treating of the partition between brothers by different mothers, says, that there is no provision for giving a share to the stepmother, because she is not the mother of all the sons. For this purpose there should exist the same degree of relationship among all the persons dividing, when each widow of the proprietor would have a share equal to that of her several sons. The same principle applies in assigning a maintenance." And then the Pundits go on to state that the son of her contemporary wife is, in the first instance, bound to maintain his stepmother; in default of him, some person whose relationship is not very clearly described by them, but who may have been intended to be the son of the daughter of the rival wife; and in his default, the son's son of the rival wife, according to the proximity of their several relations; but they should not be required simultaneously to support her, as that would be a deviation from the spirit of the law. They then proceed as follows: "In the opinion of Jimutavahana, the assignment of a share to the widow of the original proprietor, and of maintenance, are to be considered as resting with the person who is nearest in degree of relationship, and not with the more remotely connected coparceners. The son of a rival wife, whether he has received the whole of his father's estate, or a part of it only, must supply his stepmother with food and raiment, and other necessary expenses for the performance of her religious duties. This view of the case is confirmed by the doctrine of Menu and other legislators, who contend that a son is bound to maintain his father and mother, and may even commit a crime to effect this object. In fine, the son of the rival wife should support his stepmother out of the ancestral or acquired property, or out of both; and, if he should be dead or unable to do so, the duty should devolve on the son of the stepson, or other parcener, but not otherwise. This opinion is conformable to the Dayabhaga, Dayatatwa, Dayakrama Sangraha, Vivada Bhangarnava, and other books of law current in Bengal."* LECTURE VI.

The suit† in which the above opinion was given was brought by a widow for maintenance, under circumstances which necessitated a discussion of the stepmother's claim. After her husband's death, his brother entered upon the hereditary estate, and maintained all the members of the family. Afterwards he, with the widow's three stepsons, partitioned the estate, and the four obtained separate possession of their shares. In the suit for maintenance brought by the widow, the defendants were first, one of her three stepsons; second, the son of another stepson; and lastly, the widow of the third. The Zillah Court of Rung-

* See the authorities referred to in Kishnanund Chowdhree and others *v.* Mussamut Rookeenee Debia, 3 Select Reports (new edition), p. 96.

"Here, since the term mother relates to the natural parent, the stepmother does not participate, but she must be maintained with food and raiment."—*Dayakrama Sangraha.*

"When partition is made by sons, no shares need be alloted to the stepmother who has no male issue, but food and raiment must be assigned, for the late owner of the property was bound to support her." —*Vivada Bhangarnava.*

"In childhood must a female be dependent on her father; in youth, on her husband; her lord being dead, on her son."—*Menu.*

"All the wives of the father are considered mothers."—*Vasistha.*

"Thus if, among all the wives of the same husband, one bring forth a male child, Menu has declared them all, by means of that son, to be mothers of male issue."

"All the paternal grandmothers are declared equal to mothers."—*Vyasa.*

† Kishnanund Chowdhree *v.* Mussamut Rookeenee Debia, 3 Select Rep. (new edition), p. 96.

LECTURE VI.

pore decreed maintenance to her, to be paid by all of the defendants, *viz.*, by the surviving stepson and the heirs of the two deceased stepsons, who were in possession, and who were directed to contribute.

The case ultimately came to the Sudder Court, and there the Pundits declared that, if the plaintiff's stepson, the widow of her stepson, and the son of her stepson, obtain possession of the zemindaree left by her husband, the wife and son of her stepson are not liable to the payment of maintenance; inasmuch as uterine brothers, on succeeding to and dividing their father's property, are not enjoined by the shasters to give a share to their childless stepmother, but they are enjoined to allow her food and raiment. The maintenance of a stepmother rests on her stepsons alone, and not on their sons or widows. The final decree was that the surviving stepson alone should pay the maintenance proportioned to his share of the estate as respects the extent of the widow's claim to maintenance.

General observations.

The claim of one person to be maintained by another is one which it is certainly, for the interests of society, should be strictly defined. The duty of a parent to maintain his child until the child is *sui juris*, and of a husband to maintain his wife, is one which almost any society would undertake to enforce. But in the Hindu family system, with its community in food, worship, and estate, the right to receive, and the obligation to afford, maintenance did not spring from a purely personal relation, but from the relationship of the individual to the family. Where there is family property, no difficulty arises; all the members must be maintained out of it, unless the right be in any particular case forfeited. But when there is no joint property, the difficulty arises of distinguishing between those claims which can be enforced by a Court of law and those which appeal to a merely moral obligation. LECTURE VI.

Besides the wife and mother the dependent members of the family include the stepmother, the grandmother, the son's widow, the daughter and sister who still remain unmarried, and are not, therefore, otherwise provided for. They include also those who by reason of some incurable mental or physical disease, are disqualified for inheritance, as also their childless wives or unmarried daughters. With regard to outcasts and their issue, the authority of Yajnavalkya may be cited in favor of their right to maintenance; but in their case, it is restricted to food and raiment.

All these, in the absence of a family fund, have, nevertheless, a right to be maintained. But the difficulty is to say on whom and to what extent is the legal duty imposed and enforced of providing that maintenance. It is impossible, having regard to the decided cases, to lay down a definite rule; but in general terms it may be said that a man is personally liable at law to maintain, besides his wives and children, those who, by reason of sex or other disability, have been or would have been excluded in his favor as heirs to any ancestral estate.

Guardianship.

Although the obligation to maintain his dependents was the primary duty of the Hindu as laid down in the shasters, yet there are some provisions also for the exercise of authority and the rights of guardianship. The nature and extent of the paternal authority seems to have very little to do with the idea of a right to dominion, but seems rather to be founded upon the son's present need of support controlled by the father's expectations of future services. Sancha* and Lićhita say:—"Since the family is

* Dayabhaga, Chap. III., Sec. I., verse 7.

LECTURE VI.

supported on the inheritance, sons are not independent, but as it were under the authority of a father; so long as the mother lives, they are not independent of their mother; they are not competent to make a partition." And Vyasa* adds:—"For brethren a common abode is ordained, so long as both parents live; but after their decease, the religious merits of separated brethren increase." Commensality is prescribed so long as the parents live; but according to the Mitakshara, sons can compel their father to partition the estate and separate the family; and whether they do so or not, they can always control and even prohibit his dealings with the family property.

Position of women.

Women have always occupied a very dependent position, both in Hindu society and also in the joint family. Originally Menu† declared that married women must be honored: where females are honored, there the deities are pleased; where not being honored, they pronounce an imprecation, such families utterly perish. But, notwithstanding this ordinance of Menu, all the sages agree that women must be held in a state of subjection,—first by their fathers, then by their husbands, next by their sons, and lastly by their kinsmen; and according to Vrihaspati, they should be guarded day and night by their mothers-in-law and other venerable matrons. The mind of the sages is occupied and perplexed by the difficult duty of prescribing the method of guarding them and preserving them from the consequences of those depraved dispositions which, it is said, are implanted in them by the lord of creation. Superfluous as it may seem, the sages go on to prescribe,

* Dayabhaga, Chap. III., Sec. I., verse 8.

† 3 Menu, 55 to 58.

even in the minutest detail, the duties of life to those for whose close guardianship and supervision they so carefully provide; and a large portion of their attention is occupied by a disquisition upon the routine of daily observance, both in the presence and absence of the husband.

Lecture VI.

Hindu women were, and are still to a great extent,* supposed to be destitute of any degree of mental capacity, and are accustomed to refer to their sex, as implying a natural and inevitable inferiority. The happiest lot that under the former state of the law could have befallen them, was to die in the married state, and thereby escape the evils formerly incident in Hindu society to the position of a widow—a position, of which I shall in a subsequent lecture endeavour to trace the history. Such a lot was considered to be the reward of good deeds done in a former state of existence.

Paternal male kindred preferred as guardians.

The dependent position which women occupied in a Hindu family, did not lead to any very definite ideas upon the subject of guardianship. Practically, the individual child, or female, whether single or married, was lost sight of; the joint family collectively, rather than its individual members, being chiefly regarded by law. It rests with the sovereign† to take care of the infant and his property, and to appoint a guardian for that purpose. So far as the personal relation of guardian and ward is concerned, the performance of the initiatory rites, and the giving a female child in marriage, is the duty chiefly discussed; and with regard to that, the paternal male kindred are preferred. The female‡

* Abbé Dubois's Customs and Manners of the Hindus, p. 217.

† 8 Menu, 27; see Colebrooke's Digest, B. V., C. VIII., Sec. I., sl. 449, 450, 451.

‡ 1 Macnaghten's Hindu Law, p. 103.

LECTURE VI.

kindred, even the child itself, if capable of any discretion, should be consulted in the appointment. Women could not, strictly speaking, be appointed guardians, for, under the old rules of Hindu law, they were themselves in perpetual tutelage; if married, under their husband or his male descendants, or his paternal male kindred; and if unmarried, under their own paternal male kindred. Besides, they are unable to perform the initiatory rites, which is of course an objection of great importance. But, nevertheless, the claims of the mother were in practice seldom overlooked, and are now unquestionable. In a case decided in 1847 by the Bengal Sudder Court, the mother* of a minor was held to have a preferential right of guardianship to the † brother, under the shasters, and according to Regulation I. of 1800, which was then in force, and acccording to the provisions of which "guardianship was in no instance to be entrusted to the legal heir of the ward, or other person interested in outliving him." While, however, the father ‡ lives, he alone is entitled to give the daughter in marriage, but he can delegate his authority to another. The duty of giving a daughter in marriage in the proper season, which is before maturity, is enforced by all the sages from Menu downwards. The right or duty of doing so, and of performing the ceremony of gift, devolves successively upon the father, paternal grandfather, brother, and other relations in their order as far as the tenth degree;

The mother's claim recognized at the present time.

* Kooldeep Narain v. Rajbunsee Kowur, 7 S. D. R., p. 395.

† But it seems that the half-brother will be preferred as guardian, to the mother, if she be disqualified by loss of caste, and also to the grandmother. Mussamut Mahtaboo v. Gunesh Lall, 10 S. D. Dec., p. 329.

‡ Golamee Ghose v. Juggessur Ghose, 3 S. W. R., p. 193.

and the mother and maternal* grandfather and the relatives in order in the maternal line. LECTURE VI.

But, although the mother has undoubtedly a right to the guardianship of the child, especially a female child, next to the father, it does not follow that she has the right to give her in marriage. That would appear to belong exclusively to the father's male kindred, if any; the grandfather,† brother, uncle, and uncle's son, all ranking in that respect before the mother. Excluding the right to give a daughter in marriage, and the right to perform the initiatory ceremonies, the guardianship of a minor belongs to the father, then, by‡ long and general custom, to the mother, and afterwards to the male paternal relations, in order of proximity.

Paternal grand-mother preferred to the stepmother.

A question arose not long ago in the High Court of Bengal, as to the comparative claims of the stepmother and the paternal grandmother to be the guardian of the infant. The Court decided§ that the latter had the preferential right; and that, as a rule, it was more fitting that she should be related, because her appointment is more likely to be for the minor's interests, and is most in accordance with the general principles of Hindu law. "When we find," the Court proceeded, "that, under no circumstances can a stepmother inherit from her stepson,‖ and that, on partition, the stepmother does not get a share, because she is not included in the term 'mother;'¶ and when we find that the grand-

* See Shamachurn's Vyavastha Darpana, p. 651.

† 2 Macnaghten's Hindu Law, p. 204.

‡ 1 Macnaghten's Hindu Law, pp. 103, 104; 1 Strange's Hindu Law, pp. 70, 71; See Shamachurn's Vyavastha Darpana, pp. 651, 652.

§ Maharanee Ram Bunsee Koonwaree *v.* Maharanee Soobh Koonwaree, 7 S. W. R., p. 321.

‖ Lalla Joteeloll *v.* Mussamut Dooranee Koer, W. R., F. B., p. 173.

¶ Dayabhaga, Chap. III., Sec. 2, C. 29, 30.

LECTURE VI.

mother can inherit from her grandson (a point on which there can be no dispute, and on which it is therefore unnecessary to refer to authorities), we cannot but come to the conclusion that, according to Hindu law, the connection between the paternal grandmother and her grandchild is to be deemed closer than the connection between the child and its stepmother. Blood relationship, especially on the father's side, is usually preferred by Hindu law. In the case of the paternal grandmother, we have that relationship; in the case of the stepmother, we have it not."

In disposing of the minor in marriage by the grandmother, to whom, under the circumstances of the case, it was held that the right to give in marriage belonged, the assent of the nearest male kinsmen on the father's side is advisable.

Recent legislation.

By an Act passed in 1858 by the Legislative Council of India (No. XL of 1858), for making better provision for the care of the persons and property of minors in the Presidency of Fort William in Bengal, it was provided* that "every person who shall claim a right to have charge of property in trust for a minor under a will or deed, or by reason of nearness of kin, or otherwise, may apply to the Civil Court for a certificate of administration, and no person shall be entitled to institute or defend any suit connected with the estate of which he claims the charge, until he shall have obtained such certificate." When, however, the property is of small value, or there is any other sufficient reason, any Court having jurisdiction may allow any relation of a minor to institute or defend a suit on his behalf, although a certificate of administration has not been

* See Section 3.

granted to such relation. Such certificate may be granted to any person entitled to it by virtue of a will or deed, or to any near or other relation or friend of the minor who is willing and fit to be trusted with the charge of his property.

There is a later Act, *viz.*, Act IX of 1861, which amends the law for hearing suits relative to the custody and guardianship of minors, and which applies to the whole of the British territories in India. It does not, however, interfere with the jurisdiction exercised under the laws in force by any Supreme Court of Judicature or the Court of Wards, or under Act XXI of 1855, which applies to the Madras Presidency (the provisions of which are extended by Act XIV of 1858); or under Act XL of 1858, which applies to the Bengal Presidency. There is a further Act, *viz.*, Act XX of 1864, which provides for the care of the persons and property of minors in the Presidency of Bombay.

LECTURE VII.

THE MEMBERS OF THE FAMILY.—THEIR CIVIL STATUS.

Civil Status of Hindus—Caste—Ceremonies of Regeneration—Anaprasana—Tonsure—Upanayana—Regeneration for Sudras, Women, and Brahmins—Marriage—Relation of Husband and Wife—Who may Contract Marriage—Former Restrictions to a great extent removed—Adultery—Illegitimacy—Rights of Illegitimate Children—Age of Majority—Bengal Regulation XXVI of 1797—Act XL of 1858. Full Bench Ruling in *Muddosoodun Manji* v. *Debee Gobinda Newgi*—Results of Legislative Enactments.

In my last lectures I have referred to the Hindu family and endeavored to trace its true character as the primitive institution of Hindu society. The principle upon which each family is separated from the rest of the community, and its limits ascertained, is disclosed to us in the rules which have been handed down from the remotest times for the celebration of the great religious observances called the *shraddha*. Within the family so formed as a separate aggregation of beings, the authority of the *kurta*, controlled by the wishes and opinions of adults, and guided by the *guru* and the *purohit*, was the ultimate rule of life. Without the family, its relations to other families and to the ruling power were determined by the joint will expressed through the representative of the body; and law originally accepted this aggregate responsibility, and did not hasten to interfere with the self-government, which more or less prevailed within its limits. But long as the institution prevailed, it at length gave signs of decay, and the doctrines of the Bengal school are a protest against a system which overwhelmed the individual in communal life. The advance thus made has been fostered and strengthened by the growth of a more energetic society, and by recent administration of their law which has always been ready, when opportunity offered, to define individual rights, and to set limits to joint responsibility. I have traced the efforts made to define this legal power of an adult member of the family, especially of the *kurta*, to bind by his acts the family and its possessions; and the manner in which the family has been rendered free to select its own ministers of religion, and its members free to give or withhold their contributions towards defraying the expenses of worship. And penetrating within the precincts of the family, the rules of law are being gradually developed, which determine the rights of its individual members to maintenance, and the extent to which they can be enforced; and which also regulate the authority and duties of guardianship.

Civil *status* of Hindus.

I shall now pass from the joint family and the considerations to which it gives rise, and proceed to the subject of the personal rights and duties which devolve upon individuals. The rules which determine the civil *status* of each, that is his position in the eye of Hindu law, *e. g.*, his age of majority, his legitimacy, his marriage, his capacity to be adopted and so forth, are derived from the doctrines of religion, and it is not always easy to distinguish the precepts which have the sanction only of religion from the rules which have the force of law.

Caste.

At his birth there is ascribed to him by law the state or position involved in the possession of a particular caste.

LECTURE VII.

The *caste* to which he belongs influences his legal position, for each *caste* has its special rules, still to some extent and for some purposes recognized by law, which affect only its own members. Religious teaching separates the regenerate or twice-born Hindu from the unregenerate Hindu, who is still affected by the taint of sin which he contracted in the womb. The only regenerating ceremony for a Sudra, or a woman of whatever caste, is marriage. In the other three castes, marriage is the final ceremony which completes the regeneration of a male Hindu. It unalterably fixes him as a member of the family in which he was born, after which, under no circumstances whatever, can he be affiliated in any other family, or to any other father; away from and destroying his affiliation to his natural father.

It originally marked the period at which a Hindu attained his majority.

Ceremonies of regeneration.

There are eight successive ceremonies which are necessary in order that a Hindu boy of the three superior castes, *viz.*, the *Brahmana*, the *Kshatriya*, and *Vaisya* castes, may attain regeneration. Though Hindu law, especially as recognized and administered in English Courts, does not in general regard their performance or omission as affecting the legal position of a Hindu, yet they are all of more or less importance. Besides completing the work of regeneration, they successively strengthen the tie which binds the boy to the family in which they are performed; and two of them, the ceremony of tonsure and the ceremony of investiture with the Brahminical thread, have often been discussed in Courts of law, especially with reference to their effect on a boy's capacity for adoption, *i. e.*, the legal ability to be transferred to and affiliated in a family other than that of birth.

The three first ceremonies are,* I believe, of slight importance, being, first, the *jatacarana*,† a rite ordained on the birth of a male before the section of the navel-string, and which consists in making him taste clarified butter out of a golden spoon; second‡ *namacarana*, a ceremony on giving a name, performed on the tenth day after birth; or on the eleventh, twelfth, or one hundred and first day; third, *nishcramana*, carrying the child out of the house to see the moon on the third lunar day, of the third light fortnight from his birth; or to see the sun in the third or fourth month.

Annaprasana.

The fourth ceremony, or *annaprasana*, is an event of some celebrity in the life of a child. It means the feeding him with rice in the sixth or eighth month, or when he has cut his teeth. Generally it is a time of family festival at which relatives assemble, and the child is publicly recognized as a member of the family; presents being made to it by those nearest connected with it. Next comes the important rite of *churacarana*, or ceremony of tonsure, performed in the first or third year after the birth in the case of the three first classes.§ The rite of tonsure is an important one in securing the affiliation of a child in the family of his birth, or to his natural father. In case of adoption, it is important that it should be performed in the family of the adopted, in order to secure his sonship to the adopted father. The family name is used in the rite, and its use is essential to its efficacy. "The coronal locks,"

Tonsure.

* Colebrooke's Digest, Book V., Chapter III., Section 134, note.

† 2 Menu, 29.

‡ *Ibid*, 31. The first part of a Brahmin's name should signify holiness; of a Kshatriya's, power; of a Vaisya's, wealth; and of a Sudra's, contempt.

§ 2 Menu, 35.

it is said, "of the boy must be made with the enunciation of his patriarchal tribe."* And according to Nanda Pandita, "that son, who is initiated under the family name of his natural father, unto the ceremony of tonsure, does not become the son of another man."

Upanayana.

The sixth ceremony, or *upanayana*, consists of the investiture of the child by the father with the marks of his class.† Different seasons are prescribed for the performance of this ceremony on a Brahmana,‡ Kshatriya, and Vaisya respectively. The fifth year is the principal season, at least for a Brahmana, and the sixth or eighth for the other two castes respectively.§ But if that season be neglected, then a secondary season is allowed, *viz.*, according to a text of Yajnavalkya, interpreted according to the commentary in the Mitakshara:—"For a Brahmana, the eighth year from conception, or the eighth year of his age; for a Kshatriya, the eleventh year; for a Vaisya, the twelfth." So also is the rule as laid down by Menu.‖ It is still in force, the custom of families however determining whether the periods are reckoned from the birth or from the conception. Another text of the author of the Mitakshara¶ relative to the extent of the period for the performance of this rite is to the following effect:—"The period for the performance of this *upanayana* rite of a *Brahmana, Kshatriya,* and *Vaisya*

* 4 Dattaka Mimansa, p. 28. But see Lecture XIV. on the subject of the Capacity to be received in Adoption.

† These consist of three thick twists of cotton hanging from the left shoulder to the right hip, in honor of Brahma, Vishnu, and Siva, which are increased to nine at marriage.—*Abbé Dubois*, p. 92.

‡ 2 Dattaka Chandrika, pp. 30, 31.

§ 2 Menu, 37.

‖ *Ibid*, 36.

¶ 2 Dattaka Chandrika, p. 31, note.

respectively extends to the sixteenth, twenty-second, and twenty-fourth years. Subsequent thereto, should the rite be unperformed, they become outcasts and uninitiated persons, excluded from the participation in religious rites, and incapable of being taught the *savitri;* except on the performance of a sacrament denominated *vratyastoma.*"

The seventh ceremony is the *savitri* first referred to, or ceremony of investiture hallowed by the Gyatri.* It must not be delayed for a Brahmana beyond the sixteenth year; nor in the two other castes beyond the twenty-second or twenty-fourth year respectively. Unless the investiture takes place within those periods, the youth becomes degraded from the Gyatri, and contemned and excommunicated by the virtuous, *i. e.*, by *Brahmanas.* The eighth is the ceremony of *samavartana,* performed on the return of a student from his preceptor's house. To these eight ceremonies must be added one, which precedes conception, entitled *garbhadhana;* and the last ceremony of all, marriage, which completes the regeneration of the twice-born classes.

Regeneration for Sudras, women, and Brahmins.

Marriage and the *annaprasana* are the only ceremonies enjoined or permitted in the case of Sudras and women. "The nuptial ceremony," says Menu,† "is considered the complete institution of women, ordained for them in the Vedas." By it a Brahmana who has completed his period of studentship, becomes a *grihastha,* or house-keeper. Marriage, therefore, is, in the case of all four castes, the ceremony which finally secures regeneration of both man and woman, and also effects the final affiliation of the son in the family to which he belongs. In the

* 2 Menu, 38.

† *Ibid*, 67.

LECTURE VII.

life of a *Brahmana*, there are four distinct periods.* The first one commences with the *upanayana*, by which he becomes a *brahmachari*, or religious student. This may be, but seldom is, prolonged through life, there being a distinct religious order of perpetual studentship. The second begins with marriage, when a man becomes *grihi*, or married man. The third begins at a time when, withdrawing from the pleasures and occupations of life, he becomes a hermit, or *vánaprastha*. The fourth is the period when, as a *sanyasi*, or ascetic, he becomes absorbed in the divine essence. With the two last however, we have nothing to do. When the regenerating ceremonies are concluded, a Brahmana becomes fully invested with the signs of his class: until which time he may not, according to Menu,† pronounce any sacred text, except what ought to be used in obsequies to an ancestor.‡

Marriage.

The institution§ of marriage therefore remains to be

* 4 Menu, 1.—Let a Brahmana, having dwelt with preceptor during the first quarter of a man's life, pass the second quarter of human life in his own house, when he has contracted a legal marriage. And see 6 Menu, 87.—The student, the married man, the hermit, and the anchorite, are the offspring, though in four orders, of married men keeping house; also see 1 Strange, p. 35, note.

† Colebrooke's Digest, Book V., Chapter III., Section 133.—Till he be invested with the signs of his class, he must not pronounce any sacred text, except what ought to be used in obsequies to an ancestor, since he is on a level with a Sudra before his new birth from the revealed scripture.

‡ There are some other ceremonies, making sixteen in all, for which see Steele's Synopsis of the Law of Castes, p. 23.

§ The nubile (*a*) age is twelve years for a girl to be married to a man aged thirty; and eight years to one aged twenty-four; of still younger age, to a youth. The girl remains with her family after the ceremony until she reaches maturity, of which the mother gives notice. By the

(*a*) Dayabhaga, Chapter I., verse 39; 9 Menu, 95.

considered since the act of receiving the bride effects death of the husband, in the interval, she is condemned to virgin widowhood (*a*) for her life; but in practice, a second marriage is not uncommon, under such circumstances, amongst the lower orders.

There are eight forms of the nuptial ceremony, but only four are legal for a *Brahmana*, namely, those called *brahma*, *doiva*, *arsha*, and *prajapatya* (or caya). They are described by Yajnavalkya: the *brahma*, where the bride is given by her father to the bridegroom whom he has himself invited; the *daiva*, where she is given to the family priest employed in performing the sacrifice; the *arsha*, where she is given to the bridegroom in return for a bull and cow given for religious purposes, and on no account, according to Menu, to be considered as a bribe; and the *prajapatya*, where she is given to any person asking her, the giver pronouncing "perform all duties together." The two ceremonies, called *gandharva* and *rákshasa*, are permitted to men of the Kshatriya or military class; upon the same principle, as suggested by Mr. Macnaghten, on which soldiers have, both in civil and English law, been permitted to dispense with the orthodox legal formalities, both in making wills and disposing of their property. They signify marriages contracted respectively by reciprocal amorous agreement, or by seizure in war. The *assura* nuptials are peculiar to *Vaisyas* and *Sudras;* the giver of the bride taking from the bridegroom at his own choice, without authority of law, wealth, other than the pair of kine, which we have seen, are legally demandable in the *nuba* ceremony (*b*). This ceremony, which is held in odium as mercenary, is good as (*c*) concerns the contracting parties; but the giver of the bride, who receives the gratuity, comes within the curse of Menu, directed to those who tacitly sell their daughters; a practice, he says, condemned by ancients and moderns, and even in former creations. The *paisacha* ceremony is forbidden to all classes and *castes* alike, and signifies a marriage contracted through deceit practised upon the bride (*d*).

The contract itself is considered to be complete and irrevocable, after the bride and bridegroom have joined hands, after having walked seven steps hand in hand, during the recital of certain prayers (*e*).

(*a*) See Shamachurn's Vyavastha Darpana, p. 647.

(*b*) Colebrooke's Digest, Book IV., Chapter IV., Section III., verse 173.

(*c*) 3 Menu, 51. (*d*) *Ibid*, 21, 25, 34.

(*e*) Neither by water poured on his hands, nor by verbal promise, is a man acknowledged as husband of a damsel; the marital contract is complete, after the ceremony of joining hands, on the seventh step of the married pair.—Colebrooke's Digest, Book IV., Chapter IV., Section III., verse 175.

LECTURE VII.

the final regeneration. It is an indissoluble contract, as well as a religious sacrament.* Only one wife is enjoined, the principal deities of the Hindus having been married each to one wife; Brahma to Saraswati; Vishnu to Lakshmi; Siva to Parvati. But whatever prohibition there may be against a pluralty of wives, except under the circumstances of the first wife's infidelity, bad temper, barrenness, and production only of daughters, the rule is† only directory, and not imperative. There is nothing in Hindu law or usage to render polygamy illegal, whatever may be urged against its morality.

The precepts against it are of the character and meaning of such texts as these:—"With sorrow does he eat," says Dachsa, "who has two contentious wives; dissension, mutual enmity, meanness and pain, distract his mind." "Let mutual fidelity," says Menu, "continue till death; this in a few words may be considered as the supreme law between husband and wife."

Relation of husband and wife.

According to Devala,‡ a woman may forsake her husband, if he be impotent or degraded, or absent from her for a sufficient period of time, which, in the case of a Brahmana wife with children, is eight years. He who forsakes a wife, says Yajnavalkya, though obedient§ to his commands, diligent in household management, mother of an excellent son, and, speaking kindly, shall be com-

* Colebrooke's Digest, Book V., Chapter III., verses 132 and 133.

† Virasvami Chetti *v.* Appasvami Chetti, 1 Madras, p. 375.

‡ A husband may be forsaken by his wife if he be an abandoned sinner, or an heretical mendicant, or impotent, or degraded, or afflicted with phthisis, or if he have been long absent in a foreign country.—Colebrooke's Digest, Book IV., Chapter IV., Section II., verse 151.

§ Colebrooke's Digest, Book IV., Chap. I., Section II., verse 72.

pelled to pay a third of his wealth; or if poor, to provide* a maintenance for his wife. If afflicted with illness, she must never be disgraced, though she may be superseded with her own consent. Supersession without her own consent, is justified by her immorality, disease, extravagance, temper, barrenness, or giving birth to daughters only.†

Vrihaspati‡ says that the wife is considered as half the body of her husband, equally sharing the fruit of pure and impure acts. Of him whose wife is not deceased, half the body survives; a doctrine which would tend to render marriage indissoluble, and the re-marriage of widows illegal.§ "Half his body perishes, whose wife drinks intoxicating liquors:" which implies the principle upon which supersession is permitted. According to Vijnyaneswara's‖ commentary on the text of Yajnavalkya, a wife superseded by a second marriage on the part of her husband, has a right to receive from him as much as is expended in jewels, ornaments, and the like for the second marriage, unless such property has already been bestowed upon her, and then only half should be given.

A similar rule is laid down by Jimutavahana, who explains that the object is to obtain a second wife with the first one's consent.

The wife's power to pledge her husband's credit, or to render him liable on her contracts, on the ground of an im-

* Colebrooke's Digest, Book IV., Chap. I., Section II., verse 72.

† Menu; see Colebrooke's Digest, Book IV., Chapter I., Section II., verse 67; Colebrooke's Digest, Book IV., Chapter III., Section II., verse 132.

‡ See Dayabhaga, Chapter II., verse 5.

§ Colebrooke's Digest, Book IV., Chapter III., Section II., verse 132.

‖ Mitakshara, Chapter II., Section XI., Verse 35; Dayabhaga, Chapter IV., Section I., verse 14.

LECTURE VII.

plied agency, is the same in Hindu or in English law. "A person dealing with a Hindu wife and seeking to charge her husband must show either that the wife is living with her husband and managing the household affairs, in which case an implied agency to buy necessaries is presumed, or he must show the existence of such a state of things as would warrant her in living apart from her husband and claiming support and maintenance, when of course the law would give her an implied authority to bind him for necessaries supplied to her during such separation, in the event of his not providing her with maintenance." It has been held by the Madras High Court that the supersession* of a wife by a second marriage does not justify her separation from her husband, and cannot of itself, give her implied authority as his agent to bind him for debts incurred for necessaries.

Who may contract marriage.

The restrictions upon the right to contract a marriage depend upon considerations of relationship or caste. A woman may not marry a man of a caste beneath her; a man may marry in his own caste, or an inferior one.† A Sudra therefore may only marry a wife of his own caste. But Menu denounces the marriage of a man of priestly rank with a Sudra; a Brahmin who so offends sinks to a region of torment; and‡ as regards the son of such an union, he is a living corpse, equally incapable of fulfilling the purpose of obsequies, whether his Sudra mother were or were not lawfully married to his father. The father, too, loses his priestly rank, and no expiation will restore him to his lost

* Virasvami Chetti v. Appasvami Chetti, *per* Scotland, C. J., 1 Madras, p. 375.

† Menu, ix, 157.

‡ *Ibid*, ix, 178.

position.* In the present age, according to Mr. Sutherland,† marriage with one unequal in class is prohibited.

And the High Court of Bengal affirmed that principle in a case‡ where a Dome-Brahmin was alleged to have been married to a girl of the Haree tribe. As those were two distinct castes, the Court ruled that local custom distinctly proved alone could sanction and render valid a marriage of that description. But the Chief Justice of Madras took a different view; and having regard to the decreasing influence of caste, a more reasonable view of the law, as applicable at the present day, when he observed in the course of a judgment in a case§ in which the question of illegitimacy was under discussion. "The general law applicable to all the classes or tribes does not seem opposed to marriage between persons of different sects or divisions of the same class or tribe; and even as regards marriage between individuals of a different class or tribe, the law appears to be no more than directory. Although it recommends and inculcates a marriage with a woman of equal class, as a preferable description of marriage, yet the marriage of a man with a woman of a lower caste or tribe than himself, appears not to be an invalid marriage rendering the issue ille-

* A Brahmana, if he takes a Sudra to his bed, as his first wife, sinks to the regions of torment; if he beget a child by her, he loses even his priestly rank.

His sacrifices to the gods, his oblations to the manes, and his hospitable attentions to strangers, must be supplied principally by her; but the gods and manes will not eat such offerings, nor can heaven be attained by such hospitality.

For the crime of him who thus illegally drinks the moisture of a Sudra's lips, who is tainted by her breath, and who even begets a child on her body, the law declares no expiation.—3 Menu, 17, 18, 19.

† Sutherland's Synopsis, Heading ii.

‡ Melaram Medyal *v.* Tenuram Banum, 9 S. W. R., p. 552.

§ Pandaiya Tilava *v.* Puli Telava, 1 Madras, p. 478.

LECTURE VII.

gitimate." Moreover, when the prohibitions of religion were directed against marriage between individuals of a different class, the class referred to must be taken to mean one of the four great castes recognized in the time of Menu and the earlier legislators. To hold that such prohibition is one having the force of law, and refers not merely to inequality as respects the four historical classes, but also to inequality as respects the numerous sub-divisions of those classes introduced in the progress of time, is to introduce a new and irrational rule, which can only tend to encourage and stereotype the existing sub-divisions of Hindu society in a manner which is mischievous and unreasonable.

Former restrictions to a great extent removed.

Whether or not the restrictions upon marriage originally pronounced should be now regarded as obsolete prohibitions of religion, having no force of law at the present day, is a matter for judicial discretion. The authority of the Madras case, which I have just referred to, establishes a useful precedent; and if generally followed, at least as respects the twice-born classes, the impediment of inequality of caste will only follow the fate of other impediments which have been singularly placed in the way of marriage by legislators who in doctrine regarded it as a ceremony of the first secular and religious importance. Menu,* for example, originally declared that, if the younger brother or the younger sister married before the elder, the wife of the younger brother so married, the giver of her in marriage, and the performer of the nuptial sacrifice, all sink to a region of torment. Notwithstanding this sweeping prohibition, subsequent sages provided a number of exceptions to it, and no one would dream of

* 3 Menu, 171 and 172.

giving effect to it at the present day. On the other hand, another prohibition of the same legislator is valid now,* *viz.*, against marriages with women who are descended from the same paternal or maternal ancestors within the sixth degree, that is, who come within the degree of relationship, which I have already described, as "sapindas for the purpose of mourning and purification." Beyond that degree of relationship, he says that women are eligible for twice-born men for nuptials and holy union. LECTURE VII.

Adultery. A wife may be deserted on the ground of adultery,† which is regarded as a criminal offence, but, Nareda says that a husband who deserts an affectionate or faultless wife, shall be brought to his duty by the king with severe chastisement. In Bombay, however, there is a practice of deserted or divorced wives marrying again, under a form of marriage which is of sufficiently frequent occurrence to have a name of its own ‡ *viz.*, *natra.* But in 1864, in an appeal from a conviction by the lower Court on a charge of adultery, which, under the Penal Code, is a criminal offence, a defence that a *natra* marriage had been solemnized between the prisoner and prosecutor's wife, was considered by the Bombay High Court.§ It was alleged to be a custom amongst the caste to which the parties belonged that a woman may, without the consent of her husband, leave him, and contract a valid marriage with another man. "We are of opinion," said the Court, "that such a caste custom as that set up, even if it be proved to exist, is invalid, as being entirely opposed to the spirit of the Hindu

* Menu, 5.

† See Shamachurn's Vyavastha Darpana, p. 679.

‡ 1 Strange's Hindu Law, p. 52.

§ Reg. *v.* Kassan Goja; Reg. *v.* Bai Rupa, 2 Bombay High Court Reports, p. 125.

LECTURE VII.

law, and we hold that a marriage entered into in accordance with such a custom is void."

And, generally, according to Hindu law, adultery, though a penal, is an expiable offence, at all events, if the parties be of the same *caste*. The ancient law prescribes* the penance for adulterous connexion. The provisions as to the son of concealed birth being entitled to inheritance† to the husband of the mother, show clearly‡ that neither adultery nor illegitimacy is, in the eye of the Hindu lawgivers, the disabling stigma, which codes, based upon Christianity, have made it. But a woman divorced for adultery who has continued in adultery during her husband's life, and in unchastity after his death, is not entitled to maintenance after his death.

Illegitimacy.

There is no disabling stigma about adultery amongst Hindus, and it follows that illegitimacy does not confer disgrace. Sonship confers so great advantages upon fathers, that the question of legitimacy§ is one which originally had no effect, even in excluding from inheritance.‖ The son whether of concealed birth, or born before marriage, belonged to the husband.¶ He could perform the obsequies, and therefore could succeed. The *paunerbhava*, or illegitimate offspring,** were entitled to inherit on failure of legitimate or other preferable issue, or to an inferior portion, if there were a legitimate son. That, however, as a general rule of law, has long become obsolete,

* 9 Menu, 178 and 179.

† 2 Colebrooke's Digest, pp. 249-250.

‡ 2 Madras, p. 196.

§ 9 Menu, 159-160, 180.

‖ Mitakshara, Chapter I., Section XI., verses 6 and 7.

¶ 2 Strange, pp. 205, 207.

** Mitakshara, Chapter I., Section XI., verses 1—8.

except as regard Sudras,* with regard to whom the Privy Council† recently held that their illegitimate children may inherit and have a right to maintenance. And, although the pundits gave it as their opinion that the child of an illegitimate father amongst Sudras was of no caste at all, and could not contract a legal or valid marriage, the Privy Council disregarded it as entirely without authority or decision in its favor.

Rights of illegitimate children.

In 1799, the Sudder Court held that an illegitimate son could succeed only when his right to do so was established by local usage, and not otherwise. And in a much later case,‡ when the dispute was between a daughter's son and an illegitimate son born of a low woman of the Dhanook tribe, it was held that the illegitimate son was not entitled to any specific share, but that he had a right to maintenance; it being provided by law that the son by a Sudra woman, of a man belonging to any of the three superior classes, should be allowed a sufficiency for that purpose. The same rules that apply to illegitimate children by Sudra women, are applicable also to the spurious offspring of women in the inverse order of the classes. The claim of the illegitimate son, in the particular case, was partly rested on the ground of its being the usage of the family that an illegitimate son should succeed in default of a legitimate one, but the Court held that the most satisfactory evidence should be adduced to justify a belief in the existence of a usage which confounds all distinction between lawful and unlawful issue.

* Mohun Singh v. Chummun Rai, 1 Select Rep. (new edn.), p. 37, note.

† Inderpan Valumgputty Taver v. Ramaswamy Pandia Talser, 3 B. L. R., P. C., p. 4.

‡ Persad Sing v. Ranee Muhesee, 3 Select Reports (new edition), p. 176.

LECTURE VII.

The distinction so existing and recognized, availed at first to give to legitimate issue merely a preferable right of inheritance over illegitimate. All* the analogies of Hindu law are against the view of a bastard taken by the law of England, which law in that respect is founded upon the doctrine of Christianity. The right of inheritance to their father's estate, which formerly belonged† to illegitimate sons in the Sudra caste, is still retained by them, according to a very recent decision of the Privy Council. But in the three superior castes, an illegitimate son has long ceased to possess a right to inherit. Nevertheless, he is not, as in English law, *quasi nullius filius*, but his *status* as a son in the family, and his right to maintenance, are secured to him. Further than that, illegitimacy is no taint or disqualification for *caste* in the individual and his children.‡ But it depends upon the *caste* of the father, whether it disables a man from inheriting. If that father's caste is above the Sudra, the illegitimate son cannot inherit, even though the caste is one of the mixed classes between the second and third of Menu's divisions.

This rule led in one case§ to a desperate attempt to establish that the second and third castes have ceased to exist in a particular part of India, and that all Hindus were either Brahmins or Sudras. On the death of one of the Rajahs of Ramnugger leaving three widows and a brother of the half blood, the brother of the half blood, by arrangements with the eldest of the three widows, obtained and kept

* 2 Madras, p. 196.

† Mitakshara, Chapter I., Section XII.; 1 Strange's Hindu Law, p. 132.

‡ Pandaya Telayer *v.* Puli Telava, 1 Madras H. C., p. 478.

§ Churturya Run Murdhun Sing *v.* Sahab Purhidan Syce, 4 S. W. R., P. C., p. 132.

possession of the Raj and estates until his death, when his illegitimate son claimed the inheritance. The deceased Rajah was a Rajpoot, and was alleged to belong to the Khatri caste, but it was contended on behalf of the illegitimate son, who was the appellant before the Privy Council, that the Kshatriya and Vaisya classes had ceased to exist, and were sunk into the Sudra class, amongst whom illegitimacy is no bar to inheritance; and that there were now two classes only, the Brahmin and the Sudra, and many authorities were quoted in support of that contention. The Privy Council, however, decided that the Kshatriya class must be considered as subsisting; that the Rajpoots are considered to belong to that class; and that the illegitimate son of any one of the three regenerate sons cannot succeed to the inheritance of his father.

Age of majority.

The completion of the regenerating ceremonies marks, according to Hindu law, the period at which the boy ceases to be under tutelage, and is considered to have attained the age of discretion. The completion of the sixteenth year generally throughout India is the age at which, according to the original shasters, a Hindu attains majority. In Bengal, the commencement of the sixteenth year, *i. e.*, the completion of the fifteenth, is the age at which the disabilities of minority cease. Various authorities, including Raghunandana, the great authority of Bengal, concur in fixing the end of the sixteenth year as the limit of minority. And Jagannatha, in his Digest,* expressly mentions the end of the fifteenth year; for the annotation of Srikrishna†

* Colebrooke's Digest, Book I., Chap. V., verse 188; see 2 Strange's Hindu Law, p. 76.

† Dayabhaga, Chap. III., Section I., verse 17.

LECTURE VII.

to the Dayabhaga, seems to have fixed the rule as applicable in Bengal*

During minority, the disabilities may be considered to be the same amongst Hindus as amongst those subject to English law.† They are so held to be in practice.

Hindu law therefore confers independence at a somewhat early age; but in practice, it has not been found convenient to adhere too strictly to the rules laid down by the old authorities. When the rules for the decennial settlement of the three provinces were first issued, minors were declared disqualified for the management of their estates; and subsequently minority was by Bengal Regulation X of 1793, Section 28, declared to be, in conformity with those rules, limited with respect to Hindus and Mahomedans to the expiration of the fifteenth year. In fixing this period by the rules which they issued, the Government were, it was stated in the preamble to a subsequent Regulation, guided by legal considerations. But the inexpediency of vesting proprietors with the charge of their lands at so early a period was soon discovered; and by the Bengal Regulation XXVI of the same year, followed by a similar Madras Regulation, a few years later, the age of eighteen was fixed upon as the age of majority, in respect of those to whom the Regulation applied. "The rule contained in Section 28 of Regulation X of 1793, which limits the minority of Hindu and Mahomedan *proprietors of estates paying revenue to Government* to the expiration of the fifteenth year, is hereby rescinded, and the minority of such proprietors is declared to extend to the end of the eighteenth year."

Bengal Regulation XXVI of 1793.

* Debiamoye Dossee *v.* Jugessur Hathi, 1 S. W. R., p. 75.

† Shamachurn's Vyavastha Darpana, pp. 396, 397; and the texts there cited.

Subsequently in 1858, by Act XL of that year, "for making better provision for the case of the *persons* and *property* of minors in the Presidency of Fort William in Bengal," it was enacted that, except in the case of proprietors of estates paying revenue to Government, who have been or shall be taken under the protection of the Court of Wards, and who, of course, still remain subject to the provision of the Regulation of 1793, "the case of the persons of all minors (not being European British subjects), and the charge of their property, shall be subject* to the jurisdiction of the Civil Court." Further on, by the 26th section, it is enacted that, "for the purposes of this Act, every person shall be held to be a minor who has not attained the age of eighteen years." The purposes of the Act being to subject to a particular jurisdiction, the care of the persons of all minors, with specific exceptions, and the charge of their property; it follows that all minors to whom the Act applies retain their disabilities till the age of eighteen years.

LECTURE VII.

Act X of 1858.

It seems, however, in practice, to have been taken for granted, that the Act only applied to those cases in which the jurisdiction of the Court was actively enforced, and the charge of the person and property and the general duties of guardianship were assumed by the Judge. The question whether a much wider change had not been effected in the law which regulates the personal *status* of Hindus and Mahomedans was discussed by the High Court of Bengal in the case of *Muddoosoodun Manji* v. *Debee Gobinda Newgi*,† where the plaintiff endeavoured to exempt himself from

* Section 2.

† 1 Bengal Law Reports, 1 F. B., p. 49.

LECTURE VII.

the operation of the Statute of Limitations by alleging that his age of majority, that being the date from which the statutable period would run, was not attained until he reached the age of eighteen years. The suit was to recover possession of his ancestral property. The first Court held that the plaintiff who was subject to Bengal law became a major at the age of fifteen years, because, though he was a proprietor of land paying revenue direct to Government, he was owner of only a share in a revenue-paying estate. The Judge on appeal held that, as he was a landowner paying revenue directly to Government, be the estate large or small, so his minority did not cease till he was eighteen years of age.

Full Bench ruling in *Muddoosoodun Manji* v. *Debee Gobinda Newgi.*

The case was referred to a Full Bench of Judges who, on the 7th day of August 1868, delivered through the Chief Justice the following judgment:—

"This case appears to me to be very clear when we look at the whole of Act XL of 1858. The recital declares that it is expedient to make better provision for the care of the persons and property of minors, not brought under the superintendence of the Court of Wards, treating those whose estates have been brought under the Court of Wards as minors. Certain Regulations are repealed; and then by section 2 it is enacted that, "except in the case of proprietors of estates paying revenue to Government, who have been or shall be taken under the protection of the Court of Wards, the care of the persons of all minors, not being European British subjects, and the charge of their property, shall be subject to the jurisdiction of the Civil Court." By this section, also, proprietors of estates paying revenue to Government, who have been taken under the care of the Court of Wards are treated as minors; for such persons are excepted out of the general term 'all minors,' as if it had been said 'all minors, except those who are under the care of the Court of Wards.' Section 26 declares that 'for the purposes of this Act, every person shall be held a minor who has not attained the age of eighteen years.'

"Every person, therefore, not being a European subject, who has not attained the age of eighteen years, is a minor for the purposes of the Act, and unless he is a proprietor of an estate paying revenue to Government, who has been taken under the jurisdiction of the Court of Wards, the care of the person and the charge of his property are subject to the jurisdiction of the Civil Court.

"Then, can it be said that, being a minor subject to the jurisdiction of the Civil Court, he is not a minor, unless proceedings are taken in the Civil Court for the protection of his property, or for the appointment of a guardian. His relatives may neglect his interests, but he is still a minor. There may be a minor whose interests are neglected, as well as a minor whose interests are looked after and protected. The exception of the Statute of Limitation in the case of minors is more necessary for the former than for those who have some one to look after their interests.

"Being a minor, the plaintiff came within Sections 11 and 12 of Act XIV of 1859, and was under a disability, until he attained the age of eighteen. As pointed out by Mr. Justice E. Jackson, if the law were otherwise, this anomaly would follow that a minor may have attained his majority on one day, and become a minor on the next. A man cannot be said not to be under a disability as a minor, when he is liable as a minor to have his property and person put under the charge of a guardian. If he is

Lecture VII.

a proprietor of an estate paying revenue to Government, and has been taken under the protection of the Court of Wards, he is still a minor up to the age of eighteen (Regulation XXVI of 1793, Section 2). It cannot be said that he is not a minor when, on account of his minority, his estates have been taken under the charge of the Court of Wards, under the provisions of Regulation X of 1793; when by Section 22 of that Regulation, he is to have a guardian of his person; and by Sections 7 and 15, a manager of all his estates, real and personal; and by Section 32, he cannot sue in the Civil Courts for any cause of action."

Again, in a case* before a Division Bench of the Bengal High Court, it was held that, under Act XL of 1858, eighteen years is the age of majority, not only for persons paying revenue to Government, and taken under the Court of Wards, but for all other persons not European subjects. There is an Act XX of 1864 which applies to Bombay, and is in terms similar to that of Act XL of 1858, and therefore a Hindu in the Bengal and Bombay Presidencies, whether male or female, attains to independence at the age of eighteen; but in other parts of India, sixteen is the age of majority, except in the Madras Presidency, where a Regulation provides the age of eighteen as the period of majority for those who are proprietors paying rent to Government.

Result of legislative enactments

Questions however must and do arise as to the applicability of the Act in case of the individual whose personal *status* is under discussion. Although eighteen is possibly the age of majority according to the Indian Succession Act for all persons domiciled in India, except Hindus, Mahomedans, and Buddhists; and although various

* Lakhikant Dutt *v.* Jagabandhu Chuckerbutty, 3 B. L. R., App., p. 79.

Regulations and Acts have provided that, with respect to a large number, perhaps the majority of Hindus and Mahomedans, eighteen shall also be the age of majority; yet there is another portion of the Hindu and Mahomedan community to whom those Acts and Regulations do not apply; and a residuum still left of those communities to whom it is a matter of doubt and perplexity what is the age at which their disabilities cease.

For instance, it might well be that, under the 27th Section of Act XL of 1858, minors, whose fathers or husbands are living, and are not minors, would not be liable to any of the provisions of the Act; and then they might probably be held to attain the age of majority at fifteen or sixteen as the case may be. On the other hand if, after they had attained the age of fifteen or sixteen, and before they reached the age of eighteen, their husbands or fathers died, they would in that case come within the purposes of the Act, and return to a status of minority. According to the Full Bench Ruling, the Act must be so construed as to avoid this result, and it is difficult to say what that construction may be. Then it has been contended that Act XL of 1858 does not apply to the High Court in its Original Civil Jurisdiction, and also that Regulation XXVI of 1793 does not so apply; and the High Court expressing* its opinion that the general question was "in a complicated and unsatisfactory state," abstained from deciding the point so raised, considering it unnecessary to do so in the particular case. That is to say, the question whether that portion of the Hindu and Mahomedan communities whose

* In the goods of Gungaprasad Gosain.—*Per* Macpherson, J., 4 B. L. R., App., p. 43.

LECTURE VII.

age exceeds sixteen, or in some cases fifteen, and is under eighteen, is a responsible body of citizens capable, in the eye of law, of entering into business transactions with their fellow men, is a matter of such difficulty and perplexity, is governed by so many complicated considerations, capable, moreover, of being differently decided by different Courts, that the highest Court in the empire finds it a matter of insuperable difficulty to lay down a rule upon the subject.

Further than that, the Indian Succession Act will probably be held to have introduced a similar difficulty with regard to the domiciled inhabitants of British India, not Hindu, Mahomedan, or Buddhist. It is nowhere enacted in that Statute that eighteen shall be the age of majority. It is provided in the interpretation clause that whenever the word "minor" is used in that Statute it shall mean one who has not completed the age of eighteen years; and that "minority" means the *status* of such person.

But that leaves untouched the general *status* of such persons in matter in respect of which the Indian Succession Act does not apply. In respect of those matters their age of majority will probably be held to be the age according to English Law, *viz.*, twenty-one. As a general rule, it may be said that no one domiciled in British India can say, with absolute certainty, at what particular date his disabilities cease, and when, in the eye of law, his responsibilities commence.

Such a state of things ought not to be allowed to exist. The law of personal *status* ought always to be clear and well-defined. How a valid marriage can be created or dissolved, whether a child is legitimate or illegitimate, whether a man is under the disabilities of minority or not, ought to be plain to the commonest understanding, not merely in the interests of the parties themselves whose *status* is in question, but in the interests of all who may deal with them, whether they are fellow subjects, or the subjects of other Powers. By dealing with the subject of minority, in a partial and incomplete manner, and for special purposes, the Legislature has unwittingly thrown the subject into confusion, and introduced doubt, where is neither occasion nor excuse for it. If the age of eighteen, which the Indian Succession Act probably intended should be the age of majority, were expressly declared to be so in case of all to whom the Act applied, and if such rule were also extended by legislative enactment to the three great populations who are excepted from its operation, the alteration so effected would obviate much difficulty and inconvenience, and would, under the circumstances created by recent legislation and decisions, be undoubtedly a useful and beneficial measure.

LECTURE VIII.

THE HINDU WIDOW.

Precepts in favour of Suttee—Suttee not sanctioned by all the Sages—Decline of the practice of Suttee—Principle on which the practice was based—Opposed to the teaching of the earlier Sages—Position assigned to the Widow in the Shasters—By English administration of Hindu Law—Suppression of Suttee—Remarriage of Hindu Widows expressly permitted—Widow's succession to her husband's Estate—According to Mitakshara Law—According to the Dayabhaga—Nature of the interest which she possesses in her deceased husband's property—Power of Alienation—Reversionary Heirs, even the Crown can prohibit or set aside her authorized alienation—Power of alienation under the Mithila School—Under the Bengal School—The Hindu Widow's Estate held to be a restricted estate of inheritance—Power of alienation of her own Estate—As defined by the Full Bench—Right of Widows where there are more than one.

In treating of the members of the joint family, especially with respect to the subjects of maintenance and guardianship, and also in a future discussion upon the questions of inheritance and partition, the position and rights of the Hindu widow relatively to others cannot be overlooked. But the condition of widowhood amongst Hindus has a peculiar and separate history, one which is full of tragical and striking incident, and which has attracted a large share of attention from civilized nations. The comparatively modern practice of suttee and the well grounded suspicion that that practice rested largely on a foundation of crime and fraud, instead of religious feeling, rendered the

Hindu widow an object of especial interest to western nations; and the practical result indirectly attributable, no doubt, to that circumstance, has been to effect a considerable change in recent years in her position and to secure to her personal independence, rights of property, and an established position in her family.

Precepts in favor of Suttee.

The early teaching of the sages is by no means consistent upon the subject.* "That woman," says Angiras, "who, on the death of her husband, ascends the same burning pile with him is exalted to heaven as equal in virtue to Arundhati, and expiates the sins of three generations on both sides of her husband's family; and as long as in her successive transmigrations she shall decline to do so, she shall not be exempted from springing again to life in the body of some female animal." Angiras was one of the sons of Menu,† "one of the ten lords of created beings, eminent in holiness," and he taught in the most primitive times. The sum of his doctrines upon the subject is that "no other effectual duty is known for virtuous women at any time after the death of their lords except casting themselves into the same fire."‡ Vyasa, the reputed author of the *Puranas*, adopted the same doctrine, and declared that with the widow it rested to redeem by self-sacrifice her husband from torment, and that her reward would be to share his felicity "as long as fourteen Indras reign."

Not sanctioned by all the sages.

On the other hand Menu, whose code is of the highest authority amongst Hindus, and is singularly humane except when Brahmanas are to be protected, or adultery to be repressed, and whose sanctions are mostly derived

* Colebrooke's Digest, Book IV., Chap. III., Sec. I., verse 123.

† 1 Menu, 34, 35.

‡ Colebrooke's Digest, Book IV., Chap. III., Sec. I., verse 123.

LECTURE VIII.

from the terrors of a future state, nowhere enjoins a practice which is admittedly the greatest blot on the history of Hindu civilization. Menu, therefore, could never have been cited in support of a practice which nevertheless prevailed for a considerable time and became rooted in the institutions of the race. Vrihaspati, moreover, who considers a wife to be half the body of her husband, declared that whether she ascended the funeral pile after him, or survived for his benefit, she was a faithful wife. He declared in explicit terms* that the widow violated no duty by refusing to burn; and he endeavoured to set limits to the practice. He forbade the mother of an infant child,† or one about to give birth to a child, to ascend the funeral pile; and declared that strict in austerities and rigid devotion, firm in avoiding sensuality, and even patient and liberal, a widow attains heaven even though she have no son.

Decline of the practice of Suttee.

In the opinion of Sir T. Strange ‡ the practice had in it more of *malus usus* than of law, and was confined in Southern India at least pretty much to the lower orders. According to the *Abbè Dubois*,§ it was by no means so frequent at the commencement of this century as in former times, and was more rare in the peninsula than in the Northern parts of India; and was never permitted by Mahomedan rulers in provinces subject to them. "If," he says,‖ "a woman choose to survive her husband, the wildest demonstrations of grief are prescribed to her, and she is afterwards constituted a widow by particular ceremony;"

* Colebrooke's Digest, Book IV., Chap. III., Sec. II., verse 132.

† *Ibid*, Book IV., Chap. III., Sec. I., verse 128.

‡ 1 Strange, p. 241.

§ Manners and Customs of Hindus, p. 236.

‖ *Ibid*, p. 227.

and thereupon, he adds, the Tahli or golden ornament worn in that part of India round the neck, as the symbol of marriage, is cut by her nearest female relations, and she is formally consigned to a state of widowhood, from which the customs of the country forbid emancipation. LECTURE VIII.

Principle on which the practice was based.

The practice of suttee was based upon the principle of the entire subjection of the wife to the husband, which runs through the whole of Hindu law, custom, and feeling. It was probably in the first instance due to that horror of remarriage which dates from the time of Menu and pervaded the whole people. The authors of Menu's code discuss the question of a childless wife or widow bearing children to the brother or near kinsman of her husband, for the purpose of such husband obtaining those who may stand* to him in the relation of offspring; a practice which dated from a still earlier period in Hindu history when *Vena* held the sovereign power. Menu forbad it, denouncing it as only fit for cattle (though he permitted it to Sudras); but he did not proceed to enjoin cremation as its remedy. But upon the subject of the remarriage of a widow, he is as explicit in his denunciations as any of the subsequent sages:—"A Brahman," he says, "who has married a widow resembles clarified butter poured on ashes as an† oblation to fire; and a widow who from‡ a wish to bear children slights her deceased husband by marrying again, brings disgrace on herself here below, and shall be excluded from the seat of her lord." The marriage of a

* 2 Colebrooke's Digest, Book IV., Chap. IV., Sec. I., verses 146, 147, 148, and 150.

† 3 Menu, verse 181.

‡ 5 Menu, verse 161.

widow was even in Menu's time a thing unknown to, and unmentioned in, the laws relating to marriage.*

Opposed to the teaching of the earlier sages.

So far from directing the widow to burn herself, some of the earlier sages carefully define her position and duties.

According to Vrihat Menu,† the widow of a sonless man keeping unsullied her husband's bed, and persevering in religious observances, that is, in the performance of religious acts beneficial to her husband's soul in the next world, shall present to him the oblation cake and obtain his entire share. Menu thus prescribes the duties of widowhood:‡ "Let her emaciate her body by living voluntarily on pure flowers, roots and fruits, but let her not, when her lord is deceased, even pronounce the name of another man. Let her continue till death, forgiving all injuries, performing harsh duties, avoiding every sensual pleasure, and practising the incomparable rules of virtue which have been followed by such women as were devoted to one husband only." "Many thousands of Brahmans, having avoided sensuality from their early youth, and having left no issue in their families, have ascended, nevertheless, to heaven; and like those abstemious men, a virtuous wife ascends to heaven though she have no child, if after the decease of her lord, she devotes herself to pious austerity. But a widow, who, from a wish to bear children, slights her deceased husband by marrying again, brings disgrace on herself here below, and shall be excluded from the seat of her lord."

Other sages insist more strongly upon strict austerities,

* 9 Menu, verse 65.

† Dayabhaga, Chap. XI., Sec. I., verse 7.

‡ 5 Menu, verses 157, 158.

rigid devotion, and harsh duties. "Only one meal each day," it is said, "should ever be made by a widow; not a second repast by any means, and a widowed woman sleeping on a bedstead would cause her husband to fall from a region of joy." She must perform the shraddas in each of the twelve successive months, and the two half-yearly shraddas, and also the first and anniversary shraddas. She is, however, forbidden to perform the *parvana* or double set of oblations.

Position assigned to the widow in the shasters.

The position assigned by the shasters to the widow, and even to women generally, both in their families and in society, is a state of abject dependence and submission, one wholly inconsistent with English notions of freedom. They were in fact crushed by the weight of the joint family system. The males alone had authority in those small communities, and their union tended to rivet more closely the chains of female subjection. "Day and night," says Menu,* "must women be held by their protectors in a state of dependence; even in lawful and innocent recreations, being too much addicted to them, they must be kept by their protectors under their own dominion." "Through independence," according to the text of Nareda, "even women born of noble families would swerve from their duty; hence the lord of created beings has established their perpetual dependence. Their fathers† protect them in childhood; their husbands protect them in youth; their sons protect them in age; a woman is never fit for independence." "In no instance," says Yajnavalkya, "is it allowed." "Left to the guidance of her own will,"

* Colebrooke's Digest, Book IV., Chap. I., Sec. I., verse 3.

† 4 Colebrooke's Digest, Book IV., Chap. I., Sec. I., verse 5.

LECTURE VIII.

says Dacsha,* "and unrestrained by affections, she afterwards becomes ungovernable as a neglected disease becomes incurable."

By English administration of Hindu law.

Such may be the Hindu law on the subject according to the shasters, but practically the whole of it is abrogated as unsuited to the present age. Increased education and the altered circumstances of their lives may have done much to effect a change in their position. But the refusal of English Courts to interfere for the purpose of securing that dependence and submission; the application in fact of English law, to so far as it has been practicable, to protect their individual freedom; and the decay of the communal system, have established the free agency of women as well as men. Only the other day a Hindu† widow of seventeen years of age asserted her right to go wherever she pleased, in spite of her mother and brothers and her deceased husband's relations, and elected to join the house of the missionaries, and to abandon her religion, family and customs.

Actual legislation has had very little to do with the change which has been effected. The virtual legislation of the Courts, enabling them to keep pace with the growing wants and the changing circumstances of society, the application of English law to Hindus in all matters in respect of which their own laws are not expressly reserved to them, and the separation of religious obligations from the legal rights and duties of individuals have been hitherto found sufficient for the purpose. The Legislature, it is true, interfered authoritatively to suppress the practice of Suttee. But it did so with great hesitation and re-

* 4 Colebrooke's Digest, Book IV., Chap. I., Sec. I., verse 27.

† *In re* Gunnesh Soondery Dabee, reported in "Englishman newspaper," May 19, 1870.

luctance.* The fear of the resentment and resistance which the innovation would produce for a long time prevented their interference. But at length in 1829, while Lord William Bentinck was Governor-General, and in a large degree owing to his influence, Regulation XVII of 1829, was passed; the preamble of which recited that the practice of Suttee was revolting to the feelings of human nature; was nowhere enjoined by the religion of Hindus as an imperative duty; and by a vast majority of that people was not kept and observed. "It is notorious," the preamble goes on to recite, "that in many instances acts of atrocity have been perpetrated, which have been shocking to the Hindus themselves, and in their eyes unlawful and wicked." And by that Regulation the practice of Suttee was at length declared to be illegal and punishable by the Criminal Courts; provision was made casting responsibility on the zemindars, talookdars and police officers in the neighbourhood to give intelligence and assist in dispersing the assembly; and all persons convicted of aiding and abetting in the sacrifice of a Hindu widow, by burning or burying her alive, whether the sacrifice were voluntary on her part or not, were declared to be guilty of culpable homicide, the punishment to extend to that of death, in case the unfortunate victim should appear to have been under a state of intoxication, or stupefaction, or other causes impeding her free will.

Suppression of Suttee.

A still further innovation was made by the Legislature upon the law affecting the personal *status* and rights of Hindu widows, by an Act intituled XV of 1856. Although there had been a difference of opinion amongst the earlier

Remarriage of Hindu widows expressly permitted.

* Mill's History of British India, Vol. IX., p. 191.

LECTURE VIII.

sages as to the merit of the practice of Suttee, there had been none as to the duty of the widow to abstain from a second marriage, and to preserve a life of chastity, retirement, and privation. But the Act to which I have just referred, recited in its preamble that the legal incapacity imputed to Hindu widows of marrying again, though in accordance with established customs, was believed by many to be not in accordance with a true interpretation of the precepts of their religion, and that many Hindus desired that they should not be prevented by law from adopting a different custom, if so minded. The Act then proceeded to legalize the marriage of Hindu widows, and to legitimate the issue of such marriage, "any custom, and any interpretation of Hindu law to the contrary notwithstanding." This is the greatest innovation upon orthodox Hindu sentiment and practice that the Legislature has yet made. And if general custom and feeling are any proof of the interpretation put by the community on their own shasters for countless generations, the Act was a direct innovation upon Hindu law, made by the Legislature in the exercise of their undoubted powers, and with the approval of the more intelligent of the community.

Widow's succession to her husband's estate according to Mitakshara law.

Next with regard to the position of a widow, in reference to the property of which her husband died possessed. Vriddha Menu declared her right to the whole of it, on failure of male issue. Vrihad Vishnu,* Catyayana and Vrihaspati, concur in that view; "let the widow succeed to her husband's wealth, provided she be chaste." On the other hand passages occur which are adverse to the widow's claim. Nareda†

* Dayabhaga, Chapter XI., Section I., verses 43, 44. Mitakshara, Chapter II., Section I., verse 6.

† Mitakshara, Chapter II., Section I., verse 7.

is in favor of the succession of brothers, and directs the assignment of maintenance to the widows. Passages are quoted also from Menu and Sancha in support of the text of Nareda. The contradictory nature of these texts is explained by the author of the Mitakshara, who deduces from them the rule that the succession of a widow to her sonless husband is limited to the case of the widow of a separated brother. If the husband be joint with his brothers, the right of the widow to succeed is denied. The right interpretation is declared to be that* "when a man who was separated from his co-heirs and not re-united with them dies leaving no male issue, his widow, if chaste, takes the estate in the first instance."

According to the Dayabhaga.

According to the Dayabhaga† on failure of heirs down to the sons' grandson, the wife being inferior in pretension to sons and the rest, because she performs acts spiritually beneficial to her husband, from the date of her widowhood, and not like them from the moment of her birth, succeeds to the estate in their default. Vyasa says: "After the death of her husband, let a virtuous woman observe the duty of continence, and let her daily, after the purification of the bath, present, from the joined palms of her hands, water mixed with *til* (sesamum) to the manes of her husband; let her, day by day, perform with devotion the worship of the gods, and the adoration of Vishnu, practising constant abstemiousness. She should give alms to the chief of the venerable, for increase of holiness, and keep the various fasts which are commanded by sacred ordinances. The woman who is assiduous in the performance of duties conveys her hus-

* Mitakshara, Chapter II., Section I., verses 30-39.

† Dayabhaga, Chapter XI., Section I., verses 43, 44.

LECTURE VIII.

band, though abiding in another world, and herself, to a region of bliss." Since by these and other passages it is declared that the wife rescues her husband from hell, and since a woman, doing improper acts through indigence causes her husband to fall to a region of horror, for they share the fruits of virtue and vice; therefore the property devolving on her is for the benefit of the former owner; and the wife's succession is consequently proper.

In the Dayabhaga,* the question is discussed why the wife as half the body of her husband may not exclusively take his wealth, although sons or other male descendants be living. The reason assigned is that a person's own soul is born to him as a son; that the son or other descendant is con-substantial with the father and other ancestor. The continuance of race and attainment of heaven, according to Yajnavalkya, depend on a son, grandson, and great-grandson. Such descendants produce great spiritual benefit to their father or ancestor from the moment of birth, and they present the oblation cake at the Parva to their deceased father.

But although the widow succeeds to her husband's estate in the absence of male issue, she does not represent her husband, so as to succeed to an estate, which he would have taken by inheritance† had he survived the owner.

* Dayabhaga, Chap. XI., Section I., verses 31, 32, 33. *Vrihaspati.*—In scripture, in law, in sacred ordinances, in popular usage, a wife is declared by the wise to be half the body of her husband, equally sharing the fruit of pure and impure acts: of him whose wife is not deceased, half the body survives; how should another take the property while half the body of the owner lives? And see Colebrooke's Digest, Book V., Chap. VIII., Section I., verse 399.

† Colebrooke's Digest, Book V., Chap. VIII., Section I., verse 414.

Then with regard to the nature of the interest which the widow takes in the estate of her husband to which she succeeds. She does not obtain a full proprietary right of inheritance, but is only entitled to enjoy the estate under the guardianship of the next heirs of the deceased. At her death the estate does not devolve upon her heirs, but goes to the nearest heir or heirs of her husband living at her decease.

LECTURE VIII.

Nature of the interest which she possesses in her husband's property.

A widow can only enjoy the estate subject to the control of her guardians. She had originally no power of alienation, except for her own necessities, and for the performance of her husband's funeral rites, or of other religious observances for the benefit of her deceased husband's soul. Even then she could not alienate, if the reversioners supplied her with the necessary funds.* There is a note by Mr. Colebrooke in the first volume of the Select Reports,† to the effect that it has been declared by the law officers of the Courts, in other suits, that a widow's gift of the estate of her husband to the next heir is good in law, though she be restrained from making any other alienation of it. This opinion, he says, though not founded on any express passages to that effect in books of authority, seems reasonable; as such a gift is a mere relinquishment of her temporary interest in favor of the next heir. It may, however, happen that the person who would have been entitled to take the inheritance at her decease may be different from the one who obtained it under the gift or relinquishment to him as presumptive heir; and if the title be either preferable or equal, it may invalidate such gift in whole or in part.

* Shamachurn's Vyavastha Darpana, pp. 57, 69; Dayabhaga, Chap. XI., Section I., verse 56.

† Select Reports (new edition), p. 85.

LECTURE VIII.

Power of alienation.

With the consent of the reversionary heirs, the widow can, of course, aliene her husband's estate, but unless she obtain that consent, they, *i. e.* the next in reversion, are entitled to interfere and prevent such alienation. And conversely if a Hindu widow in possession of her husband's estate borrow money for any purposes, of the nature of those under which the woman was authorized by law to alienate a portion of the property, such as to pay his debts or perform his funeral obsequies, the reversioners on succeeding to the estate are liable to pay thereout the debts so contracted. But they are not liable to do so when the debts incurred by the widow are entirely personal and for purposes of her own.* Further, a widow should not alienate the accumulations† of her husband's estate, nor her own acquisitions made by means of that estate.

Suppose, however, there are no reversionary heirs, it has been contended that, in that case, the fetters on the widow's power of alienation drop, and she takes an absolute interest in the estate. Such a contention, however, was overruled by the Privy Council, in the case of *the Collector of Masulipatam* v. *Cavaly Vencata Narrainapah.*‡ The following passage of the judgment contains an important discussion on the subject:

Reversionary heirs, even the Crown, can prohibit or set aside her unauthorized alienation.

"It is clear that, under the Hindu law, the widow, though she takes as heir, takes a special and qualified estate. Compared with any estate that passes under the English law by inheritance, it is an anomalous estate. It is a qualified proprietorship, and it is only by the principles of the Hindu law that the extent and nature of the qualification can be determined.

"It is admitted on all hands, that if there be collateral

* Bungsee Dhur Hajra *v.* Thakoor Pyrag Sing, 7 S. D. R., p. 114.

† See *post*, p. 202.

‡ 8 Moore's I. A., p. 550.

heirs of the husband, the widow cannot, of her own will, aliene the property except for special purposes. For religious or charitable purposes, or those which are supposed to conduce to the spiritual welfare of her husband, she has a larger power of disposition than that which she possesses for purely worldly purposes. To support an alienation for the last, she must show necessity ; on the other hand it may be taken as established that an alienation by her which would not otherwise be legitimate, may become so if made with the consent of her husband's kindred. But it surely is not the necessary or logical consequence of this latter proposition that, in the absence of collateral heirs to the husband, or on their failure, the fetter on the widow's power of alienation altogether drops. The exception in favour of alienation with consent may be due to a presumption of law, that where that consent is given, the purpose for which the alienation is made must be proper.

"Nor does it appear to their lordships that the construction of Hindu law, which is now contended for, can be put upon the principle of '*cessante ratione cessat et ipsa lex.*' It is not merely for the protection of the material interests of her husband's relations that the fetter on the widow's power is imposed. Numberless authorities from Menu downwards may be cited to show that, according to the principles of Hindu law, the proper state of every woman is one of tutelage ; that they always require protection, and are never fit for independence. Sir Thomas Strange* cites the authority of Menu for the pro-

* See 1 Strange's Hindu Law, p. 245. But, on failure of kindred on both sides, the king is the ruler and protector of a woman. Colebrooke's Digest, Book IV., Chap. I., Sec. I., verse 7.

Nareda.—But if the kindred on both sides fail, the king is considered

LECTURE VIII.

position that, if a woman have no other controller or protector, the king should control or protect her. Again all the authorities concur in showing that, according to the principles of Hindu law, the life of a widow is to be one of ascetic privation.* Hence, probably, it gave her a power of disposition for religious, which it denied to her for other, purposes. These principles do not seem to be consistent with the doctrine that, on the failure of heirs, a widow becomes completely emancipated, perfectly uncontrolled in the disposal of her property; and free to squander her inherited wealth for the purposes of selfish enjoyment.

"Their lordships are of opinion, that the restrictions on a Hindu widow's power of alienation are inseparable from her estate, and that their existence does not depend on that of heirs capable of taking on her death. It follows, that if, for want of heirs, the right to the property, so far as it has not been lawfully disposed of by her, passes to the crown, the crown must have the same power which an heir would have of protecting its interests by impeaching any unauthorized alienation by the widow."

Power of alienation under the Mithila school.

There seems to be some difference between the Mithila and Bengal schools as to the widow's power of disposition. According to the Ratnakara and the Vivada Chintamoni, the widow has power to consume, give, or sell the moveables which may have devolved upon her by the death of the husband, but has no power over the immoveables beyond a moderate enjoyment of them. And the High

as the protector of the woman, he shall guard her and shall chastise her if led away from the path of virtue. Colebrooke's Digest, Book IV., Chap. I., Sec. I., verse 13.

* Colebrooke's Digest, Book IV., Chap. III., Sec. II., verses 133, 134, 135.

Court of Bombay said in a reported case* that the spirit and practice of Hindu law, as recognized in Western India, would be best construed by treating the widow as having uncontrolled power over the moveable estate, but as having nothing more than a life-use in the immoveable estate. And when a Hindu inhabitant of Bombay died without male issue, leaving a widow, four daughters, a brother, and the male issue of other deceased brothers, it was held, with regard to the immoveable property, that the daughters took absolutely from their father, after their mother's death, to the exclusion of the collateral heirs. LECTURE VIII.

The Pundits, however, of the Supreme and Sudder Courts of Bengal, upwards of half a century ago, not without some opposition from other Pundits, established the doctrine that "the widow, in Bengal, has the entire right of property vested in her both in the moveable and immoveable estate;† for there is no distinction between them taken in the books in respect of the husband's estate devolving upon her as heir, as there is in the case of male succession to ancestral property; and as there is also in respect of real property given to her by her husband in his life-time, which she is declared incapable of alienating from his heirs as she may alienate a personal property so given; but that she is legally prohibited from wasting the property so vested in her, and cannot make away with it except for certain allowable and declared purposes, without the consent of her husband's next male heir; and further considering, that, even in the use and enjoyment of the property so vested, she is religiously and morally enjoined Under the Bengal school.

* Toolsey Doss *v.* Doocowerban, 1 Bombay, p. 230.

† Per East, C. J. (1819), in *Kasheenath Bysack* v. *Hurrosoondery Dossee*, Shamachurn's Vyavastha Darpana, p. 93.

LECTURE VIII.

to use moderation and take the advice of her husband's kindred in her manner of living, but is under no legal disability if she do not take or follow such advice."

Further * it was declared by the Privy Council in the same case, that, whatever may be the extent of the widow's power or control over the moveable or immoveable property of her husband, she is entitled to the possession of both, and cannot be deprived of it by the husband's relations. Her right to the possession is absolute, and cannot be restricted. With regard to the extent of her interest in it, and right of dominion over it, the Privy Council laid it down that "she was only entitled to enjoy it according to the rights of a Hindu widow, which rights, (that is the extent and limit of her power of dispostion, it was absolutely impossible to define,) because it must depend upon the circumstances of that disposition, whenever such disposition should be made, and must be consistent with the law regulating such dispositions."

The widow's estate held to be a restricted estate of inheritance.

In a later case† it was said by the Sudder Court that not merely was the widow prohibited from alienating, but that her life-interest in the estate was not transferable, in fact she could be considered in no other light than as a holder in trust for certain uses.‡ If they said, she be convicted of alienation for other than justifiable purposes, she is guilty of a breach of trust, and no further confidence can be placed in her; in such cases the proper course is to remove the widow from the management of the property, to allow her a fitting maintenance, and to entrust

* See Shamachurn, p. 99, *per* Lord Gifford.

† *Ibid*, p. 139. See Macnaghten, p. 19.

‡ Macnaghten's Hindu Law, p. 19.

LECTURE VIII.

the reversioners with possession, they being controlled by and accountable to the Court. After the Privy Council judgment, in *Kasheenath Bysack* v. *Hurrosoondery Dossee,* the Hindu widow's estate was no longer regarded as a mere life-estate, but as a restricted estate of inheritance; and on proof of waste or wrongful alienation by her, the next heirs or the Court would be put in possession as receivers.

Power of alienation of her own estate.

Next arises the question, whether an alienation by the widow will hold good for her life-time, or whether the reversionary heirs can at once set it aside, assuming it to be made for causes other than those allowed by Hindu law; in other words, whether she has what is known as "a life estate" in her husband's property with absolute power of disposition over such life estate. It is scarcely to be supposed, that the notion of "an estate," of whatever duration, in the property, of which her husband died possessed, was present to the mind of the Hindu legislators, when they used such expressions as these: "But the wife must only enjoy her husband's estate* after his demise; she is not entitled to make a gift, mortgage or sale of it;" and "let her enjoy her husband's estate during her life, and not as her separate property, make a gift, mortgage, or sale of it at her pleasure;" and again,† "the wife is only to enjoy the estate of her deceased husband; she must not make a gift, mortgage, or sale of it;" and "let her so long as she lives enjoy her husband's‡ estate, and not (as she is entitled to do with her peculiar property) make a will, a gift, mortgage, or sale of it."

* Dayabhaga, Chap. XI., Section I., verse 56.

† *Ibid*, verse 57.

‡ Dayacrama Sangraha, Sec. 3.

LECTURE VIII.

Originally her power to aliene her estate was not distinguished from her power to aliene absolutely.

The notion was that the widow should have the enjoyment, without power of disposition, except for certain purposes, and then over the property absolutely; her possession and enjoyment were in right of her husband, but his power of alienation was not transmitted to her. Until her death, "half the body of the husband" survived; and in the absence of male issue, the heirs could not be ascertained till her death. This theory prevailed, moreover, in several cases.

(*a*) *Sreenarain Rai* v. *Bhya Jha,*—where the Pundits of the Sudder Dewanny Adwlut (being consulted as to whether an opinion of Jagannatha to the effect that a widow's gift of her husband's estate, though immoral, is not invalid, was supported by any and what books of the Mithila, Bengal and Benares school) replied in accordance, it was said with a variety of previous *Vyavasthas* that her gift of her husband's immoveable estate, without consent of heirs, or unless for special reasons set forth in the shasters, was not only blameable but invalid.

(*b*) *Goculchund Chuckerbuttee* v. *Ranee Rajranee,*—where the widow of a childless Hindu having taken his entire estate and sold it to a third party, such sale was set aside at the suit of the next heirs *against her* as well as the vendor.

(*c*) *Mohunlall Khan* v. *Ranee Siroomunnee,*—where the Court observed "that, according to the rule laid down in the Dayabhaga, the consent of the husband's paternal kindred, as being the legal guardians and advisers of the widow, is necessary (except under special circumstances) to the validity of an alienation by the widow *of any part* of the

(*a*) Select Reports Bengal (new edition), Vol. II., p. 29.
(*b*) *Ibid*, Vol. II., p. 213.
(*c*) *Ibid*, Vol. II., p. 40.

estate devolving on her husband's death," and accordingly set aside a deed which had been executed by the widow. LECTURE VIII.

(*d*) *Nufur Mitter* v. *Ramcoomar Chattoorjya*,—where a mother's conveyance of immoveable estate, to which she had succeeded as heiress to her son, was set aside.

(*e*) *Caleekant Lahooree* v. *Goluck Chunder Chowdhry*,—a case where a sale, in execution of a decree against a Hindu widow, of her life interest in part of her husband's immoveable estate, in the absence of proof that the debt for which the sale took place was other than a personal debt of the widow, or that that debt was in any way incurred for the purposes of her necessary maintenance, was held inoperative to convey *any* title to the estate or *any* interest in it. The Court referred to authorities which it regarded as distinct and conclusive against the claim of the purchaser to the property sold. There was the opinion of Sir W. Macnaghten* "that a widow can be considered in no other light than as a holder in trust for certain uses;" and further† "a widow has no unlimited proprietary right over any part of her husband's property, but merely a general usufructuary right over the whole indiscriminately."

(*f*) *Bolabee Bebee* v. *Nundlall Baboo*,—where reversioners sued during the life of the widow to set aside her alienation of her husband's estate, and to deprive her of the management. It was held that such a suit would lie.

Defined by the Full Bench.

Finally, however, the question was reconsidered by a Full Bench of the High Court, in the case of "*Gobindo-*

(*d*) 4 Select Reports Bengal (new edition), p. 393.
(*e*) Sudder Dewanny Decisions, 1849, p. 405.
* 1 Macnaghten's Hindu Law, pp. 19, 20.
† See 2 Morley's Digest, p. 155.
(*f*) Sudder Dewanny Decisions, 1854, p. 351.

LECTURE VIII.

monee Dossee v. *Shamloll Bysack*,"* and a decision was come to which still further secured the Hindu widow from that "abject state of dependence" to which by law, happily obsolete, she was consigned, and declared her full proprietary right for the term of her life in her husband's property.

The Court, "after considering all the cases upon the subject, were of opinion that a conveyance by a Hindu widow for other than allowable causes, of property which has descended to her from her husband, is not an act of waste which destroys the widow's estate and vests the property in the reversionary heirs, and that the conveyance is binding during the widow's life. The reversionary heirs are not after her death bound by the conveyance, but they are not entitled during her life-time to recover the property either for their own or the use of the widow, or to compel the restoration of it to her."

The effect of this decision is to give the widow an uncontrolled power over the estate, so far as her life interest in it is concerned. It has been vehemently contended, and apparently with reason, that this is an innovation upon the ancient usage of Hindus; but if it be, it is consistent with the policy which has been uniformly adhered to, of releasing the strict rules of guardianship or bondage under which the widow was formerly placed.

Widow's interest in the accumulations of her husband's estate.

With regard to the widow's power of disposition, there is a further question whether she can deal with the accumulations of her husband's property as her own self-acquired property, or whether she takes them for the estate of a Hindu widow therein subject to the reversionary rights of her husband's heirs. The subject was discussed

* Sutherland's Full Bench Rulings, p. 165.

in the case of *Grose* v. *Amritamayi Dasi*,* and the following passage, from one of the judgments delivered in the High Court of Bengal, may be cited with respect to it:—

"I confess that I was under the impression that the late Supreme Court, in disposing of a matter, *In the goods of Harendranarayan Ghose, Kailasnath Ghose* v. *Biswanath Biswas*, had held that a widow might assign or otherwise dispose of accumulations. I have, however, referred to the only published report of the case which I can find, and it appears that the Court, while saying that the widow might dispose of the income at her pleasure, drew a distinction between income and accumulations, and did not decide that she could so dispose of accumulations.

"No doubt, there is, in fact, a very substantial difference between mere income and accumulations. In the present case, almost simultaneously with the recovery of the *corpus* of her husband's estate, the widow got a considerably larger sum, being accumulations accrued due since his death. Although the theory of the Hindu law is that the income of the husband's estate shall go to the widow for her maintenance, and for the performance of pious duties, that theory by no means necessarily embraces the large lump sum of accumulations. According to all the older authorities on Hindu law, accumulations should be treated in the same way as the *corpus*, and I think they should be so treated now, in the absence of any distinct authority to the contrary."

Although a widow is dependent upon her husband's relations, she does not lose her right of maintenance by visiting her own family, though according to Mr. Colebrooke,†

* 4 Bengal Law Reports, O. C., p. 40, *per* Macpherson, J.

† 2 Strange's Hindu Law, p. 401.

LECTURE VIII.

her guardians might require her to return to live in her husband's house.

According to the Madhavya, a widow who succeeds to her husband's estate is restricted from aliening the immoveables, but there does not appear to be any restriction on her power as affecting moveables; although charitable and religious objects justify alienation by a widow, yet no doubt the Court would restrain waste even on this count.*

Rights of widows when there are more than one.

With regard to the rights of widows where there are more than one, the rule applicable to Bengal is laid down by Mr. Macnaghten thus: "If a man die leaving more than one widow (three widows, for instance) the property is considered as vesting in only one individual: thus, on the death of one or two of the widows, the survivor or survivors take the property, and no part vests in the other heirs of the husband until after the death of all the widows."†

Decisions of the Madras and Bombay High Courts.

In a Madras case‡ recently decided, the rights of two or more rightfully married wives (patnis) in the estate of their deceased husband were discussed according to Hindu law of the school of Southern India. The alternative was whether each of several widows was entitled to an equal or any other proportionate share, or whether the senior widow was entitled to hold and enjoy the whole property subject only to the right of each of the co-widows to suitable maintenance. Sir Thomas Strange§ states the rule of

* 2 Strange's Hindu Law, p. 408.

† See Macnaghten's Hindu Law, p. 21.—"If there be more than one widow," he says, "their rights are equal."

‡ Jijoyiamba Bayi Saiba *v.* Kamakshi Bayi Saiba, 3 Madras Rep., p. 425.

§ 1 Strange's Hindu Law, pp. 56 and 137.

succession to be, that the senior widow by date of marriage "succeeds, in the first instance; the others, inheriting in their turn as they survive, are entitled in the meantime to be maintained by the first; it being a principle that whoever takes the estate of the deceased must maintain those whom he was bound to support." That rule had been formerly acted upon by the Madras Sudder Court, and for a period of more than thirty years was not again brought in question. Notwithstanding the authority of those cases, and of Sir Thomas Strange, the High Court "came satisfactorily to the conclusion that the sound rule of inheritance according to the Hindu law of Southern India is, that two or more lawfully married wives (patnis) take a joint estate for life in their husband's property with rights of survivorship and equal beneficial enjoyment." The foundation for Sir Thomas Strange's rule was traced to the ancient law which recognized marriages with wives of different classes or castes, and which appears to have prescribed preferential qualities and privileges to the wives, according to the order and rank of their several classes. When support is given by the ancient sages to the doctrine of succession in the order of the classes, it is on the principle that only on the failure of a wife of equal class, can one of an inferior class be employed to perform religious duties with the husband, or to his manes. The Court discussed various texts, and came to the conclusion that there was no sufficient warrant for the preferential claim of the senior wife. On the contrary, this passage was referred to in the Mitakshara as favouring the joint and equal inheritance of the wives.* "When the father by his own choice,

* Mitakshara, Chap. I., Sec. II., verse 9.

LECTURE VIII.

makes all his sons partakers of equal portions, his wives to whom peculiar property had not been given by their husband, or by their father-in-law, must be made participant of shares equal to those of sons." But the Court rested its judgment specially upon a passage of the Mitakshara, which though apparently a genuine portion of the original Sanscrit text, had been omitted in Mr. Colebrooke's translation. It is a continuation of the 5th clause of the 1st section of the 2nd Chapter of Mr. Colebrooke's translation, and runs thus: "There (in that order) the first to inherit is the wife (patni); patni is she who is so made by marriage; and this from the Smriti or rule of grammar 'Patyurno Yagna Sumyogai,' (the particle 'ni' is added to Pati to signify one who partakes in the holy sacrifice),—singular number because the class is denoted. Hence if there be several, whether of the same or of different castes, they divide and take the property according to their shares." The Smriti Chandrika also says, "where there are several wives (patnis), it is proper that they should all take the inheritance of their sonless husband, by dividing the same in equal shares among them." The Mayukha and the Viramitrodaya were also cited in support of the same rule. The High Court of Bombay has also come to a similar decision.*

But although the rights of the widows in their husbands' estate were held to be equal, they were held not to be entitled to a partition thereof. They can, by agreement, provide for the distributive enjoyment of it by an apportionment as between themselves of the property. But they cannot interfere with one another's rights of survivor-

* In the goods of Dadoo Mania, deceased, Indian Jurist, 1862, p. 59.

ship, nor affect the rights of their husband's heirs to succeed to the whole estate, at the death of the last surviving widow.* LECTURE VIII.

Separate possession of a portion, it was considered, might be granted to one of several widows upon a sufficient case being made out entitling her to such relief, as the only mode of securing to her the enjoyment of her distinct right to an equal share in the benefits of the estate.

* See F. Macnaghten's Considerations of Hindu Laws, p. 55.

LECTURE IX.

THE RITE OF ADOPTION.

Son required to prevent Failure of Obsequies—Also to continue the Father's Name and Lineage—Object of Adoption—Classification of Sons in early Times—Sons by Birth and Adoption—Adoption amongst the Greeks, Romans, and Hindus—Dattaka Adoption—The Ritual of Adoption—Datta-homam—Its religious Significance—Originally two kinds of Dattaka Adoption—Character of the Hindu system of Adoption.

Son required to prevent failure of obsequies.

ALTHOUGH the leading idea of Hindu civilization is to preserve the continuity of the family, and to make the funeral cake a bond of union between successive generations, yet it must not be concluded that the doctrine upon which it rests has been at all times consistent and unchanged. In the earliest times, *puttra* was the name given to a son by Brahma himself, because he delivered his father from the region of torment named *put*, and the idea of a departed spirit being refused admission to heaven, because he had left no male issue, was forcibly impressed upon the national mind by the earlier sages. A further theory existed from the most primitive times, viz., that by the eldest son at the moment of birth, the father discharged his debt to his own progenitors;* and was by reason of that birth,

* 9 Menu, verse 100.—By the eldest, at the moment of his birth, the father having begotten a son discharges his debt to his own progenitors.

irrespectively of his son surviving him, relieved from some of his liabilities in the future world. By Sancha and Lichita, it was said that a man became entitled to heaven by the birth of his son, and was exonerated through his oblation of funeral cakes from debt to his progenitors, and that the perpetual support of a consecrated fire and other observances did not procure a sixteenth part of the benefit which arose from the birth of the eldest son. And Menu, in describing the sons who are substituted for sons of the body, says,* that they are allowed by wise legislators for the sake of preventing a failure of obsequies.

LECTURE IX.

Also to continue the father's name and lineage.

Thus far the idea seems to be that the son delivers the father from torment through the funeral obsequies, but Menu himself, as well as all the other sages, directs by whom the obsequies are to be performed in the absence of sons, devolving the duty upon kinsmen in regular gradation, declaring that, on failure of all these, certain Brahmanas must offer the cake, and thus he says the rites of obsequies cannot fail†. Here, therefore, the supreme necessity for a son seems to be lost sight of; for every care is taken that the ancestor should, in any case, be provided with the funeral cake. The author‡ of the Dattaka Mimansa distinctly abandons the theory of a son's performance of obsequies being necessary simply for the purpose of delivering from *put*, and substitutes for it the notion that it is essential merely for the acquisition of

* Colebrooke's Digest, Book V., Chap. IV., Sect. XV., verse 301.

† Colebrooke's Digest, Book V., Chap. III., Sect. I., verse 442. Menu.—On failure of all those (natural heirs) the legal heirs are such Brahmanas as have read the three Vedas, as are pure in body and mind, as have subdued their passions, and they must consequently offer the cake: thus the rites of obsequies cannot fail.

‡ Dattaka Mimansa, Sect. I., verses 58, 59; and see *ante* page 73.

LECTURE IX.

some particular heaven, which is not to be acquired by such rites as are executed by the wife and the rest. He does not therefore, refer the duty of adoption to the desire to be delivered from *put;* but quoting again from Menu, he says, that a son must be anxiously desired for the sake of the funeral cake, water, and solemn rites, and *for the celebrity of his name.* Whatever inconsistency and uncertainty may have crept into the doctrine of the spiritual advantages involved in the possession of a son, or of the superior efficacy of his performance of obsequies, there can be no doubt that the whole system and spirit of Hindu religion and law long maintained in the minds of the people an ardent desire which has not yet decayed for the perpetuation of their name and the continuance of their family.

Object of adoption.

It is probable that the spiritual efficacy of the possession of a son, which in the remote ages was the paramount idea, has somewhat given place, in later times, to the feeling, that the existence of a son is desirable, because it renders the continued performance of rites during the long period for which they are enjoined more secure, and still more, because to ensure the continuance of his name and family, is an object always dear to the mind of a Hindu. In the Dattaka Chandrika* especially, the preservation and continuance of the lineage are insisted upon as the chief objects of affiliation, and are assigned as the reasons why the rival wife may not affiliate her co-wife's son; while it is indispensable that the act of adoption should be completed in the case of a brother's son, since without it the lineage would not be preserved. This

* Dattaka Chandrika, Sect. I., verses 25, 26.

more secular motive is doubtless the prevailing motive with Hindus, at the present day, though it is coloured and perhaps in some cases strengthened by religious considerations. It is a rite, however, neglected by thousands, and no one can pretend to believe that it retains that absorbing importance which the religious significance attributed to it would lead us to expect. The tendency of later times has been to increase the legal rights and dignity of the wife, and mother, and widow, much, probably, to the advantage and happiness of the community, and to diminish the extraordinary inportance which in earlier times attached to the place and possession of a son.

Classification of sons in early times.

In the time of Menu the overwhelming importance of the subject required, and led to, a minute classification of the different modes in which the relationship of father and son might be established, so as to secure the advantages, spiritual and temporal, which were so earnestly desired. Twelve different* classes of sons were enumerated, six of whom became members of the father's family and heirs of his estate, the remaining six being admitted as kinsmen to himself but not as heirs, or even probably as kindred to his collaterals. In his list, Menu includes the son by a *sudra* woman, but as he elsewhere describes such a son as a mere living corpse disqualified for the performance of obsequies, he is omitted from the consideration of subsequent sages.

Moreover, a son begotten by a man himself in lawful wedlock, includes not merely his own son, but the son of an appointed daughter,† and thus his list is the same in

* 9 Menu, verses 158, 159, 160.

† Between a son's son and the son of such a daughter (an appointed daughter), there is no difference in law, since their father and mother both sprang from the body of the same man; and see Mitakshara, Chap. I., Sect. XI., verse 3.

LECTURE IX.

point of numbers as that of Yajnavalkya, who omits the son by a *sudra*, and specifies the son of an appointed daughter.

The first in rank was the son whom a man has begotten on his wedded wife of equal class; but equal to him, says Devala,* as well as Menu, is the son of an appointed daughter. The appointed daughter is like a son. Her offspring shall offer the funeral cake for her father as well as for his father; there is no difference in the benefits conferred† by a son and by a daughter's son. The daughter is appointed by the father saying, "The male child who shall be born from her in wedlock shall be mine for the purpose of performing my obsequies."‡ The appointed daughter is called *putrica-putra*, a term which includes four persons, *viz.*, the appointed daughter; her son who stands to her father in the place of a son's son; thirdly, her son when she was given in marriage with an express stipulation that her son should belong to her father; and, fourthly, when it was stipulated at the marriage that the child should perform the obsequies of both, that is, should belong to her father, and at the same time be retained by her husband's family. Such a son is called *dwyamushyayana.* The third is the son of a wife begotten, in the manner directed by Menu, by a *sapinda* of a husband or other person duly authorized. He is called *kshetraja.* The sages proclaim him base-born, and incapable of inheriting, if he is begotten from the impulse of unchaste

* Colebrooke's Digest, Book V., Chap. IV., Sect. III., verse 201.—The son of an appointed daughter is equal to him (the son of the body), he shall inherit as a son the estate of his father and of his maternal grandfather who leaves no male issue.

† Colebrooke's Digest, Book V., Chap. IV., Sect. III., verse 204.

‡ *Ibid*, verse 212.

desire, the sole justifiable object in view being* declared by Nareda to be that the family may be perpetuated.

The fourth in the list of sons as given by Yajnavalkya, is the son of concealed birth, that is, one secretly brought forth by a married woman in her husband's house, so that it is not known, owing to the husband's absence or other cause whose son he is. The principle upon which such son belonged to the husband, and not to the natural father, is that the husband was the owner of the wife, and therefore of her child.

The fifth is the son of an unmarried girl by a man of equal class, and is called *cáninà.* Such child belongs to her father, provided her nuptials have not been begun, but if those nuptials have begun, although she remains in her father's house, the child is considered the son of her husband.

The sixth is a son of a woman twice married; the first husband's right being annulled by his death or relinquishment.

These are the six sons whom Yajnavalkya describes as sons of the father by reason of his paternal right or by reason of his property in the mother. The remaining six are sons in whom he has no such right originally, but in whom he acquires property by the act of others; and amongst these the first in rank is the son given (*dattaka*) *viz.,* that son whom his father or his mother with her husband's assent gives for a son to a man who accepts him as a son. Through such a one, it is said, that the adopter rescues many ancestors; but Menu† added this proviso that the donee had no issue, and that the boy be of the

* Colebrooke's Digest, Book V., Chap. IV., Sect. IV., verse 233.

† Menu, Chap. IX., verse 168.

LECTURE IX.

same class. That I may not anticipate the full discussion into which it will be necessary to enter with regard to the law of adoption, I will merely say in this place that there are two kinds of sons given, the first where he is absolutely relinquished by his natural parents and accepted by his adoptive parents ; the second when he is given under an agreement to this effect "he shall belong to us both" and he is thence called the *dwyamushyayana.*

The eighth mentioned by Yajnavalkya is the son who is received by a man for the sake of male issue from the hands of his father or mother, or either of them, after paying a price, and is called the son bought (*krita*). As in the case of an adopted child, he must neither be an only son, nor an eldest son.

The ninth is the son made (*kritrima*) being enticed by the show of money and land, and being an orphan without father or mother.

The tenth is the son self-given who having lost his parents, or been abandoned by them without cause, offers himself saying "let me become thy son."

The eleventh is the son of a pregnant bride, provided that it be the child of a man of equal class with the bridegroom. He is distinguished from the son of an unmarried woman, and a son of concealed origin, because he was born after marriage, the husband having no property in him at the time of conception. Such child does not belong to the natural father.

A son deserted is the last who having been discarded by his father and mother is taken for adoption ; abandoned not for any fault, but from inability to maintain him.

Of these twelve sons, on failure of the first respectively, the next in order, as enumerated, must be considered to be the giver of the funeral oblation.* But according to a text of Vrihaspati "sons of many descriptions who were made by ancient saints cannot now be adopted by men, by reason of their deficiency of power;"† and sages pronounce that in the Kali Age, only the legitimate son and the son given are recognized as sons; that is *ourasa* (*uras*, breast) born of a wife of equal class, legally married; and *dattaka*. But on this it may be observed that the *ourasa* includes the *putrica-putra*, both Menu and Yajnavalkya having propounded that there is no difference between a legitimate son and an appointed daughter, nor between their sons. With regard to the *dattaka*, there must be added to it the later form of *kritrima* or son made, a form which is current in Mithila, but not in Bengal, never having been legalized in the Dattaka Chandrika and the other authorities of the Bengal school; but deriving its validity in the province where it is current from immemorial usage, and general and well-established custom.

Sons by birth and by adoption.

The son by birth, therefore, and the son by adoption alone remain; the rest with all the law appertaining to them being abrogated in accordance with the ideas and spirit of advancing civilization. The adopted son whether by the *dattaka* or *kritrima* form, or by any other form sanctioned by immemorial, local, or general usage, is the only substitute which the present age recognizes for one lawfully begotten. There is no other mode in which a Hindu can, in the language of the earlier sages, be delivered from *put*, or attain the particular heaven referred to by Nanda Pandita; or in which he can, speaking according to existing ideas, and in the language of the

* Mitakshara, Chap. I., Sect. XI., verse 22.

† Dattaka Chandrika, Sect. I., verse 9.

LECTURE IX.

author of the Dattaka Chandrika, preserve and continue his name and lineage.

We are thus led to the discussion of the Hindu law of adoption, which is a subject of some complication, although in reference to it there are less variations between the various schools than might have been expected from its frequent and general application. But not merely are the rules of adoption similar in the different schools of Hindu law, whose doctrines differ in so many other particulars, and whose votaries are scattered over so large a continent as India, but there is also a remarkable similarity between the institution as it prevailed in Italy and Greece and as it has endured through so many ages in the peninsula of Hindustan.

Adoption amongst the Greeks, Romans, and Hindus.

The origin of adoption, or rather the circumstances which led to the practice of it, were similar in all three of those celebrated communities. Before the notion prevailed that people might be grouped together in civil society and separated from other portions of mankind, merely upon the principle of living within the same topographical limits, blood relationship, real or assumed, was the bond which united nations, as well as families. The family is an association of kindred, confined within artificial limits. Adoption is the artificial mode of absorbing strangers within those limits, upon the principle of a simulated heirship, involving a complete separation from the family of birth, and a connection as close as that of birth and blood with the family of adoption. The tie of blood relationship thus artificially limited in one side and artificially extended on the other, united in primitive times both the family and society.

The entire separation of an adopted child from one family and his entire absorption into another were as strongly insisted upon in the Grecian and Roman systems as amongst Hindus. A Greek adopted child could, however, renounce his adoption, which a Hindu was never permitted to do. A Hindu child can no more renounce of his own will his family of adoption, than he can that of his birth. Under the Roman system, adoption was more closely watched and controlled than amongst Hindus. It was regarded as effecting an alteration in families, which was of public importance. The sanction of the curiæ was necessary if a member of the curiæ or his family were affected. It was never allowed when it would lead to the extinction of the family from which the child was to be separated. Emancipation by one father preceded adoption by another. There was nothing to prevent a subsequent emancipation by the adoptive parent, and thus the child might be without position or rights of inheritance in either family. Justinian remedied this gross neglect of the interests of the adopted child, by providing that a son given in adoption to a stranger, should retain his position in his natural family, acquiring a right of succession to his adoptive father, if such father died intestate. Hindu law is careless of the interests of the child, who is the subject of adoption, and vests in his natural father a right to dispose of him at his discretion; but it nevertheless secures to the adopted child nearly the same status and rights in his new family as a son born, except in the solitary instance of a son being born to the adoptive father after the adoption, in which case the son born takes three fourths or two-thirds (according to the school of law by which he is governed) of the inheritance which the adopted child would otherwise have obtained.

Dattaka adoption.

Now with regard to the form of adoption, there is

amongst Hindus only one form of simple absolute permanent adoption which effects a complete and irrevocable transfer of a child from one family to another, severing the tie to the natural parents and kindred, as thoroughly as nature will permit, and creating a link to the adoptive family, as firm as that created by actual birth in it; and that form alone is prevalent in Bengal, namely the *dattaka* adoption. When once this form is completed, it can never be revoked. The adopted son cannot return to his natural family, however much, when he comes to years of discretion, he may regret and disapprove of the severance. Nor can he be deprived of the advantages of being a member of the family to which he has been transferred, for any reasons short of those which would suffice to render a natural born son an outcast, or deprive him of his right of inheritance. He loses all claim to the property of his natural family, and all rights which would have accrued to him from belonging to it.

The prohibited degrees, however, continue in full force; and for purposes of marriage and mourning and the days of impurity he remains affected by the former tie. Nature is as it were stronger than the municipal rule; and the duties or obligations which she imposes remain while the rights *positivi juris,* such as those of inheritance and co-parcenership and succession, are gone. The natural family again have no claim to any property to which he succeeds; he inherits from his adoptive family, and they in turn inherit from him to the absolute exclusion of all his blood relations. The adopted Dattaka son performs the obsequies of his adoptive father and his ancestors, assumes his name, and continues his lineage.

The full meaning and significance of the rite of adoption are to be gathered from the ceremonies attending it, and from the directions which are carefully insisted upon with regard to those ceremonies of regeneration, which religion requires should be performed in the adoptive family, if the child affected by them is to be completely severed from his own parents, and finally and irrevocably transferred to others. But a still more important question then remains: how far the Courts of Justice, as now established, will, having regard to the principles of public policy on which they proceed, and to the course and effect of their own decisions, distinguish between the civil and religious nature of the rite; and how far, while effectuating the civil purposes in view, they will undertake to enforce, and therefore ultimately to superintend the due performance of religious observances.

Ritual of adoption.

Looking upon the subject of adoption in the first place, irrespective of the action of Courts of Justice, the first authority to refer to is the Code of Menu. According to that authoritative compilation "he* whom his father, or mother with her husband's assent, gives to another as his son, provided that the donee have no issue, if the boy be of the same class and affectionately disposed, is considered as a son given, the gift being confirmed by pouring water." A simpler ritual could not have been devised. But considering the importance of the rite, both in a religious point of view, and also in its social and domestic consequences, and considering the great influence and authority of the Brahminical caste, whose interest it is to multiply ceremonials, and to insist upon their efficacy, it was not very probable that that simplicity would be long main-

* Menu, Chap. IX., verse 168.

LECTURE IX.

tained. And, accordingly, in later times we find that whatever of sacrifice, oblation, and prayer might seem to add dignity and interest to its performance were strictly enjoined as proper to be observed; but it will scarcely be denied that Hindu practice on those points is very loose, and much is omitted "through laziness" or indifference which a firm adherence tó the shasters would have rendered essential.

The text of Vasishta must be referred to as a leading authority upon the ritual of adoption.* "He who means to adopt a son must assemble his kinsmen, give humble notice to the king, and then having made an oblation to fire with words from the Veda, in the midst of his dwelling house, he may receive as his son by adoption a boy nearly, allied to him, or on failure of such, even one remotely allied."

Here, again, simplicity is not lost sight of. But in the fifth section of the Dattaka Mimansa and the second section of the Dattaka Chandrika, we find that the forms and religious ceremonies connected with the rite of adoption have been elaborately expanded. The authors of those two celebrated treatises have treated the subject with a minuteness of detail which proves the growing importance of the ceremonial observance.

I will refer, however, to Jagannatha's Digest for an account of the ceremonies which should be performed.

"Having given humble notice† to the king, and after making an oblation to fire with holy words from the Veda, giving gold and winter corn in conformity with usage, let the adopter ascertaining his name, family, and class in the presence of kinsmen, receive a boy for whom the

* Colebrooke's Digest, Book V., Chap. IV., Sect. VIII., verse 275, note.
† *Ibid.*

ceremony of tonsure and the like has not been performed, whose age does not exceed five years, and who is given by his father, or by his mother with the assent of her husband, provided that they have another son. Let him next perform the sacrifice on adopting a boy (*pootrooishto*); this *pootrooishto* sacrifice, say experienced lawyers, must be performed by one who maintains a consecrated fire; but by him who does not maintain such a fire, an oblation must be made with the mysterious words from the Veda, as directed by Vasishta. In fact, the oblation to fire, with holy words from the Veda which is directed by Vasishta, should precede adoption; the *pootrooishto* sacrifice ordained in the Calica Purana should be performed after adoption; this appears from the form of expression used in the texts; 'having made an oblation, he may receive a son, and having, aken a boy of five years old, he should perform a sacrifice.' At present some omit through laziness the sacrifice called *pootrooishto*, in the same manner that the ceremony of combing a wife's tresses is not now practised. This author directs the ceremonial of adoption."

The ceremonies at present in use in Bengal are described at length in the Vyavastha Darpana* of Baboo Shamachurn Sircar, but need not now be detailed.

With regard to later authority upon the same subject, I will refer to the opinion of the Pundit quoted by Sir Thomas Strange† to the effect that, when a Brahmin boy is to be adopted, the adopter should invite the relations of either party, and entertain them at his house, giving notice to the king or principal authority of the place of his intention, and then the husband and wife, waiting upon the

* Vyavastha Darpana, p. 866.

† 2 Strange, p. 87.

LECTURE IX. parents of the boy, and stating that they have no son of their own, should ascertain if they are willing to give them one of theirs, to which they assenting, the *datta-homam* must be performed. The same ceremonies, with the exception of *homams*, are to be performed in the other castes, and the water called *manjenum* should be drunk in the presence of relations.

Datta-homam.

Mr. Ellis observes that, with respect to Sudras, there exists strictly no ceremonial for adoption; since by the *datta-homam*, the adopted son is converted from the *gotra* of the natural to that of his adoptive father, and Sudras have no *gotra*. Besides, the proper *datta-homam* can only be performed by those castes which use the texts of the Vedas in their religious ceremonies. Sudras cannot perform it, though they may perform an imitation of it with texts from the Puranas.

Its religious significance.

Now, with regard to the ritual of the *datta-homam*, which, notwithstanding the silence of Menu, appears to be insisted upon as important, if not absolutely indispensable, in a religious point of view in the case of a child belonging to an entirely distinct *gotra*, or family, from that of his adoptive parents, there is a description of it given from the Datta Mimansa of the Savara Swami, in the second volume of Sir Thomas Strange's Hindu Law.* The essential part of it is that the natural father, with the utmost publicity, transfers his son, seating the boy on the thigh of the adoptive father, who accepts him with prayer and holy texts; and after the performance by the giver of the remaining ceremonies pertaining to an oblation to fire, the adoptive father, seated on the same

* Strange's Hindu Law, Vol. II., p. 218.

seat with his wife and the child whom he has received, declares his acceptance of the child, performing at the same time the rite of *datta-homam,* in confirmation of him as his son. But this ceremony is unnecessary when the adopted child is taken, as, in the great majority of cases, it is from the adoptive father's *gotra.* The general result appears to be that in no case can the omission of the ceremony affect an adoption in other respects valid; but that if not performed, and the adoption is from another *gotra,* it would seem that the son so adopted must be *anitya datta,* and is not finally and absolutely dissevered from his natural family.

In a case which is reported in the second volume of Sir T. Strange's Hindu Law, upon* a question whether the *upanayana* for a plaintiff's son should be solemnized in his adoptive or his natural *gotra,* it was contended that the plaintiff had not been duly adopted by means of *homams,* as well as by the performance of his *upanayana* by his alleged adoptive father, whose *gotra,* moreover, was different from his own. It was further contended that, if one of a different *gotra* from the adopter be adopted, his sons should revert to their natural *gotra.* The Pundit's opinion was that, inasmuch as it appeared that the plaintiff had been adopted by *homams,* his son, as well as himself, belonged to the *gotra* of his adoptive father.

Originally two kinds of *Dattaka* adoption.

Adoption, he said, was of two kinds, *viz., nittya datta* and *anitya datta.* The former performed with *homams,* or offerings before fire, is permanent; the latter temporary only, being without the same formalities. In the former case, the son of one so adopted must be invested with the Brah-

* 2 Strange, p. 120.

LECTURE IX. minical thread in the *gotra* of his father's adoption; in the latter case, it may be performed, either in his father's adoptive or natural family. But upon this, Mr. Colebrooke remarks that he is not aware of any authority that the issue of *anitya datta* may be initiated in either family. It is true that a man may become a *dwyamushyayana;* but in whatever *gotra* he receives his initiation, his issue must remain in it. The real distinction between *nitya datta* and *anitya datta* is that the latter is equivalent to the *dwyamushyayana*, is adopted from a different *gotra* after he has received the tonsure in his natural *gotra*, remains while he lives in his adoptive family, but his son returns to his natural one. It would seem from this that the *datta-homam* must have been omitted from the ceremony of adopting a *dwyamushyayana*.

Character of the Hindu system of adoption.

Nothing is said of any restrictions being placed upon the full exercise by the parents, natural and adoptive, of their own discretion and judgment in effecting the transfer of a child. No machinery is provided by which the interests of the child are guarded. Adoption, according to the *dattaka* form, as understood in Hindu law, is essentially a contract between parents who assume to give and take the absolute property in a child. And if by any mischance the child* should be dissevered from his own family, without being perfectly inducted into the family of the adopter, his *status* would be one of slavery in the new family. The same anxiety to obtain children which led to this facility of adoption, has also, as was pointed out by Lord

* Dattaka Mimansa, Chap. IV., verse 40.—Should the ceremony of tonsure and the rest not be performed (by the adopter), or should one be adopted on whom the ceremony of tonsure and other rites have been performed, a servile state ensues, not that of a son.

Wynford,* operated prejudicially in another way, since very imperfect securities have been provided against fabricated adoptions. "The having three children conferred advantages on Roman citizens which induced them to adopt sons: and when they had got the honors or offices which they desired, they often turned the adopted children loose on the world again. Such frauds have been wisely provided against by the Romans and other nations who incorporated the civil with their municipal laws. By the civil law the sanction of the Magistrates was essential to the validity of the adoption of an infant. The Magistrates were authorized to enquire whether such adoption would be for the benefit of the infant having regard to the circumstances in which both the child and the proposed adoptive father were respectively placed. According to the Code de Napoleon, adoptions must be registered in the Court of first instance and in the Imperial Court; and in the latter an opportunity is afforded to the relations of the person proposing to adopt a child of showing that the adoption proposed ought not to be allowed, such Court having authority either to confirm or to annul any adoption."

According to Hindu law, neither registration of the act of adoption, nor any written evidence of that act, nor any written evidence of the grant of an authority in that behalf, when such act is done in pursuance of authority, nor the sanction of any Court of Justice or any ruling power, is essential to its validity. The consent of the child, though he may be of an age to have attained some discretion, is wholly unnecessary; nor can he question the transaction, even though his interests

* Sutroogun Sutputty *v.* Sabitra Dye, 2 Knapp's Reports, p. 289; S. C., 5 S. W. R., P. C., p. 108 (1835).

and wishes are wholly disregarded. Although the act is irrevocable, and although it may defeat the just expectations of the relations of a deceased person, it is dependent entirely upon his caprice. It may be proved by verbal testimony, at any distance of time, after it is supposed to have taken place, and it may take place even fifty years after his death, in pursuance of an authority supposed to have been given by him, and which authority itself may also be proved by parol evidence.

But, although neither registration, nor written acknowledgments, nor attested agreements, nor the performance of any religious ceremonial are essential to the validity of adoption, nevertheless the utmost publicity is usual, and its absence suspicious. The ceremonial observed at the time, the assembling of the members of the family and their friends, and the notice which is frequently given to the ruling power, guarantee the genuineness of the act; and there is this further security, that some of the most important ceremonies of regeneration ought to be performed upon the child in the name and family of his adoptive father. Although they might be neglected, it is scarcely probable that they would be so, in the case of a *bonâ fide* adoption.

LECTURE X.

THE CONTRACT OF ADOPTION.

Secular Ceremonies of Adoption—Religious Ceremonies—Datta-homam—Actual Gift and Acceptance of the Child constitutes Adoption—Constructive Gift and Acceptance not sufficient—Datta-homam not essential for civil purposes—*Bhairabnath Sye* v. *Mahesh Chandra Bhadury*—Madras High Court Doctrine on the same subject—Religious Obligations of the Adopter—Tonsure and Upanayana connected with Affiliation—Doctrine of the Dattaka Chandrika—Kritrima Adoption—Its Character and Consequences—No Ceremonies are required—*Krita*, a Son bought.

Secular ceremonies of adoption.

BESIDES the detail of the ceremonial enjoined to be observed in performing the rite of adoption, according to the Dattaka form, the important question remains how far that ceremonial or any portion of it is necessary in the eye of the law, as administered at the present day, in order to effect a valid adoption. I think it may be laid down that, if once the fact of adoption is established, the Courts will certainly not enquire into the performance of the secular, and possibly not even into the performance of religious, ceremonies merely for the purpose of testing its validity. The former are required simply for the purpose of securing publicity and preventing imposition; and though their absence is suspicious, the fact of adoption may, nevertheless, be susceptible of proof. According to

LECTURE X.

Sir T. Strange,* there must be gift and acceptance manifested by some *overt* act, that overt act, as prescribed by Menu†, being the pouring of water. Beyond this, he says, it does not appear that anything is absolutely necessary. "For, as to notice to the Raja, and invitation to kinsmen, they are agreed not to be so, being merely intended to give greater notoriety to the thing, so as to obviate doubt regarding the right of succession." The authorities seem to be agreed upon that point, *viz.*, that those secular ceremonies are not legal essentials to the validity‡ of the adoption, but are merely intended to secure publicity. This view, moreover, has been adopted by the late Sudder Court of Bengal, and may, I believe, be taken to be one of the settled points in the law of adoption.

In 1828, a widow sued her husband's brother to recover her husband's estate.§ The defendant alleged that her husband had adopted his younger son, and appointed him guardian by will. The Judge dismissed the suit, but the Sudder Court's Pundit declared that initiation and convention of near kinsmen, and the representation to the Raja, were formalities merely for the sake of securing evidence, but that the affiliation was secured by sacrifice.

Religious ceremonies.

With regard to the religious ceremonies, especially the sacrifice to fire, a distinction is taken; and though, in many of the authorities, it would appear to be placed on the same footing with the secular ceremonies, and included in a rule which is directory, and not imperative; and although there has been considerable conflict of opinion on the subject,

* Strange's Hindu Law, Vol. I., Chap. IV., p. 94.

† 9 Menu, verse 168.

‡ Sutherland's Synopsis, Head III., Note XIII.

§ Alank Manjari *v.* Fakir Chand Sircar, 5 S. D. R., p. 356.

yet it would seem that the balance of authority is in favor of regarding the performance of at least the *datta-homam*, or sacrifice to fire, as essential to the validity of an adoption in a religious, but not in a legal, point of view. LECTURE X.

Datta-homam.

Sir Thomas Strange* has recorded a decided opinion upon the point. He says that, "even with regard to the sacrifice of fire, important as it may be deemed, in a spiritual point of view, it is so with regard to the Brahmin only; . . . and even with regard to Brahmins, admitting their conception in favor of its spiritual benefit, it by no means follows that it is essential to the efficacy of the rite for civil purposes, but the contrary is to be inferred;† and the conclusion is that its validity for these purposes consists generally in the consent of the necessary parties, the adopter having at the time no male issue, and the child to be received being within the legal age, and not being either an only son, or the eldest son of the giver; the prescribed ceremonies not being essential."

The direct authority of Jagannatha at any rate may be quoted, and the silence of Menu, who only enjoins a ceremonial of pouring water, may be referred to in favor of the rule that that ceremony is not absolutely essential. Jagannatha says‡ that the *homam* is an unessential part of the ceremony, no one having declared that filiation is null without it. Adoption, he says, is the object of that act of the will called acceptance, and is valid, without oblation to fire, though no special perfection arises. The concurrence

* Strange's Hindu Law, Vol. I., Chap. IV., p. 95.

† See Strange's Hindu Law, Vol. II., p. 114.—Mr. Ellis's opinion is given to the effect that the Datta-homam is indispensably requisite only amongst Brahmins, and then only to produce spiritual benefit.

‡ Colebrooke's Digest, Book V., Chap. IV., Sec. VIII., verse 273, note.

LECTURE X.

of European authorities,* proceeding upon the texts of Menu and the commentary of Jagannatha, is to the effect that, in order to constitute adoption, there must be gift and acceptance manifested by some overt act, and that nothing further in the eye of a Court of law is necessary, however much a Brahmin may insist upon the importance of a sacrifice to fire amongst those of his own caste, and even amongst Sudras, through the intervention of an officiating Brahmin.

The antecedent performance of some of the rites of regeneration in the natural family would invalidate an adoption by rendering the child ineligible for that purpose, but the neglect of them in the adoptive family, though a matter of inference or evidence in a case of disputed *factum*, is not a subject into which the Courts, as constituted in this country, are in the habit of enquiring, whether that neglect is intentional or inadvertent. It would appear to be equally convenient and reasonable that the performance of religious ceremonies enjoined at, as well as after, the adoption, should be left to the conscience of individuals; and that the public or well-ascertained gift and acceptance, with the intention that he should be a son, by those qualified to give and accept, of a child eligible to be given and accepted, should alone be legally sufficient for the validity of an adoption.

Actual gift and acceptance of the child constitute adoption for civil purposes.

In a case† which arose between Sudras, the question was raised how far the prescribed ceremonial was necessary when the gift and acceptance of an eligible child had been

* See Strange's Hindu Law, Vol. I., Chap. IV., p. 94; Macnaghten, p. 69, note; Mr. Ellis, Strange's Hindu Law, Vol. II., p. 87.

† Dyamoye Chowdhrain v. Rasbcharee Sing, 8 S. D. Dec., p. 1001.

ascertained. The plaintiff, a Sudra, sued a woman whom he alleged to be his adopting mother, on the allegation that, acting under permission and authority from her deceased husband, she had adopted him. The defendant repudiated his title, and declared that the necessary ceremonies, according to the shasters, were never completed. The action was brought upon a *hibbanameh,* which recited that the deceased husband, agreeably to the consent of his two wives, had adopted the plaintiff; and then it went on to say, "the ceremonies *of pootrooishtojag, &c.,* have not been performed; you will perform them; when he becomes major, and you shall in your judgment think he has become a fit person, you will cause his name to be registered as proprietor of the zemindaries included in the deed." The plaintiff admitted that the ceremonies *pootrooishtojag,* including oblation by fire, and even the important ceremony of tonsure, had never been performed, and he prayed that the Court would award him the property, and cause his mother to perform the ceremonies. The defendant relied, amongst other things, chiefly upon the non-performance of the ceremonies; and upon that point, *viz.,* whether their performance was essential to the validity of an adoption in Bengal, the decision of the Court was taken. The majority of the Judges held that the ceremonies were not essential; that the legal giving and legal taking were all that were necessary to constitute adoption in a Sudra family; and although the Dattaka Chandrika and the Dattaka Mimansa prescribe certain forms to be observed, they refer to the form of giving and taking, and not to the subsequent performance of the sacrifice by fire, the shaving of the head, or the naming of the child, which may be deferred to any period, or altogether neglected.

LECTURE X.

The same doctrine was adhered to a short time afterwards in another case,* which also arose between Sudras, and in which it was also ruled that the giving and taking of the son was all that was necessary to adoption.

Although the parties to these cases were Sudras, the reasoning on which the decisions proceed, and the rule so laid down, equally apply to the three other castes. According to the doctrine so laid down, whatever may be the effect of the neglect of ceremonies upon the position of a Hindu in the eye of his *caste*, and those who exercise authority in matter of *caste*, it does not affect the validity of his adoption in point of law, or diminish his legal rights as a member of his adoptive family and of inheritance therein. The rule, however, as to Brahmins, was not left to inference from those cases. The opinion has been adhered to from the time of Jagannatha, or at all events, from the time of Sir Thomas Strange,† that, with regard to Brahmins, the efficacy of the rite of adoption for civil purposes is not affected by the non-performance of the religious ceremonial. It seems to have been so considered both by Mr. Ellis and Mr. Colebrooke. And the Sudder Court of Bengal, in 1859,‡ affirmed that view, and laid it down in a suit which arose between Brahmins that, if the operative part of the ceremony of adoption, *i. e.*, the giving and receiving, has been properly performed before kinsmen, the omission, even of oblation to fire, being an unessential part of the ceremony, does not invalidate the adoption.

Constructive gift and acceptance not sufficient.

But although the Courts have, in cases of disputed adoption, investigated the question of the gift and acceptance

* Perkaschunder Roy *v.* Dhunmonee Dossee, 9 S. D. Dec., p. 96.

† 1 Strange, p. 96; 2 Strange, p. 114.

‡ See S. D. Dec. (1859), p. 229.

merely as a matter of fact, and have regard to the legal capacity of the parties to the adoption, and to the legal eligibility of the child as matter of law; yet they strongly insist upon an actual bodily transfer of the child being proved, and altogether refuse to recognize anything in the nature of a constructive giving and taking. The ceremony of gift must be not merely a form; it must be a fact patent to all beholders, the natural parent in person must actually with his own hand transfer the body of the child to the adoptive parent in person.

In a suit,* which was brought to have it declared that neither of two boys was the adopted son of the testator, and of his widow, the plaintiff, the question arose whether the acts and ceremonies which had been done and gone through, with a view to constituting both of them such adopted sons, were sufficient for the purpose or not. The secular portion of the ceremony took place during the life-time of the testator; the religious ceremonies, prescribed for adoption, were not carried out till full twelve months after his death; nothing had occurred meanwhile to connect the two ceremonies together; and inasmuch as they were completely disjoined, each was held to stand or fall by its own merits, and neither of them could be regarded as constituting a valid adoption. It was held, with regard to the secular ceremonies, that there must be an actual, and not a constructive, giving and receiving. The boy must be absolutely transferred from the one father to the other, he must be actually present, and given over from one parent to another. But at the time of the alleged giving and taking, the boys were hundreds of miles away from

* Siddessorry Dossee *v.* Doorgachurn Doss, 2 Ind. Jur., N. S., p. 22.

LECTURE X.

the place of the transaction; and, under such circumstances, the legal transfer of the proprietary interest in them was not effected. The religious ceremonies were performed wholly without the directions of the testator, and without the intervention of the widow. It was a case of an alleged simultaneous adoption, which, of course, was another and a totally distinct objection to their validity. The judgment, however, proceeded chiefly on the ground of there being no actual transfer, and not on account of a defect in the religious ceremonial.

Again, in the case of *Srinarayan Mitter* v. *Srimati Krishna Soondari Dassee,** it was contended that the execution of two deeds of agreement to give and receive a child in adoption amounted to an actual giving and acceptance of the child, and constituted a valid adoption. But the Court held that the execution of the two deeds did not amount to an actual transfer, and that even the change of name supposed to be evidenced by the deed was not a sufficiently overt act to show that the child was given or received.

In *Sabo Bawa* v. *Mahajun Maiti,*† although allusion was made to the absence of proof of formal ceremonies, the decision proceeded upon the ground that the gift and acceptance of the child in adoption had been proved, and the adoption recognized for a series of years.

Datta-homam not essential for civil purposes.

Thus far the balance of authority seems to be in favor of regarding the sacrifice to fire as unessential, at least to the validity of the rite for civil purposes. But in the Dattaka Mimansa,‡ there occur these passages:

* 2 Bengal Law Reports, A. C., p. 279.

† *Ibid*, Appendix, p. 51.

‡ Dattaka Mimansa, Chap. V., verses 45, 46, 55, and 56.

"The same author propounds a special rule, should the due form for adoption not be observed: 'he who adopts a son, without observing the rules ordained, should make him a participator of the rites of marriage, not a sharer of the wealth.'

"The meaning is, the marriage only of one adopted, without the form for adoption, is to be performed; no wealth is to be bestowed on him; on the contrary, in such case, the wife and the rest even succeed to the estate; for, without observance of form, his filial relation is not produced.

"Although it may be used like the word Indra and so forth, still since the prevailing sense proceeds from popular recognition, and the production of a son is ordained in holy writ, the general acceptation 'of son', like the general acceptation 'of wife' and the like, must be understood. By the purport of this and other passages, Mid'ha'tit'hi also declares the filial relation in adopted sons to be occasioned only by the proper ceremonies.

"It is therefore established that the filial relation of adopted sons is occasioned only by the proper ceremonies of gift, acceptance, *a burnt sacrifice,* and so forth; should either be wanting, the filial relation even fails."

And in the Dattaka Chandrika,* we find these :—

"In case no form, as propounded, should be observed, it will be declared that the adopted son is entitled to assets sufficient for his marriage."

"It is declared by this that, through the extinction of his filial relation from gift alone, the property of the son given in the estate of the giver ceases; and his relation to the family of that person is annulled."

* Dattaka Chandrika, Chap. II., verses 17, 19.

LECTURE X.

Baboo Shamachurn Sircar, the author of the Vyavastha Darpana, argues from these passages that the rule propounded by Jagannatha* which, as I have shown, has decided the law upon this point for a considerable time, is inaccurate; for that it has been conclusively laid down in the Dattaka Mimansa, and intimated in the Dattaka Chandrika, that filiation is null without "gift, acceptance, power, and so forth;" and the High Court of Bengal recently, in the case of *Bhairabnath Sye* v. *Mahesh Chandra Bhadury*, has upheld this view, and confirmed a decision of the Judge of Mymensing, in a case between Sudras, that ceremonies other than giving and taking were necessary to render an adoption valid even amongst parties of that caste.

Bhairabnath Sye v. Mahesh Chandra Bhadury.

The High Court in part relied upon this, that evidence had been adduced by the plaintiff, in support of the adoption, to prove that ceremonies which were considered necessary did take place, and that, therefore, in the opinion of the parties, something more than mere giving or taking was necessary to a valid adoption even amongst Sudras. In other words, the parties admitted the necessity of the ceremonies, and the question of fact depended upon the proof of their performance. No doubt, the absence of them is always suspicious, and where the parties by their conduct admit the absence to be fatal, and then fail to prove them, an adoption, under such circumstance, could scarcely be upheld. But the High Court did not rest the decision upon that ground alone. They examined the question whether any ceremonies were essential. Referring to the passages in Strange which I have quoted, and to the opinion of Mr. Ellis, they considered that the law there laid down

* Vyavastha Darpana, 874.

was successfully attacked by Baboo Shamachurn Sircar in his Vyavastha Darpana, and that the passages from the Dattaka Mimansa and Dattaka Chandrika, on which he relies, show that Sir Thomas Strange's rule is incorrect, when he says that all that is legally necessary for an adoption is "gift and acceptance manifested by some overt act;" for that the filial relation is authoritatively stated to fail if either gift, acceptance, sacrifice, or so forth, as described in the fifth section of the Dattaka Mimansa, should be wanting. The Court also, upon the authority of Baboo Shamachurn Sircar, held that Sudras could employ Brahmins to perform the rite of the *datta-homam* for them, and that the performance of it was necessary also in their case for a valid adoption.

This decision recognizes that even now, notwithstanding the opinions which have prevailed for the last forty years, and the decisions which have been made, the performance of the *datta-homam* at adoptions by all castes is, according to strict Hindu law and in a religious point of view, essential. It cannot, therefore, be safely neglected for the future. But the point was never argued or decided whether, assuming that the ceremonies were essential in a religious point of view, the performance of them was a duty which the Courts would undertake to enforce, as essential to the legal validity of an adoption, for civil purposes. All the ceremonies mentioned in the fifth section of the Dattaka Mimansa stand* on the same footing as the sacrifice to fire; and "he who adopts a son, without observing the rules ordained, should make him a participator of the rites of marriage; not a sharer of the wealth,"

* Dattaka Mimansa, Chap. V., verses 45, 46, and 56.

LECTURE X. the meaning of which is declared to be that the marriage only of one adopted without the form of adoption is to be performed; no wealth is to be bestowed on him; on the contrary, in such case the wife and the rest even succeed to the estate, for without observance of form the filial relation is not produced.

There can be no doubt that all these ceremonies prescribed at adoption, and also the subsequent ceremonies enjoined, all belong to the process of regeneration, which it is important should take place in the family of adoption. It is equally important that the ceremonies of regeneration should be performed, whether the child remains in the family of birth, or adopts a new one. But since the process is, as I have shown before, begun from the time of natural birth, Hindu law is careful to direct how far that process must be re-commenced in the adoptive family, and what additional ceremonies must be performed to secure that filial relation which shall authorize the adopted son to perform the funeral obsequies. But the Courts have never been in the habit of interfering with the performance or non-performance of any portion, either of regenerating ceremonies or of funeral obsequies. Their performance has never been insisted upon as a legal duty. The Courts have always inquired whether they have been so far performed in the family of birth as to render a child ineligible for adoption, for if they have been so performed, there is, as we shall see hereafter, a legal prohibition against adopting him. But when it* is authoritatively declared that

* Dattaka Chandrika, Chap. II., verse 19.—It is declared by this, that through the extinction of his filial relation by gift alone, the property of the son given in the estate of the giver ceases, and his relation to the family of that person is annulled.

by gift alone the extinction of the filial relation is caused, and the property of the son given in the estate of the giver ceases; and his relation to the family of that person is annulled; it is obvious that the rite has held good for civil purposes; that the transference of the boy from one family to another is complete, and the only question remaining is as to his *status* in the family of adoption, whether it should be one of sonship or of slavery. That depends purely upon the performance of ceremonial more or less connected with the work of regeneration. The Courts have always declined to supervise religious ceremonials or to insist in any way on their performance. They are left, and properly so, to the conscience of individuals, or to the influence of the priests or of the opinion of the caste or community to which the parties belong. The weight of judicial authority has never been thrown into the scale to secure their observance or to prescribe their necessity.

The case, however, in the Bengal Law Reports, to which I have referred, has undoubtedly thrown uncertainty upon the rule laid down by Sir T. Strange which has obtained for a considerable time, and which, it is submitted, is the correct one,—*viz.*, that for civil purposes the rite of an adoption is complete by the actual gift and acceptance of a child manifested by some overt act. It is admitted that the gift destroys the *status* of the child in one family; it is reasonable therefore that the acceptance should, as Jagannatha laid it down, establish it in the other, and the religious ceremonies may be left for their support to other influences than those of Courts of Law.

Otherwise the position of an adopted son is to the last degree insecure. I have already pointed out that no pro-

LECTURE X.

vision whatever is made to secure his interests, and if he must always be ready to make good his title against his adoptive family, who would be more ready to attack than defend it, by proving the due performance of a ceremonial made when he was a child, with the alternative not of reverting to his family of birth, but of remaining a mere dependent on his family of adoption, his position would be one of the most precarious imaginable. The rule laid down by Sir T. Strange, and supported by Mr. Macnaghten, and never impugnedfor a long space of time, but, on the contrary, acted upon by the Courts as I have shown, is I believe the correct one, and one which cannot safely be departed from in the administration of justice.

Madras High Court rule upon the same subject.

The Madras High Court has recently adhered to that rule, although such rule is at least more opposed to the Dattaka Mimansa than it is to the Dattaka Chandrika, which is the leading Bengal authority. In the case of *V. Singamma* v. *Vingamuri Venkatacharlu*,* the plaintiff sued as adopted son to the deceased husband of one of the defendants. The Judge of the lower Court found that it was not proved that the *datta-homam*, or any other ceremony except giving and receiving, was performed at the time of the adoption. The parties were Brahmins, and the High Court of Madras, after an examination of the authorities, came to the conclusion that proof of the performance of the *datta-homam* is not essential in order to establish a valid adoption.

" In the two celebrated treatises on adoption," the Court observed, " *viz.*, the Dattaka Mimansa and the Dattaka Chandrika, the observance of the prescribed solemnities

* 4 Madras High Court Reports, p. 165.

(including a burnt sacrifice and recitation of the prayers denominated *Vyakrit*) is certainly treated as essential to the validity of the adoption, and to the establishment of the filial relation, in the case at all events of the son given. But the writers of these treatises depend mainly upon the texts of Vasishta and Saunaka as the authorities for their position, and these texts enjoin in similar terms the observance of various other solemnities on the occasion of an adoption, some of which appear not to be regarded as essential by the commentator." The Madras High Court then passed in review the opinion of Jagannatha; of Sir Thomas Strange expressed in his judgment in *Veerapermal Pillay* v. *Naraina Pillay* and in his work on Hindu law; the opinions of Mr. Colebrooke and Mr. Ellis; and the dictum of Lord Wynford*—"neither written acknowledgments nor the performance of any religious ceremonial are essential to the validity of adoption." The High Court further considered that view of the case to be more consistent with its own previous decisions. Although there was no case in which the point before them had been formally decided, yet there are several decisions by that Court which I have already quoted, and shall hereafter quote, which are distinctly in favor of separating the legal and religious aspects of Hindu institutions, and of confining the attention of Courts of law to the civil purposes of the various acts and engagements which are prescribed, no doubt, by religion for religious purposes, but whose secular importance far outweighs their religious significance.

Religious obligations of the adopter.

Besides the ceremonies which are performed at the time of adoption, and which, as I have shown, have so little

* See Sutroogun Sutputty *v.* Sabitra Dye, 2 Knapp, P. C. Rep., p. 290.

LECTURE X.

effect upon the legal validity of the rite, there are other ceremonies which bear upon the subject of affiliation. The religious obligation to perform them is thrown upon the adopter, but there is, of course, no legal liability to do so which the Courts would enforce. I have already described the long ceremonial process of regeneration through which every Hindu of the three superior castes must pass. It is essential that some of these should be performed in the family of the adopter, it being necessary that the work of a second birth should be carried out, as far as possible, in the family of which the child must for life remain a member. Further, it is important that some of those ceremonies should not have been performed in the family of birth and by the natural father, for after the regeneracy of a Hindu has passed a certain stage, the child is so far affiliated to his natural parents, that he is incapable of being dissevered from them, and is therefore ineligible for adoption. And the question who is eligible to be adopted is, on that very account, one not free from difficulty or uncertainty.

Tonsure and *upanayana.*

The ceremonies, which it is essential to the completion of an adoption, in the fullest sense of the term and, with due regard to its religious significance, should be performed in the family of the adopter, are *tonsure* and the *upanayana*, or investiture with the Brahminical thread. In the ceremony of tonsure the family name is used, for a text expresses: "The coronal locks of the boy must be made with the enunciation of his patriarchal tribe."* Besides, an essential component of the initiatory rites is the ceremonial called Vriddhi-Sraddha, in which oblations are

* Dattaka Mimansa, Chap. IV., verse 28.

offered to the manes of three sets of ancestors in the family in which it takes place. The performance of initiatory rites ending with tonsure is said to be the cause of the filial relation. The most preferable object of adoption is a child wholly uninitiated; but a child may always be affiliated before the ceremony of tonsure has been performed, and there are means, as we shall see hereafter, of effecting a valid adoption, even after that rite has been duly celebrated in the maternal family.

It has been said that a child adopted after the ceremony of tonsure has been performed becomes a *dwyamashyayana*, or child of two fathers; the absolute transfer being regarded as incapable of taking effect. Such a child belongs to both families, inherits in both, and performs the obsequies in both. If such adoption takes place by special agreement between the two fathers, the child is called *Nitya Dwyamashyayana.** If the cause of the incomplete transfer be the antecedent performance of the rites of tonsure, the child is called *Anitya Dwyamashyayana.*

Doctrine of the Dattaka Chandrika.

But, according to the Dattaka Chandrika, the authority which is recognized as supreme in the Bengal school,† if the rite of investiture merely be performed by the adopter, the previous rites having been performed by the natural father in due season, or if neglected by him, then by the adoptive father out of season, the filiation of the son given as son of the adopter is completed. This doctrine is grounded on the text of Vasishta, which says: "Sprung from one following a different Sakha (or branch of the Vedas) the given son, even when invested with the characteristic thread, under the family name of the man himself,

* Macnaghten's Principles of Hindu Law, p. 71.

† Dattaka Chandrika, Chap. II., verse 23.

according to the form prescribed by his peculiar Sakha, becomes participant of the duties of such Sakha."

But such an adoption should take place within the primary season for the performance of the *upanayana* and not be postponed till after its expiration. In Bengal, therefore, the period for adoption is extended until the season of investiture for the three higher castes, and till marriage in the case of Sudras, marriage being the only regenerating ceremony of that class. All over India the performance of the *upanayana* in the natural family in the case of the three higher castes, and marriage in the case of all four, presents an insurmountable bar to adoption. In countries where the Dattaka Mimansa is recognized as the leading authority, the performance of the ceremony of tonsure is an impediment which can only be surmounted by prescribed sacrifices and penance.

Kritrima adoption.

Another, but widely different, form of adoption, is the *kritrima* adoption, which still prevails in the Mithila country, but is rarely practised in other parts of India, and is almost, if not wholly, unknown in Bengal. It appears to have been an innovation upon the established *dattaka* form, and it was designedly, and by gradual changes, introduced into the Mithila country. Mr. Macnaghten says* that, according to Vachespati, whose authority is recognized in Mithila, a woman could not, even with the previously obtained sanction of her husband, adopt a son after his death in the *dattaka* form; and he traced to this prohibitory rule the origin of the practice of adoption in the *kritrima* form. According to a note of Mr. Colebrooke to his translation of Jagannatha's† Digest, its introduction was owing

* Macnaghten's Principles of Hindu Law, p. 95.

† Colebrooke's Digest, Book V., Chap. IV., Sect X., sl. 284, note.

to the instrumentality of two Pundits named Sridatta and Pratihasta. Their motive was, lest a child already registered in one family, being again registered in another, upon a gift of him being made by his parents, a confusion of families and names should thence ensue. A case of such nature arose, and thereupon,* and in consequence thereof, a general assembly of Brahmins was held, at which the two Pundits above named presided, and it was then agreed that for the future the practice of the *dattaka* adoption should be discontinued. It remained, it is true, unforbidden, and therefore not illegal, except so far as long discontinuance and the general prevalence of a contrary custom might render it so. But practically it has been abolished in that country, and the *kritrima* form established in its stead.

Its character and consequences.

The *kritrima* adopted son does not lose his claim to his own family, or his rights of inheritance therein. He does not even take the name of his adoptive father, but he succeeds to his estate and performs his obsequies, although he does not continue in the family. Such a mode of affiliation is widely different in its character and objects from the ordinary form of Hindu adoption. It does not serve the purpose of effectuating the predominant motive of preserving and continuing the lineage of the adopter. Nor does it provide effectually for the performance of the obsequies, for the Kritrima's son returns to his father's natural family. It would appear to be in general a merely temporary arrangement, one which exists between the individual parties to the transaction and does not extend beyond them. A son so obtained† is not initiated in any rites in the family of his adoptive parent, nor does he assume any

* Sutherland's Synopsis, Note XV.

† *Ibid*, Note XVII.

LECTURE X.

relationship whatever to the adopter's father. Such an adoption can only be held to be legal, according to Hindu law, where it is in accordance with the uniform and well established custom, agreeably to the text of Vrihaspati, in which it is declared that immemorial usage legalizes any practice. It requires no ceremony to complete it and is instantaneously perfected by the offer of adopting and the consent of the adopted party. A husband may adopt one *kritrima* son, and the wife another. The simple form according to which this kind of affiliation takes place is* described on authority by Mr. Sutherland. "At an auspicious time, the adopter of a son having bathed, addressing the person to be adopted, who has also bathed, and to whom he has given some acceptable chattel, says—'Be my son.' He replies—'I am become your son.' The giving some chattel to him arises merely from custom. It is not necessary to the adoption. The assent of both parties is the only requisite; and a set form of speech is not essential."

No ceremonies are required.

No ceremonies are ever enjoined with regard to a *kritrima* adoption, but the fact of giving and accepting must be proved. There again also it must be an actual contract between parties present together, in person expressing to one another their consent.

In a suit brought by a widow† to recover certain property by right of succession to her husband, who died without issue, the defendant pleaded a title as adopted son of the deceased; who it appeared a short time before his death made a verbal declaration of adoption in his favor in the presence of several persons, but without any religious

* Sutherland's Synopsis, Note XVI.

† Kullean Sing *v.* Kirpa Sing, Select Reports (new edition), Vol. I., p. 11.

ceremony or observance; and that the defendant performed the obsequies, and was acknowledged as the heir. It was insisted that a sufficient form to constitute adoption had not been observed; but the adoption was held to be valid, it being ruled that by the Shasters the consent of the *adopter and adopted* was alone essential, and that the outward form was one which was merely sanctioned by custom, and was only required in order to establish the fact of an adoption having duly taken place. LECTURE X.

Again, where a plaintiff sued* as the adopted (*kritrima*) son of the deceased husband of the defendant, who admitted the fact of the adoption, but contended that it had been made solely for the due performance of funeral obsequies and not for the purpose of conferring any right of inheritance, the estate having been conferred upon her by her husband previously to his death. The adoptive father was a Mithila Brahmin, and being on the point of death, made a verbal nomination of the absent plaintiff to be his *kritrima* son. The Pundits declared it was invalid, because the proposal 'Be you my son' and the consent 'I will become your son' are both requisite. The prescribed form for adopting a *kritrima* son is as follows:— In an auspicious hour let him bathe, and also cause the person whom he wishes to adopt to be bathed, let him present something at his pleasure and say 'Be you my son,' and let the son answer 'I am become your son.' Then let him, according to custom, give a suit of clothes to the son. These are the legal conditions of adoption. The consent of both parties is the only requisite; neither the gift nor the set form of speech is essential. The *kritrima* son will

* Mussamut Sutputtee *v.* Indranund Jha, Select Reports (new edition), Vol. II., p. 221.

LECTURE X.

inherit the property of his adoptive father even although the latter leave a widow. It was held in this case that the adoption was invalid, and the plaintiff's suit was dismissed.

According to Sir T. Strange* the ceremonial usual at a *kritrima* adoption is the same with that of the *dattaka*, omitting the sacrifice, or burnt offering, which is not performed at it. Initiation into the family of the adopter is not practised; for the connection with the natural family is seldom wholly relinquished. The rite falls far short of the *dattaka* adoption, both in its religious significance and its civil importance. It is in the nature of a secular contract between the adopter and adopted for a temporary purpose.

Krita, or son bought.

Although the *dattaka* and *kritrima* adoptions are the only forms in use at the present day as a general rule, yet an exception must be allowed in favor of any particular usage which may be proved to have had immemorial usage.† One example of this is the *krita*, or son bought, a mode of adoption which was said by Mr. Ellis‡ to be uniformly practised by some particular castes in Southern India. Such a mode is admittedly unlawful amongst Brahmins; and even amongst the other castes, the better opinion appears to be that a child cannot pass from one family or father to another by virtue of a pecuniary dealing. To constitute adoption by purchase there must be an express and specific acceptance of the boy *as son*, the child being surrendered by his parents in consideration of a price paid. The purpose must be distinctly understood that by reason of the transaction the child is imme-

* Strange's Hindu Law, Vol. II., p. 204

† Macnaghten's Principles of Hindu Law, p. 101.

‡ Strange's Hindu Law, Vol II., p. 156.

diately to become son to the buyer. There must in fact be a gift and acceptance of the child in adoption, the passing of money from one hand to another being an unessential part of the ceremony. The Gosswamies and other devotees who lead a life of celibacy are referred to by Mr. Macnaghten as in the habit of buying children for the purposes of adopting them in the form termed *krita*, or son bought.

LECTURE XI.

THE RIGHT TO ADOPT.

Three Branches of the Law of Adoption—Who may adopt—Sonless Men—Minors—Unmarried Men may adopt—Impotent and excluded persons may adopt—Except perhaps under Mitakshara Law—They must perform Penance—The Husband's right to adopt is absolute—Legal capacity of Women to adopt—The Wife—The Widow—Her right to adopt a *Dattaka* Son—*Collector of Madura* v. *Muttu Ramalinga Sathuputty*—Whose assent is necessary to a Widow's adoption, in the absence of her husband's consent—Judgment of the High Court of Bombay—The Mother—The Wife and Widow in Mithila—Conflicting Opinions as to their right to adopt—Decided Cases.

Three branches of the law of adoption.

ALTHOUGH the Hindu is subject to but few restrictions when he comes to exercise the right of adopting a son, and although he is in no way fettered by any provisions of law introduced to secure the interests of any child whom he may wish to obtain, it must not be concluded that the law of adoption is either meagre or simple. It chiefly concerns the right to give a son and the right to receive him, and the eligibility of the child to secure to his adoptive parents the objects for which they had recourse to the expedient of affiliation. The circumstances which, on the one hand, give birth to those rights of giving and receiving, and on the other secure the objects in view, are somewhat complicated in their character, and require the closest attention; and thus the law relating to adoption, though nearly uniform throughout India, forms one of the most difficult subjects in the whole of Hindu jurisprudence.

In dealing, therefore, with the law of adoption, an inquiry must be directed to ascertain, first, the circumstances under which the right to receive a child as a *dattaka*, or given son, accrues to either man or woman, and the rules which guide him in the exercise of that right. Next comes the question, who is entitled to give a child in adoption, and by what law his discretion is controlled and guided. Thirdly, what are the circumstances which render the child a fit and proper subject for affiliation, capable of being absolutely transferred from one family to another. In discussing these subjects, I shall also refer, when necessary, to the *kritrima* adoption.

Who may adopt.

With respect to the first of these questions, as to the circumstances under which a right to adopt arises. On this subject, the general rule is in the words of Atri* that "by a man destitute of a son only, must a substitute for the same always be adopted; with some one resource for the sake of the funeral cake, water, and solemn rites." The rule is also given by Menu in very similar words.

Sonless men.

It must be understood that the destitution referred to is at the time of the adoption. A man to whom no son has been born, or whose son has died, is within the meaning of the term *aputra*, and may adopt. The son referred to includes the son's son, and son's grandson, for either of these is denoted by the term male issue (the absence of which is a bar to the entrance of heaven), and is capable of performing the funeral obsequies.† Sir Francis Mac-

* Dattaka Mimansa, Chap. I., verse 3.

† Dattaka Mimansa, Chap. I., verse 13.—By a man destitute of a son. The word "son" here used is inclusive also of the son's son and grandson, for through these the exclusion from heaven denounced in such passages as "Heaven awaits not one destitute of a son" is

naghten* has expressed a doubt whether the *aputra* man does not also mean one destitute of a daughter's son, but such doubt is said to rest on no solid foundation.† A daughter's son, however, performs the obsequies of his maternal grandfather, in fact of three male ancestors, in right of his mother. But he is not a son, and does not continue the name and lineage of his maternal grandfather, except when, as in old times, he was *putrika putra,* or son of an appointed daughter.

Minors.

It is, therefore, the *aputra* man who may adopt; and the only other qualification, besides sonlessness, is that, in the case of a man adopting, he should be of age; and that, in the case of a woman adopting, it should be with the consent of her natural protector, who in Bengal is exclusively her husband, while in other provinces it may be his kindred. Minority, therefore, is the first limitation to the *aputra* man's legal right to adopt. No decision, however, to that effect has yet been made, nor is such limitation anywhere expressly laid down in the shasters. But the act of adopting may reasonably be held to be one which falls within the scope of the ordinary disabilities of minority, and of those ordinary provisions of law which refuse to minors the capacity to bind themselves or their property by contract or other engagements. It can scarcely be considered at the present day that the act of adopting is exclusively a religious rite which minors should be allowed to perform irrespective of

removed, since it is declared in the text subjoined that the mansions of the happy are attained through the grandson and the other. "By a son a man conquers worlds; by a son's son, he enjoys immortality; and afterwards by the son of a grandson he reaches the solar abode." (9 Menu, 137).

* Considerations of Hindu Law, p. 150.

† Macnaghten's Principles of Hindu Law, p. 66.

the civil consequences which they are presumed to be incapable of appreciating.

For however strong the religious obligation to adopt may be, regard being had to the strict word of the shasters, the fact that ample provision is made for the performance of obsequies independently of the son, and the superior advantage of the son's performance being left so extremely indefinite, the obligation referred to cannot be regarded as so essential or indispensable as to over-ride the provisions of law. As pointed out by Mr. Colebrooke,* in a note to Sir T. Strange's work, passages of law recommend, but do not enjoin, adoption. An omission to adopt is nowhere declared to be a sin, and no longer involves a man in the terrors of *put,* but is merely said to deprive him, on the mere suggestion of the author of the Dattaka Mimansa, of a particular heaven. Although a minor may perform obsequies, he can have no other qualifications, except such as are especially allowed by the shasters or by law. And there is no reason for presuming adoption to be within his legal capacity, before he is by law able to contract, since on the one hand it is merely an optional religious rite, probably neglected by thousands, and on the other, is a civil act of momentous importance, altering the devolution of property, whether large or small, to the exclusion of those who claimed by right of inheritance in succession to the adoptive infant. Such legal capacity, if it existed, would obviously be liable to great abuses; and it would be impossible to maintain it, except upon the ground that adoption was an essential religious observance, which the shasters and general consent re-

* Strange's Hindu Law, Vol. II., p. 83.

LECTURE XI.

garded as absolutely indispensable; a view which has never yet been taken by the Courts, nor sanctioned by Hindu practice and by general belief, as evidenced by that practice.* A minor is competent to appoint a substitute for the performance of the *shraddhas* of his ancestors, and is probably also competent to appoint a substitute for the performance of his own *shraddhas* as well as those of his ancestors after his death. But he cannot complete the act of filiation so as to break the legal order of succession.†

Although minority is a bar to a man performing the civil act of adoption, it has nevertheless been decided that a wife, while an infant, can adopt a son under her husband's authority, the reason of which is that in doing so she is the mere instrument of her husband's‡ will, the act being in reality that of the husband.

Minority, however, is almost the only disability imposed by law in respect of the right to adopt. It is not even provided that the adoptive father should be one who, in the ordinary course of things, might be considered to be supplying or remedying his reasonable expectations. For Jagannatha, in his Digest, declares that no law is found expressing that a son shall not be adopted by one who§ has not contracted a marriage. There is no argument, he says, to support the conclusion that because a man has no

Unmarried men may adopt.

* Shamachurn's Vyavastha Darpana, p. 775.

† Dattaka Mimansa, Chap. V., verse 46—The meaning is: the marriage only of one adopted without the form for adoption is to be performed; no wealth is to be bestowed on him; on the contrary, in such case, the wife and the rest even succeed to the estate; for, without observance of form, his filial relation is not produced.

‡ Shamachurn's Vyavastha Darpana, p. 770.

§ Colebrooke's Digest, Book V., Chap. IV., Sec. 8, verse 273 note.

wife, and is therefore excluded from the order *grihastha*, or householder, therefore he cannot adopt a son. LECTURE XI.

Whether a man has abstained from contracting a marriage, or having married has lost or forsaken his wife, or whether he has not completed the ceremonies which perfect twice-born men, and therefore belongs to no order, it is declared by the commentator to be contrary to common sense, that although the form of adopting a son given has been observed, the adoption should be void. But as celibacy is scarcely ever observed amongst Hindus, marriage being the essential ceremony to complete the religious scheme of regeneration, the law enabling an unmarried man to adopt is not of frequent application. There are some passages referred to by Mr. Sutherland, in a note to his Synopsis* of the Law of Adoption as contained in the Dattaka Chandrika and Dattaka Mimansa, from which it might be argued that an adoption by an unmarried man was illegal, but they are not sufficient to outweigh the express authority of Jagannatha. And, accordingly, it has been held by the Madras High Court, that an adoption by a widower does not present any exception to the general rule of Hindu law which allows the privilege of making such adoption to any one destitute of legitimate male issue.†

Impotent and excluded persons may adopt.

Further, if an unmarried man, who voluntarily remains in the position of one incapable of having legitimate issue, is under no disability to adopt, another question arises whether an impotent man may adopt, and if so, whether such disability attaches in the case of those persons who

* Sutherland's Synopsis, Note 4.

† Nagappa Udapa *v.* Subba Sastry, 2 Madras High Court Rep., p. 367.

LECTURE XI.

are excluded from inheritance by reason of some incurable mental or physical disease.

Such disability is nowhere positively declared, but sons adopted by such persons are alluded to by the authors of the Dattaka Chandrika* and the Dattaka Mimansa, without any expression of a doubt respecting the propriety of such adoption, and it is declared that they have no right to succeed to the estate† of the paternal grandfather, but are only entitled to maintenance. In fact, the disability to inherit, which they are supposed to derive from their adoptive father, is avowedly a mere matter of inference from a text of Yajnavalkya, which, although it expressly declares that the sons of an excluded person are entitled to allotments, if free from defects, nevertheless, by introducing the descriptive clause "whether legitimate or the offspring of the wife by a kinsman" is supposed by this specific mention impliedly to disinherit their adopted sons, or even to forbid their adoption.

Such is the interpretation of the text which is accepted by the author of the Mitakshara. A case once arose in Bengal, in which the question was mooted, but nothing was decided which would throw light on the course which the Courts would take in case of an adoption by an outcast or other person suffering under disability. It was a case

* Dattaka Chandrika, Sect. 6.

† See also Dattaka Mimansa, Section I., verse 4; Sutherland's Synopsis, Head I., 9 Menu, 201, 203.—Eunuchs and outcasts, persons born blind or deaf, madmen, idiots, the dumb, and such as have lost the use of a limb, are excluded from a share of the heritage; . . . If the eunuch and the rest should at any time desire to marry, and if the wife of the eunuch should raise up a son to him by a man legally appointed, that son and the issue of such as have children shall be capable of inheriting.

in which* the plaintiff sought to cancel an adoption made by the defendant, on the ground that she was debarred from inheriting by divers acts of impurity. The Court refused to listen to that charge, no proof having been given that the defendant had been excommunicated by her tribe for having been guilty of any impurity which would, according to the shasters, have rendered her an outcast.

Except perhaps under Mitakshara law.

Notwithstanding, therefore, that the right of the impotent man and of others (who are excluded from inheritance) to adopt, seems to be admitted by the author of the Dattaka Chandrika, which is of paramount authority in Bengal, such rule would probably not apply where the Mitakshara was implicitly followed. It is, however, reasonable, and may be considered to be law, that adoption by one excluded from inheritance would confer no right of succession greater than the adopter himself possessed; and that although a legitimate son of an excluded person born in his grandfather's life-time is heir to the grandfather, the adopted son can claim nothing further than the maintenance to which his adoptive father was entitled. Vriddha Gautama† refers to the impotent man as one who is capable of adopting.

Vachespati‡ declared the incompetence of Sudras to adopt from their incapacity to perform the sacrament of the *homa* and prayers prescribed for adoption; but Vriddha Gautama refers to a Sudra adoption, when prescribing the nature of the gratuity payable by the members of each caste at the performance of the ceremony, and directs that a Sudra upon that occasion should pay to the extent of

* Koonwarree *v.* Tewaree, 1 Sudder Dewanny Dec., p. 240.

† Dattaka Mimansa, Section V., verse 3.

‡ 1 Dattaka Mimansa, Section I., verse 26.

LECTURE XI.

his means, and in some cases even the whole of the year's earnings.

They must first perform penance.

Penance, however, must be performed by persons under disability produced by incurable disease before they proceed to adopt, since otherwise they would not be capable of performing the religious rites, but they may authorize their wives to adopt without performing penance.*

There are two cases given in the second volume of Macnaghten's Hindu Law,† in one of which it was decided that a person afflicted with leprosy is incapable of adopting; and in the other that, if he has performed the prescribed penances, that, incapacity is removed. Expiation is said to be necessary to enable a polluted person to perform the religious acts ordained in the Vedas. And before the Privy Council‡ it seems to have been taken as admitted law that adoption by a person while under pollution in consequence of the death of a relation, would be invalid.

The husband's right to adopt is absolute.

The husband's power of adoption is never dependent upon the consent of his wife, since as between him and her it is absolute in him. He can, by his mere act of adoption, affiliate a child both to himself and his wife. Where a widow sought to recover her husband's estate§ in the Moorshedabad Court, as her husband's heiress, her claim was opposed on behalf of a child to whose adoption by her husband she did not appear to have assented. It was

* Shamachurn's Vyavastha Darpana, p. 757.—A man afflicted with leprosy or such other sinful disease, is however required to perform penance previous to his adopting a son. . . . . But to authorize his wife to adopt, he is not indispensably required to perform the penance in question.

† See Volume II, page 201, cases xx and xxi.

‡ Ramalinga Pillai v. Sinisapa Pillai, 1 W. R., P. C., p. 25.

§ Alank Munjari v. Fakir Chand Sirkar, 5 Sudder Dewanny Decison, p. 351.

considered that the assent of the wife of an adopter was not indispensable to legalize adoption, and the widow's suit was dismissed.

LECTURE XI.

Legal capacity of women to adopt.

Next comes the question of the legal capacity of a woman to adopt a son. Upon this subject, with regard to adoption in the ordinary and full meaning of the term,—that is, adoption in the *dattaka* form, the text of Vasishta*—"Let not a woman either give or receive a son, unless with the assent of her husband"—declares a prohibition, which is in full force at the present day. The rule of law may be laid down that a woman, whether wife or widow, is unable to adopt a son in the *dattaka* form as son to herself exclusively. In either capacity her only power to adopt is a vicarious one—a power to adopt a son to her husband, who *ipso facto* becomes a son to herself. Both wife and widow may so adopt with the permission or direction of the husband however given. In Bengal the husband's consent is indispensable; according to the doctrine of the other schools it is always sufficient, but may be dispensed with in the case of a widow if in lieu of it the consent of a majority of his *sapindas* or other near kindred is obtained.

It is not apparent, at first sight, from the doctrine of the text books why the Hindu law should deny to a woman the capacity to receive a son in adoption. According to the author of the Dattaka Chandrika,† a woman is excluded from heaven, as much as a man is, if destitute of male issue; and if this be the case it would seem to follow that her right to adopt, on failure of that issue, should be co-ordinate with his. But from Menu and the author of the Dattaka Mimansa, it would appear that a woman does not derive the same

* Colebrooke's Digest, Book V., Chap. IV., Section VIII., verse 273.
† Dattaka Chandrika, Section I., verse 25.

LECTURE XI.

spiritual benefit from adoption as a man does; that it is not in her case indispensable to future happiness.* "Many thousands of Brahmins," says Menu, "having avoided sensuality from their early youth, and having left no issue in their families, have ascended nevertheless to heaven; and like those abstemious men, a virtuous wife ascends to heaven though she has no child, if after the death of her lord she devote herself to pious austerity."

Menu and Vrihaspati provide for the difficulty, if there be any, in the way of refusing to her the capacity to adopt, by the doctrine that in the son of her co-wife she is provided with male issue, who can perform her funeral obsequies; which assumes that her husband has already begotten or adopted a child. Menu pronounced that, if among several brothers of the whole blood, one had a son born, all were fathers of a male child, and that the uncles would have no power to adopt; and that similarly if among all the wives of the same husband one brought forth a male child, all the wives by means of that son become mothers of male issue.†

With regard to a brother becoming father of male issue through the brother's son, the text of Menu is expounded to mean that a man cannot adopt another while a brother's son is living and can possibly be adopted, but his affiliation must take place by means of adoption.‡ But such act of affiliation is unnecessary as between a wife and her co-wife's son; and therefore assuming that the husband has acted in accordance with the precepts of the shasters and provided himself with a son, the woman's

* 5 Menu, verses 159, 160; Dattaka Mimansa, Section I., verse 29.

† 9 Menu, 182, 183.

‡ Dattaka Mimansa, Section II., verse 73.

incapacity to adopt would not prejudice her interests. It only has this practical consequence, that she is by reason of that incapacity unable to anticipate, and thereby to prevent the free exercise of his discretion. LECTURE XI.

With regard, therefore, to a Hindu wife, she is absolutely incapable of adopting in the *dattaka* form, according to the doctrine of all the schools, except with the consent, by the authority, and on behalf of her husband. The wife.

But with respect to the widow's power of adopting, that is a subject which formerly was open to considerable doubt, but is now satisfactorily settled. Nanda Pandita* insisted upon the disqualification of women, whether as widows or wives, from their incompetency to perform the sacrament of *homam ;* but that, as we have seen, was also assigned as a reason for refusing the right of adoption to Sudras, who nevertheless may, and constantly do, adopt. This doctrine, however, being enforced by Vachespati prevailed in Mithila, and led, as we have seen, to the *kritrima* form being introduced. In all the other provinces more attention was paid to the insurmountable and often quoted text of Vasishta, in consequence of which it seemed impossible to deny to a woman, who had obtained the assent of her husband, a power to receive in adoption. But the author of the Dattaka Mimansa nevertheless sought to limit this right to the case of a wife who had so obtained her husband's assent, and denied the extension of the same privilege to the case of a widow; for in her case he said it was impossible for her to obtain his assent. Still, however, according to the Dattaka Chandrika, a widow may adopt with the previously obtained sanction of her husband, in the absence of male The widow.

* Dattaka Mimansa, Section I., verses 23, 24.

LECTURE XI.

issue, and such is the doctrine of the Bengal school at the present day.

Her right to adopt a *dattaka* son.

The widow's right to adopt in the *dattaka* form, therefore, is not absolute, but is dependent upon the permission of others. The three rules which embrace the whole law upon the subject are: (1) that the husband's permission is always a sufficient authority to his widow to enable her to adopt, except in Mithila, where the *dattaka* form has in practice been abolished; (2) that such permission in Bengal is essential, and cannot be dispensed with under any circumstances; (3) that by the followers of the Mitakshara, both in the Benares and the Maharashtra schools, the consent of the husband's kindred may be substituted, when the husband has expressed no prohibition, and has merely failed or omitted to give his sanction.

The widow, however, must not be disqualified by being under pollution, or degradation, for performing the religious ceremony of receiving a son to her husband. It has been held* in the case of an unchaste widow, who assumed to adopt, while living in concubinage, and being in a state of pregnancy resulting from such concubinage, that such adoption was invalid.

The husband's assent† has always been and is now necessary, according to the Bengal school, to the validity of an adoption by a widow. The same rule was originally observed in the Benares school,‡ according to a case reported in the second volume of the Select Reports. In that case the Provincial Court, at Benares, affirmed the lower Court's

* Shamloll Dutt *v.* Sreemutty Sowdaminee Dossee, *per* Norman, J., see *Englishman* Newspaper, June 27, 1870.

† Strange's Hindu Law, Vol. II., p. 96.

‡ Rajah Shumshere Mull *v.* Ranee Dilraj Konwar, Select Reports (new edition), Vol. II., p. 216.

decision that the husband's assent was necessary. And the Pundits of the Sudder Court, when the case went up in appeal, declared that it was written in the Vera Mitrodoya and Sunskar Kustoobha, that a widow can adopt a son, without authority from her husband, provided she obtain the consent of her husband's heirs; but that that doctrine was overruled in the Dattaka Mimansa, and that therefore the adoption in the case was illegal and invalid.

Collector of Madura v. Muttu Ramalinga Sathuputty.

But in support of the three rules, which I have given, it is only necessary to refer to a single case, for scarcely any doubt can now rest upon them. The judgment to which I refer is one pronounced by the Privy Council in 1868, in the case of the *Collector of Madura* v. *Mutu Ramalinga Sathuputty.** It was on an appeal from a decision of the High Court at Madras, and concerned the title to a zemindary which was of the nature of a Raj or principality descendable to a single heir. The principal question at issue in the appeal was the validity of an adoption made by the widow of the last undisputed owner of the zemindary. That last owner had, in a document executed shortly before his death, directed that his mother should exercise chief control over and enjoy possession of the zemindary, and that his brother should manage its affairs until his daughters should attain their proper age. He gave no authority to his widow, the respondent, to adopt. The elder daughter died without issue; the widow quarrelled with her mother-in-law, and was subsequently appointed guardian of her surviving daughter in the stead of her husband's mother, and assumed the management of the estate. She finally succeeded to

* 1 Bengal Law Reports, P. C., p. 1.

LECTURE XI.

the estate as heiress to her younger daughter, who died without issue. A long litigation intervened between herself and her mother-in-law, and shortly after her succession to the estate by right of inheritance, she asserted apparently, for the first time, a right to adopt a son to her husband. This right was claimed in the alternative either under an alleged authority from him in the event which had happened of both his daughters dying without issue: or under a more general power of adoption said to be consistent with Hindu law as current in the Dravida country, according to which a widow, without the authority of her husband, but with the consent of his kindred, may adopt a son to him. The alleged authority from the husband was never proved; if it had been it would have disposed of the case.

But the Court of first instance, under an issue directed by the High Court of Madras, had found that the adoption by the widow had taken place with the consent of her mother-in-law, and of all the surviving kindred; and the High Court declared that there was no doubt, as a matter of fact, that it had been made with the assent of the majority of her husband's *sapindas*. The Privy Council treated as an admitted proposition that a widow has the power to receive a son in adoption to her husband according to all the schools of Hindu law, except that of Mithila; but that such power is subject to conditions. According to the Bengal school it is established beyond all doubt that she must have the formal permission of her husband, given in his lifetime, verbally or in writing, but clearly proved. Other schools extend the right of the widow to adopt, to cases where although the husband has abstained from giving his permission, his kindred, after his death, *bonâ fide* authorize or consent to the act. The point in dispute was, whether the doctrine of the assent of the husband's kindred being of sufficient authority to the widow, was limited to the Mahratta school in which the treatise called the Mayakha is the predominant authority; or whether it was common to the followers of the Mitakshara in the Benares, as well as in the Mahratta school, and as such to be receivable as the law current in Vizagapatam, where the litigation had arisen. Balambhatta, who was a commentator of the Benares school, contends that a woman's right of adopting, as well as of giving, a son is common to the widow and to the wife, and does not enforce the usual restrictions; and Mr. Colebrooke's note to the Mitakshara,* and several notes of his in the second volume of Strange's Hindu Law, were quoted to show that, according to his opinion, all the followers of the Mitakshara, whether of the Benares or of the Mahratta school, recognized a widow's adoption when made with the consent of her husband's kindred. The Privy Council also cited and approved the following statement of the law by Sir Thomas Strange:† "Equally loose is the reason alleged against adoption by a widow, since the assent of the husband may be given to take effect like a will after his death; and according to the doctrine of the Benares and Mahratta schools, prevailing in the peninsula, it may be supplied by that of his kindred, her natural guardians; but it is otherwise by the law that governs the Bengal Provinces."

Whose assent is necessary to a widow's adoption, in the absence of her husband's consent.

And the further question disposed of by their lordships which appears to be all that was necessary to complete the rule of law upon this subject was, who are the kinsmen whose assent will supply the want of positive authority from the deceased husband in the provinces,

* Mitakshara, Chap. I., Sect. XI., verse 9.

† Strange's Hindu Law, Vol. I., p. 179.

LECTURE XI.

when such want of authority may be supplied at all? When the husband's family is undivided, then it was said that under the law of the schools which admit this disputed power of adoption (*i. e.* all the schools except those of Bengal and Mithila) the father of the widow's deceased husband, if living, or at least the surviving brothers, who in default of adoption would take the husband's share, would obviously be the persons whose consent would be necessary; inasmuch as it would be unjust to allow the widow to defeat their interests by introducing a new coparcener against their will; the widow, according to those schools, not herself succeeding to a share of the joint estate. When, however, as in the case before the Council, the deceased husband was separate in estate, the widow takes it by inheritance, and then there is greater difficulty in laying down a rule. The reason, however, for the necessity of the assent of kinsmen, being the presumed incapacity of women for independence, rather than the necessity of procuring the consent of all those whose possible and reversionary interest in the estate would be defeated by the adoption, their lordships held that the consent of every kinsman was not essential. While ruling that every case must depend upon the circumstances of the family, their lordships laid it down that there should be such evidence of the assent of kinsmen as suffices to show that the act is done by the widow in the proper and *bonâ fide* performance of a religious duty, and neither capriciously, nor from a corrupt motive.

Further, their lordships pointed out that, inasmuch as the authorities in favour of the widow's power to adopt, with the assent of her husband's kinsmen, proceed in a great measure upon the assumption that his assent to this meritorious act is to be implied wherever he has not forbidden it; so the power cannot be inferred when a prohibition by the husband either has been directly expressed by him or can be reasonably deduced from his disposition of his property, or from the existence of a direct line competent to the full performance of religious duties, or from the other circumstances of his family which afford no plea for a supercession of heirs on the ground of religious obligation in order to complete or fulfil defective religious rites.

LECTURE XI.

Judgment of the High Court of Bombay

The case of the *Collector of Madura* v. *Mattu Ramalinga Satthuputty* must be read in conjunction with that of *Rakhmabai* v. *Radhabai*,* in which the High Court of Bombay held that, according to the authorities applicable in that part of India, a Hindu widow, in the Mahratta country, may, *without* the permission of her husband, and *without* the consent of his kindred, adopt a son to him, if the act is done by her in the proper and *bonâ fide* performance of a religious duty, and neither capriciously nor from a corrupt motive. The Court referred to two cases in which that doctrine had been clearly recognized. One was where an adoption made by a widow, without the express consent of her relations, but confirmed by the Emperor of Delhi and the local authorities, had been held to be valid. In another, an adoption by a widow of a son of her husband's brother had been held to be valid without proof of the consent of any of her relations except the father of the person adopted.

The mother.

In conclusion, it nowhere appears that the Hindu law permits a man to delegate to his mother a power to adopt a son for

* 5 Bombay High Court Reports, A. C. J., p. 181.

him where the widow is a minor. In such a case the mother,* like the widow, would act as deputy for her son, the act of adoption being his and not hers. The competence even of a widow to adopt for her husband has been denied and has only been established after considerable controversy and discussion. Adoption by a mother on behalf of her son cannot be regarded as legal or valid. The wife and widow are the only persons who may be deputed for that purpose.

The wife and widow in Mithila.

Now, with regard to adoption in the *kritrima* form, and according to the law of the Mithila school, the case is different, and having regard to the peculiar characteristics of that form of adoption, which effects no change of *gotra*, and is a mere temporary arrangement between two contracting parties, the capacity to receive a *kritrima* son would seem to be necessarily co-equal with the capacity to contract. I am not aware, however, of any decision of the Courts in India in which a *kritrima* adoption by a Hindu wife has been upheld. And, in the absence of authority, the matter is left in doubt by the expressed opinions of the leading text writers.

Conflicting opinions as to their right to adopt.

Mr. Sutherland† points out that the prevailing custom in Mithila of widows adopting in the *kritrima* form is due to their desire to obtain the performance of their *sapindakarana* by a person especially obtained for that purpose, and thereby to exempt their other relatives who are unable to celebrate that ceremony from the duty of observing in lieu thereof (as failing such adoption they would have to do) twelve monthly funeral repasts. A man's purpose in adoption, according to Vachespati Misra and other sages, whose authority is paramount in Mithila,

* Strange's Hindu Law, Vol. II., p. 94.

† Sutherland's Synopsis, Note V.

is that he may be preserved from the hell called *put*; the woman's purpose is that some one may exist capable of performing her *sapindakarana*. The right to adopt, therefore, will only accrue to either man or woman in the absence of any one capable of promoting the purpose which he or she has in view. Consequently the wife cannot adopt, for her husband is capable of performing her *sapindakarana*; and on the other hand, should the husband leave an adopted son who would necessarily be filially related to his wife, the widow could not adopt a peculiar son to herself. LECTURE XI.

Mr. Macnaghten, however, says that it does not appear that the prohibition in Mithila which prevails against a widow receiving a son in *dattaka* adoption, even with the previous sanction of her husband, extends to her receiving a boy in adoption according to the *kritrima* form; and the son so adopted will perform her obsequies, and succeed to her peculiar property, though not to that of her deceased husband. It is not uncommon, he says, in the province of Mithila, for the husband to adopt one *kritrima* son, and the wife another. According to the authority of Balambhatta and the author of the Vyavahara Mayakha, a woman, whether wife or widow, can adopt, in her own right and for her own sake, a son in the *kritrima* form.*

The opinions of the Pundits attached to the late Sudder Court of Bengal was taken in the year 1810 in the case of *Sreenarain Rai* v. *Baja Jha.*† The question, however, Decided cases.

* Mitakshara, Chap. I., Section XI., verse 9, *note.*—"Balambhatta contends that a woman's right of adopting, as well as of giving, a son is common to the widow and to the wife. This likewise is the opinion of the author of the Vyavahara Mayakha, but while he admits that a widow may adopt a son without her husband's previous authority, he requires that she should have the express sanction of his kindred."

† Select Reports (new edition), Vol. II., p. 29.

LECTURE XI.

was not determined, for the case was decided upon a different point. It appears from the report that the plaintiff (respondent) sued in the Zillah Court of Purneah as the adopted son of a deceased Ranee to recover her estate. The defendants were in possession thereof as heirs-at-law to her deceased husband. The parties were subjected to Hindu law as expounded in the shasters current in the Mithila country. The defendant having denied the authority of the Ranee under these shasters to give away any of the property, the Provincial Court, without entering into the question of adoption, adjudged to the plaintiff a moiety of the estate, on the footing of a deed of compromise which it held to be proved to have been executed by the Ranee in her lifetime. The Sudder Court in appeal eventually upheld the Provincial Court's decision, and decreed in the terms of the deed, also without reference to the adoption. But in the course of the hearing they referred the proceedings with the following questions to their Pundits: (1) if the Ranee, some years after the death of her husband, regularly adopted a son, will such adopted son be entitled to take her husband's estate? (2) if the Ranee, with or without authority from her husband, adopted a son to herself and her husband, according to the shasters current in Mithila, will the estate of the husband pass to such adopted son?

The Pundits gave the following answers: If a man adopt, his son so adopted is heir to his estate, and offers his funeral oblations, but the person so appointed does not become the adopted son of the adopter's wife. So also a woman may adopt one who thereby becomes son to herself, but not to her husband. According to the usage of Mithila, husband and wife may jointly or separately adopt, but the separately adopted son of either is not heir to the property of the other.

Secondly, it is not according to the usage of Mithila that a person adopted by a wife or widow, with or without the permission of her husband, becomes the adopted son of the husband.

The law which prevails in the province of Mithila is unaffected by the judgment of the Privy Council in the appeal brought by the Collector of Madura, to which I have already referred. I will however cite two other cases which illustrate the widow's capacity to adopt according to the Mithila school. First that of *The Collector of Tirhoot* v. *Huropershad Mohunt*,* where it was laid down that, according to Hindu law as current in Mithila, a widow has power to adopt a son in the *kritrima* form, with or without her husband's consent; but such son would not, by virtue of such adoption, lose his position in his own family, nor would he succeed to the property left by the husband of his adoptive mother, but would be considered her son and entitled to succeed to her property only. According to Mr. Macnaghten,† a person adopted by a widow in the *kritrima* form, even though in pursuance of a permission given by the husband, does not become thereby the adopted son of the husband, and the son so adopted will perform her obsequies and succeed to her peculiar property, but not to that of her deceased husband. A widow in Mithila is prohibited from receiving a son in adoption according to the *dattaka* form even with the previous sanction of her husband.

And, secondly, there is the decision in the case of‡ *Mussamut Shibo Koeree* v. *Joogun Sing*, where it was

* 7 S. W. R., p. 500.

† Macnaghten's Principles of Hindu Law, p. 76.

‡ 8 S. W. R., p. 155.

LECTURE XI.

held that a widow in the Mithila province is capable of adopting in the *kritrima* form without her husband's consent. He does not become a member of the adopting family, but he (and after him his issue) continues to be considered a member of his natural family, and takes the inheritance both of his own family and of his adopting mother or his adopting father. He has no rights of collateral heirship in the family of his adoptive parent. The relation of *kritrima* for the purpose of inheritance extends to the contracting parties only. He is necessarily the son of two fathers, but he does not prolong the line of his adopter, nor does he take his name.

LECTURE XII.

PERMISSION TO ADOPT—PLURAL ADOPTION.

Authority to adopt—How it may be given—Who may grant such authority—Conditional authority to adopt—Conditional Authority must be clearly expressed and strictly construed—Duty of a Widow who has received authority to adopt—Her heritable right before Adoption—Early Doctrine on the subject—Judgment in *Bamondass Mookerjee* v. *Mussamut Tarinee*—Plural Adoption—*Rungama* v. *Atchama*—General observations—Simultaneous Adoption.

Authority to adopt.

THE enunciation of the rules, which regulate the capacity of a Hindu woman to adopt a son to her husband, exhibiting its vicarious or derivative nature, leads us to the discussion of the circumstances under which the necessary authority may be granted to her, and of the mode in which it may be given. With reference to this latter, I have already pointed out how careless the Hindu legislators have been to provide any adequate safe-guards against frauds and imposition. A husband may give his wife authority to adopt a son after his death, and thereby to change the order of succession, and disappoint the just expectations of relatives, with as little of form or solemnity, as if the act and the occasion were of the most trivial importance. Nor does the law require that it should be evidenced in any particular way; a verbal power, so long as the Court believes the witness, or witnesses, who swear

LECTURE XII.

to it, is sufficient in law to convey the power of thus dealing with property of whatever value, to a woman who, so far as the provisions of law are concerned, may indulge her own caprice either in exercising or neglecting it, being under no sort of binding legal obligation to act, and being entitled to refuse, or to delay, till the last day of her life, the fulfilment of the object which her husband had in view. But if she exercise it, she must do so unconditionally; she must divest herself of her estate, singly and absolutely, for the good of her husband's soul; she may not stipulate for any advantages or reward to herself.

The chief subjects of attention, in dealing with what I may call vicarious adoption, are: first, in what manner an authority to adopt may be conferred; by whom it may be granted; and in what manner the rights and duties and interests of a widow, who alone can be grantee of such a power, are affected by the fact of her being entrusted with an authority of so important a nature, the exercise of which is attended by so many serious consequences both to her husband and herself.

How authority to adopt may be given.

With regard to the first point, no legal formalities of any kind are required, in order to create a valid permission or authority to adopt.

Deeds are however frequently resorted to, and, inasmuch as the permission or authority must be in all cases strictly proved,* it is always advisable to evidence the gift of it by some writing which shall clearly show the intention of the donor and the terms of the grant. Further the widow must act in pursuance of its directions and within the scope of its authority, and must expressly adopt the child to her

* Chowdhry Padum Sing v. Koer Udaya Sing, 2 B. L. R., P.C., p. 105.

husband as well as to herself. If she omits to do so and assumes to adopt to herself, omitting all mention of her husband, no affiliation to him takes place, and it is questionable whether any significance at all attaches to the ceremony, except in Mithila. In *Pritima Soonduree Chowdhrain* v. *Anund Coomar Chowdhry,** it is stated that although deeds of permission to adopt are unnecessary, and need not, if executed at all, be either registered or stamped, the early and open publication of them has always been insisted upon by the courts as essential; or at least the absence of such publication must be satisfactorily explained. No particular form for deeds of this description is necessary, and the permission may be and often is verbal. The object of such a ruling is obviously to supply a defect in Hindu law, and by the action of the Courts to place impediments in the way of fraud and imposition in resorting to unauthorized adoption.

LECTURE XII.

Who may grant such authority.

Now with regard to the legal capacity to grant a valid authority to adopt. I may remark, in the first place, that it is more extensive than the actual present power to affiliate, inasmuch as the authority may be given dependent upon contingencies, on the happening of which, a right to adopt, though not at present existing, would accrue. Any man who is able to adopt, can, in lieu of doing so, grant a power in that behalf to his widow. I will therefore deal with the cases and refer to the rules of law which enable a man, who is disqualified at the time from adoption, nevertheless to grant an authority for that purpose to his widow.

A man may give to his widow a power to adopt, in case of the failure at any time, of his legitimate male issue,

* 6 Sutherland's Weekly Reporter, p. 133.

LECTURE XII.

whether begotten or adopted. His actual right to make a second adoption in succession to the first, would not have accrued to him whilst living, unless he had survived the first. There is no such thing as a conditional adoption. But a conditional power to adopt is of frequent occurrence; and extends to justify and legalize the practice of successive adoptions.

Conditional authority to adopt.

The condition, however, must be the death of one son before another can be adopted. No other circumstances, such as disagreement between the son and his adoptive mother, or stepmother, can legally form conditions on the happening of which an authority to adopt can be granted and exercised.

An early case upon this subject is to be found in first volume of the Select Reports, *viz.*, *Mussamut Solukhna* v. *Ramdolall Pande.** The plaintiff claimed a Zemindary by right of inheritance. The defence was that, *after the death* of the son of the deceased zemindar, the defendant had been adopted by the zemindar's younger widow, who, on the death of the son, had succeeded as his stepmother to the estate. It appeared that this younger widow had authority to adopt from her husband. The Pundits, when consulted, declared their opinion, but it does not appear whether it was accepted by the Court that a Hindu can legally give to his second wife provisional authority to adopt in the event of the death of the son of the first wife, but that a similar authority in case merely of disagreement between the second wife and the first wife's son would be void.

This case, however, is an authority, if one were needed, that a widow must exercise the power, if at all, uncondi-

* Select Reports (new edition), Vol. I., p. 434.

tionally. She cannot by agreement with the son's natural father, or by any other means, secure to herself a better provision than is secured to her by operation of law—namely, her widow's maintenance. It appeared that the younger widow referred to above (the adoptive mother of the defendant), had executed at the time of the adoption, to the defendant's father, an instrument termed *Niyumputra*; in accordance with which she continued in possession, till shortly before her death she made it over to the defendant. The effect of the *Niyumputra* was that she should maintain and educate her adopted son; but that his right of succession should be postponed until after her death. An opinion was given by the Pundits that such document was illegal, and conferred no title upon the widow; and that the rights of the adopted son were not affected thereby. The obsequies and other religious ceremonies must be performed by the son and not by the widow. He alone is entitled to the possession of the estate; nor can his rights be in any way affected by any agreement of the sort made to his prejudice, antecedently to, or simultaneously with, his adoption.

As far back as the year 1807, the lawfulness of two successive adoptions by the widows of the same person, under authority for that purpose from their husband, was established. Such was the effect of the decision in *Shamchander* v. *Narayni Dibeh.*† In that suit the plaintiffs claimed as heirs to a deceased zemindar, alleging that their title accrued on the death of a son whom the zemindar's elder widow had duly adopted. The title of the defendant rested upon the validity of a subsequent adoption of a son made by the younger widow under a verbal authority to that effect from her husband, which

* Select Reports (new edition), Vol. I., p. 279.

LECTURE XII.

authority was finally held to be established. This second adoption was made after the death of the son, through whom the plaintiffs claimed title. It was contended that a second adoption under such circumstances was illegal, but the Court held, in conformity with the opinion of the Pundits, that two successive adoptions in the family of the same man are valid.

Next follows a case, which it will be important to refer to, upon the subject of plurality of adoption, but which it will be convenient to consider now in order to exhibit the gradual growth of the doctrine of the Court, the ultimate source of Hindu law.* It was a suit brought at Dacca by a younger widow on behalf of her adopted child, to obtain a moiety of her husband's estate. She had adopted her son in pursuance of an authority given to her by her husband, who, being childless, had given permission to each of his wives to adopt a son. Before his death, and after the permission, he had himself adopted a boy on account of his senior wife. The younger widow adopted her son four years after her husband's death, and it was urged that this second adoption was illegal. The Judge dismissed the suit on the opinion of the Pundit, that there was no authority for a husband adopting on account of a particular wife; that the son adopted by him renders service to all his wives, and that during the life-time of a son so adopted, none of his wives could adopt another. The Hindu law officers of the Sudder Court, when the case came before them, gave their opinion as follows:—"If a man having two wives give authority to each to adopt a son, and afterwards, in concurrence with his senior wife, adopt a son; and after his death, his second wife, in pursuance of the authority originally obtained from him, adopt a son,

* Gourcepersad Rai v. Mussamut Jymala, Select Reports (new edition), Vol. II., p. 174.

the adoption by the second wife is not legally valid. All the property of the deceased devolved on the son adopted by him. Thus far the ruling of the Dacca Court, and the opinion of the Pundits, would be upheld at the present day. The younger widow had already male issue belonging to her in the person of her husband's adopted son, and on that ground alone could not adopt another. But the Pundits went on to say, at variance with what they had already advanced, that, inasmuch as the permission granted originally by the husband was confirmed to the second wife after the adoption in favor of the senior wife, it was obvious that the desire of the adoptive father was to have many sons (which was a laudable desire), and the adoptive sons would take in equal proportions. The Sudder Court ruled in accordance with this opinion, assuming to follow the decision in the case of *Sham Chunder* and *Rooderchunder v. Narayni Debia* and *Ramkishor.** If this case laid down correct law, it would follow that a man having male issue may give a power to adopt living that issue, a proposition for which no one would now contend according to any school of Hindu law.

But although provisional authority granted by a man to his wife to adopt a second, or third, or other son, in succession, in the event of the death of each adopted son in succession, is valid, no other contingency but such death can be provided against. An attempt was once made to set up an authority to the second widow to adopt a son, on account of probable disagreement between her and the son of the first widow, if we may judge from a question put by the Sudder Court to its Pundits in a case,† the facts of which are not very

* Select Reports (new edition), Vol. I., p. 279.

† Mussamut Solukna *v.* Ramdolal Pande, *Ibid*, p. 434.

LECTURE XII. fully stated. The answer was that it was not lawful for a man to give such authority. But the Pundits went on to say that a man having a son of his body, may, with the consent of such son, or from a wish to have more sons (for the performance of religious acts) give authority to his wife to adopt a son; and that such authority, according to the shasters, is lawful. They, however, relied in respect of this latter doctrine solely on the text "many sons are to be desired, that some one of them may travel to Gaya."

Conditional authority must be clearly expressed and strictly construed.

Notwithstanding that decision, it is undoubted law at the present day that a Hindu in possession of male issue can only authorize his widow to adopt, contingent on the failure of that issue.

Such contingent authority must be given in clear and express terms, for the Court will not, even after the widow has assumed to exercise the power, extend the strict meaning of the words by which it is conferred by any inference or implication. The authority will be strictly construed. I will quote two decisions* to that effect, and I may add that, although Mr. Macnaghten† considered it when he wrote a disputed point, whether a widow having, with the sanction of her husband, adopted one son, can, on the death of that son, adopt another, without having received a conditional permission to that effect; yet that it is now clear that successive adoptions will not be upheld, unless they are authorized by the husband in distinct terms beyond all reasonable doubt. In the case of *Purmanund Bhuttacharjee* v. *Oomakunt Lahoree*,‡ a zemindar at

* See also Gournath Chowdhry *v.* Annopoorna Chowdhrain, 8 Sudder Dewanny Dec., p. 332.

† Principles of Hindu Law, p. 86.

‡ Select Reports (new edition), Vol. IV., p. 404.

Mymensingh died, leaving a son and daughter. After-wards the son died childless; but previous to his death, he executed two deeds conveying to his wife a limited permission to adopt a son. The first document was in these terms:—"I authorize you, should I be removed, to adopt Shib Kishen Kurma, second son of Joogul Kishen Roy, in order that he may perform my funeral rites, and preside over my estate. Should Joogul refuse his consent, you may adopt the son of some other Brahmin." Below the signature was written—"I have authorized her to adopt a son." The second document was confirmatory of the former, and was also addressed to the wife. "Joogul Kishen has deputed his wife to give his son in adoption; I accordingly adopt him as my son. If I recover, I will perform the prescribed rites; if not, I hereby empower you to perform the ceremonies. The investiture of the Brahminical thread must be performed by Joogul Kishen; Shib Kishen will be the lawful possessor of all my wealth."

He died the next day, and his wife adopted the boy named, who obtained possession, and died without issue. The widow then succeeded, and made another adoption under the general authority given by her husband, selecting a child named Kishennauth. The Collector and the Board of Revenue recognized it, but the suit was brought to set it aside. The Court held that the second adoption was illegal, being in excess of the authority given by the husband; that the power conferred was explicitly confined to the son of Joogul Kishen, namely Shib Kishen; or if the father was unwilling, then the son of another person, who was expressly named; that there was not a word in relation to repeated adoptions at the widow's pleasure in the event of any casualty to the first adopted son, and

LECTURE XII.

that without a distinct permission she could not legally adopt.

Again, in the case of *Joy Chandra Rai v. Bhyrub Chandra Rai,** a Hindu being on the point of death gave this authority to his widow—" moreover there being only my one son, and apprehensions in consequence arising, I authorize you to take an adopted son," which was clearly an illegal permission on the face of it. The Court decided that it could not convert it into a permission for what was altogether a distinct purpose, that is the adoption of a son after the death of the natural son then living.

A widow cannot correct or modify an illegal permission.

Duty of a widow who has received authority to adopt.

It may be convenient here to point out that the widow who is thus supposed to receive from her husband a power to adopt, has nearly always a direct interest opposed to the adoption, leading her to refuse or to delay the execution of the power which is conferred upon her solely for the purpose of fulfilling the wishes and advancing the interests of her husband.

Take for instance the case of every Hindu widow in Bengal, and of those widows in the wide provinces subject to Mitakshara law, whose husbands were without brothers or were separated from them. Failing male issue, or otherwise the power to adopt could not have been conferred upon them, they are entitled to succeed to the whole of their husbands' estates and to possess and enjoy them till their deaths. But the moment a widow exercises the power and adopts a son, she is *ipso facto* divested of the whole of the estate, which immediately devolves upon the child. As stated by the Privy Council, in† *Dhurmadoss*

* 5 Sudder Dewanny Dec., p. 461.

† 3 Moore's Indian Appeals, p. 242.

Panday v. *Mussamut Shama Soondry Debiah*, the result of an act of adoption by a Hindu widow is, that the whole property is divested from her, and vested in the adopted son. She stands to the estate from that moment simply in the relation of guardian of her son, bound to deliver over possession to him on his attaining the age of majority, and accountable to him for every act which she does in reference to it. Her interest in it is cut down to the widow's right to maintenance, which is no doubt a primary charge upon it, but bears a comparatively small proportion to its extent and value. The possession of the power to adopt involves no legal duty, and does not, so long as it is not exercised, affect in the slightest degree the interest which the widow takes. In one point of view it enables her to devote herself to the future welfare of her husband, by providing him with the advantages of sonship; on the other it arms her with a weapon against his reversionary heirs, with which she may at any moment exclude them from the inheritance.

Her heritable right before adoption.

The case* of *Bamandoss Mookerjee* v. *Mussamut Tarinee*, decided by the Privy Council in 1858, is the leading authority for the proposition that the mere fact of a Hindu widow omitting or refusing to exercise the permission to adopt given to her by her husband does not affect her heritable right. Before she adopts, she takes her husband's estate as heiress, and she is entitled to retain it in that capacity until she chooses by her voluntary act of adoption to divest herself of it. The devolution of the estate upon a Hindu widow is not affected in the least degree by a power of adoption being given and by the

* 7 Moore's Indian Appeals, p. 169.

LECTURE XII.

possibility of a third person coming into existence with the superior title of adopted son.

Early doctrine on the subject.

The doctrine thus enunciated, and ever since implicitly followed, was by no means in accordance with the previous current of decisions.

Previously to this case coming before the Courts for decision, *Beejayah Debiah* v. *Shamasoondery Debiu* was an authority to the effect that where a power had been given to a widow to adopt, the title to the husband's estate vested from the date of his death in the boy thereafter to be adopted.* And the Pundits consulted in the two cases cited in the footnote had replied distinctly that the moment permission to a widow to adopt a son was pronounced, it had the same effect as if a son had been conceived in the womb of the widow; and that her intention to adopt under the permission operated to all intents and purposes as if she were *enceinte,* and the boy adopted by her had all the rights of a posthumous child.

Judgment in Bamandoss Mookerjee *v.* Mussamut Tarinee.

The Sudder Court in deciding Mussamut Tarinee's case (which was brought seventeen years after her husband's death, for the purpose of obtaining possession of his property), declined to enter into any discussion upon such speculative questions as the possibility of the existence of rights present or contingent in a child from the moment of its conception in the womb; as to what is the precise time of vital conception and existence according to Hindu law or usage; as to analogies between a Hindu widow who has received permission from her husband to adopt and of a widow naturally

* Sudder Dewanny Adawlut Report of 1848, p. 762; and see Ranee Kishenmonee *v.* Rajah Oodurnit Sing, 3 S. D. R., p. 228.

pregnant; as to the abstract causes or grounds of inheritance; or as to modes and questions of Hindu obsequial or other ceremonies.

Referring to the admitted principles and positive texts of the Hindu law as current in Bengal, they considered that a widow in default of nearer heirs had an incontestable right to succeed to her husband's estate; that no text enjoined the suspension of her rights when actually pregnant, until it be seen whether she is delivered of a male or female child, and therefore there was no inference to be drawn from the dictum of the Pundits that a widow with permission to adopt was to be regarded as *enceinte;* and that it was still more certain that there was no express provision for divestiture of right in the case of a widow, held only to be constructively pregnant of a son through the effect of a permission to adopt. They argued from a consideration of passages in the Dayabhaga and the Dayacrama Sangraha that the after-born son's right is to his share of the estate as it stands at the time of his birth, and not retrospectively with reference to its state at any supposed period of his conception. They inferred from a text in the Mitakshara, which directed the postponement of a partition in case of the pregnancy of a brother's widow till after the delivery, that if a widow by Mitakshara law could have been heir, as she incontestably can in Bengal, she might have been admitted in her own right during pregnancy; the share devolving to her son only on his birth. In Bengal the right of inheritance does not vest in a son till after the death of his father, but in the Mitakshara it is laid down that birth is the means of acquisition, a doctrine which the commentator on the Dayabhaga is at least willing to accept when it

LECTURE XII.

is confined to the case of a posthumous child. Mr. Colebrooke* considered "that an adopted child is in most respects precisely similar to a posthumous son, and that from the moment of the adoption taking effect, the child becomes heir to the widow's husband, and the widow has no other authority than that of mother and guardian."

Although Mr. Colebrooke stated this with reference to a Madras case, the principle is of general application. Neither the Mitakshara, nor the Bengal school, considers that a legal right can vest before birth; the difference between them is that the Bengal school postpones the vesting of the right till the death of the father, while the Mitakshara considers that the rights of father and son may be concurrent from the moment of the son's birth; as in England in the familiar case of an entail. Adoption therefore divests the estate from the widow and vests it in the adopted son. The Court further observed "that the supposition of a positive and actual right vested in an embryo, which may never come into full existence, is one which must almost be rejected on the mere statement of it. It is particularly repugnant to common reason in the case of a possible adoption which may be made after the lapse of many years, or may never be made at all. If the supposition were to be admitted and acted upon, the effect would be to alter the whole course of natural inheritance; for there would be one course of inheritance as from the son to be adopted, and another (as is usual at present), from the widow's husband on her own death. The rights for instance of any daughters of the husband would, in the former case, be wholly set aside. It is true that a

* Strange's Hindu Law, Vol. II., p. 127.

widow from the continuance of her life-interest, has an interest opposed to her duty, which should lead her, if she has a permission from her husband, to adopt a son without any delay which she can avoid. But there appears to be no power under the Hindu law to compel a widow to adopt, though a case* has been referred to, where there is a mention of an incompetency in a widow to succeed, if she neglect to make an adoption. The subject, however, is only cursorily noticed in that case, and in connection with a point which appears to have been ruled upon different grounds. The question of any possible check on a widow who wilfully protracts or evades an adoption specially enjoined upon her by her husband, is not before us and what we have to decide, *viz.*, the power of a widow duly authorized to adopt, to claim under any circumstances her personal rights until she does adopt, is not affected by a consideration of what might be the proper course, if she could be proved to have violated any clear and positive legal obligation."

The Privy Council on appeal upheld the ruling of the Sudder Court, and stated that they entirely agreed with the principles laid down in the judgment.

I now pass on to the subject of double or plural adoption. Some obscurity hung over this subject at one time, on account of some passages of the commentators, drawing inferences in favor of such a practice. No single text, however, expressly affirming it, was ever produced, though in Bengal there were one or two decisions founded on the opinions of Pundits, which it was contended gave it a judicial recognition.

* Macnaghten's Principles of Hindu Law, Vol. II., p. 247.

LECTURE XII.

As the dispute upon this question was long of considerable interest, which has not yet died way, I will state shortly the effect of the authorities upon it. First of all there was the ordinance of Menu which I have frequently quoted before: "He whom his father or mother, with her husband's assent, gives to another as his son, provided that the donee have no issue, is considered as a son given." The proviso that the adopter had no issue is there enforced with the utmost distinctness and on the highest authority; and seems to be decisive in favor of there being absolute destitution of such issue at the time of adoption. In the Vivadarnava Setu, translated by Mr. Halhed (which translation or compilation is not now regarded as authority) and quoted by the Privy Council, in the leading case upon this subject, the same proviso is insisted upon and enforced as an absolute prohibition. "He who has no son or grandson or grandson's son, or brother's son, shall adopt a son, and while he has one adopted son he shall not adopt a second." Next, there is the text of Atri: "By a man destitute of a son only must a substitute for the same always be adopted," and lest any doubt should arise as to his meaning, the author of the Dattaka Mimansa† has placed it beyond a doubt, saying, in so many words "that the incompetency of one having male issue is signified by the term only in this passage."

These are direct prohibitions recorded in the texts of the earliest sages. No text is to be found enjoining such a practice. This only was relied upon, and was made by Jagannatha the main foundation of his opinion in favour of plurality of adoption, that "many sons are to be desired

* 4 Dattaka Mimansa, Section I., verse 6.

in order that one may travel to Gaya." Then there was a passage quoted by Nanda Pandita, when discussing the question by whom is a son to be given: "He who has only one son is considered by me as one destitute of male issue; one who has only one eye is as one destitute of both, should his one eye be lost he is absolutely blind." The Privy Council considered that the texts on which that doctrine rests, were not for the purpose of enabling a man with one child to receive in adoption, but for the purpose of prohibiting such a one from giving in adoption.

It is not difficult, therefore, to see how the matter stands on the authority of the ancient sages. On the other hand, there was the Bengal case to which I have already referred, *viz.*, *Goureepershad Roy v. Mussamut Jymala*, decided in 1814, in conformity with the opinion of Pundits; and the opinion of Sir Thomas Strange,* formed in favour of the double adoption avowedly upon the equivocal authority of that case and also on the authority of the case† in 1807, which in no way supports it.

Mr. Macnaghten‡ denied it in the strongest terms, saying that the desire for many sons, in order that one may travel to Gaya, refers only to natural born sons. Mr. Sutherland,§ in a note, states that a Hindu cannot have legally adopted children; and that a son, legitimate or adopted, existing, any subsequent adoption would be invalid; at least that the son so adopted would not inherit. In Mr. Steele's treatise which relates to the customs of the provinces of Bombay, he states "an‖ adoption can

* Strange's Hindu Law, Vol. I., p. 78.
† See *ante*, p. 277.
‡ Macnaghten's Hindu Law, Vol. I., p. 80.
§ Strange's Hindu Law, Vol. II., p. 85.
‖ Steele on the Law and Customs of Hindu Castes, p. 42, para. 34.

LECTURE XII.

take place only where no begotten son or grandson exists, or where the begotten son has lost caste." And again, "in* the case of the death of an adopted son (and total loss of caste is considered equivalent to death) another may be selected and given in the same manner; but a man, after adopting one boy, cannot adopt another at the desire of a second wife, &c.; only one adopted son can exist at one time." A second adoption,† he says, was permitted by the Peshwa on one occasion only, when he received a nuzzur of some lacs of rupees, but it gives great offence to the Brahmans, being considered by them to be contrary to the shasters. There seems, therefore, to be a remarkable concurrence of opinion on the part of the European authorities who have investigated the question, and very little inconsistency to be traced in the recorded texts of the earliest sages.

Rungama v. Atchama.

But, on the other hand, the Bengal Pundits had, in the case above referred to and decided in 1814, appeared to assume the validity of the plural adoption. And from the report of the celebrated case of *Rungama* v. *Atchama*,‡ which finally settled the controversy, it appears that the Pundits who were consulted by the Courts in the Presidency of Madras where the suit arose, who were at a distance from each other, and gave separate opinions at some intervals of time, without, as it appeared, any communication between them, nevertheless all agreed in holding that a second adoption, living the first adopted child, was good, and that both sons were equally entitled to inherit. Still, however,

* Steele on the Law and Customs of Hindu Castes, p. 45, para 41.

† *Ibid*, p. 183, para 41.

‡ 4 Moore's Indian Appeals, p. 89.

the opinions of the Pundits, throughout the entire Presidency, could not be said to have been unanimous; for evidence was adduced that a number of them had given their opinion against its validity, when consulted by the adoptive father previous to the adoption. The adoptive father in that case was a powerful and a wealthy Rajah who was bent upon carrying out his wishes, and in whose favour, it might be supposed, that the Pundits consulted by him would be strongly biased.

The circumstances of that case were that this Rajah, in the year 1798, when childless, adopted a son who lived to succeed to him, and about the validity of whose adoption no question ever arose. In 1807, he adopted another son, doing all that was necessary to constitute a valid adoption, if such second adoption could, by Hindu law, be valid. His object was to divide his property between them. After his death disputes naturally arose, and various suits were brought, in which the question of the validity of the second adoption was fully discussed both by the Courts in the Madras Presidency, and finally, in 1846, by the Privy Council. The Judges in the Sudder Court, proceeding entirely upon the opinion of the Pundits, ruled in favour of its validity; but the Privy Council on examining the reasons assigned by those Pundits, found that the texts which they referred to did not support their conclusion. It seemed, moreover, that Jagannatha alone was ultimately responsible for such opinion. No earlier indication of assent to it was produced, and no evidence was given of second adoptions being customary in the province where the case arose, or in any degree recognized by usage.

Although this case comes from the Madras Presidency,

the decision proceeds upon authorities which prevail throughout India, and it must be regarded as finally establishing the law upon this subject throughout the Empire; except perhaps in any district where an immemorial and well ascertained custom to the contrary could be shown to prevail.

In Bengal, in the case of *Joy Chandra Roy* v. *Bhyrub Chandra Roy,** decided in 1848, and also in a later case,† the Privy Council decision was held to be conclusive as to the law of Bengal, although it is said that second adoptions are common in that province. The Court, nevertheless, considered that Bengal authorities having been fully considered in that judgment, it should be taken as authoritatively settling the general Hindu law of India on that subject.

General observations.

Authority, therefore, has finally decided the question of the invalidity of a second adoption while the first adopted child is living. If it be necessary, in consequence of the interest which still attaches to this obsolete controversy, to criticise the result, the decision may reasonably be considered a wise and satisfactory settlement of the discussion. The doctrines of Hindu law must be sought in the religious traditions, ancient usages, and modern habits of Hindus; and when no evidence was offered as to ancient or modern practice to the contrary, it was reasonable to limit the legal capacity to adopt, by the traditional duty or anxiety of providing a delivery from *put.* The origin of the power to adopt is constantly referred to that duty, and when the necessity does not exist, a strong authority from the shasters should be quoted to show that, nevertheless, the

* Sudder Dewanny Decisions, Vol. V., p. 461.

† Sudanund Mohapatter *v.* Bonomallee and others, Marshall, p. 317.

power arises. Even, if by the ingenious comparison and discussion of ancient texts, or by a fanciful disquisition upon the speculative questions to which they may give rise, it could be shewn that the doctrine of the validity of a second adoption was after all deducible from the earliest authorities, even then the further question must be disposed of, whether a doctrine of so much importance can be allowed to rest upon mere inference from the texts, and whether it has been recognized as law by any school, and sanctioned by usage. Of this latter there is not a trace of evidence in the recorded cases, whatever may be the real feeling of the Hindu community with regard to the question. Every year that passes tends to rivet the decision of the Privy Council as the unalterable law; by fixing it with the acquiescence and approval of the community who conform to it. And when sages and commentators and Pundits differ as to the true teaching of the Hindu scriptures, a decision, which terminates the controversy, may be criticized by more secular considerations, and it may not be superfluous to enquire if the rule of law so laid down is, on the whole, likely to be more conducive than a contrary one to the social welfare of the community, having regard to their feelings and habits. Viewed in that light, it is worth while to remember that the rule so laid down is the only one in the whole of Hindu law, which tends to secure the interests of the child who is the subject of affiliation. Under the law, as it is now ascertained and declared, the adopted child, so long as he lives, is in general secure from any rival in his rights of inheritance. With a plurality of adoption recognized by law, natural parents would have no means of estimating the advantages to their child of its transfer to another family, and that consideration would tend strongly to impede the

LECTURE XII.

efforts of those who were desirous of adopting. The same ruling which is regarded in some quarters as unduly limiting the capacity to adopt, seems to give increased vitality to the institution, by rendering the terms of the contract more certain, and in general securing the adopted child from being displaced in any degree in his rights of sonship or inheritance. Besides, it is inexpedient and mischievous to entrust to one and the same person, a power to adopt many sons and a power capriciously to disinherit any one or more of them by will. If the power to adopt can only be exercised with regard to one child at a time, the same motive which led to its exercise, whether the religious desire to secure the performance of his own and his ancestor's obsequies, or the secular one of continuing his name and lineage, will strongly tend to prevent the disinherison of the child. Where the powers of alienation are more limited, there is nevertheless a scarcely diminished objection, in the interests of the adopted child or of society, unfairly to weaken the tie formed by adoption, by granting to one of the parties to it and refusing to the other a power capriciously to contract a similar relationship to others.

Simultaneous adoption.

With regard, however, to the simultaneous adoption of two or more sons, that is, the adoption of them by a man destitute of male issue, by one and the same act of the will and by one and the same performance of religious ceremonies, the matter stands upon a different footing. Such adoptions do not appear to be prohibited by any texts, and they do not contravene the doctrine which limits the right of adoption to those who are destitute of sons. Such a practice is at least in accordance with the spirit of the law which is so anxious to provide security for the performance of obsequies, and the preservation of the lineage, and which recommends a plurality of sons as desirable, in order that one may travel to Gaya. And further, it is not open to the objection, to which the subsequent adoption is liable, of rendering the transaction or contract of adoption, as between the adoptive and natural parents, a matter of hopeless uncertainty and speculation. A father who gives a child to be one of two simultaneously adopted children, knows that if his child lives, his rights of inheritance certainly extend to a moiety of the estate of his adoptive father, and will, if he survive his adoptive brother, or the widow and issue of that brother, include the whole of the estate. But, if the rule be adhered to, that the capacity to adopt is limited by the necessity or religious duty which a state of sonlessness imposes, then the doctrine of the validity of what is called the simultaneous adoption must fail. In any district of India, however, evidence of such a practice being consonant to the feelings and habits of Hindus will probably be regarded as sufficient to legalize it and to justify its recognition by the Courts.

We must first see how the matter stands upon the authority of the ancient texts and of the commentators who are followed by the various schools. In the Dattaka Tilaka by Bhavadeva Bhatta, as quoted in Shamachurn's Vyavastha Darpana,* it is said, that by the maxim "one cannot regulate according to his independent will," if many sons even are adopted by one will and by one (that is simultaneous) performance of religious ceremonies, they are certainly valid, but not those adopted with ceremonies performed at different times, though the will of

* Shamachurn's Vyavastha Darpana, p. 767.

adopting them be one; and not even if the same be done under permission. Consequently as sons simultaneously adopted at an earnest desire, by the performance of the prescribed religious ceremonies, are valid; so while there exists one adopted son free from defect, no other is valid. If out of regard to one's wives, even many sons are adopted by one will, and by the simultaneous performance of the religious ceremonies, they are good in law." This is the only direct authority which is quoted, and it is not very easy to see how it is justified by the maxim to which it is appended. The authors of the Dattaka Mimansa and the Dattaka Chandrika, who are implicitly followed by all the schools except that of Mithila, are silent upon the subject; and as the permission to adopt contained in the texts of Menu and Atri is worded in the singular number, and a son adopted in pursuance of it is declared to be son to all the wives, it would seem that those authors were opposed to the practice. The law does not prevent a Hindu from having more wives than one, but it does not encourage the practice of polygamy, although it assigns to each of several wives her proper station, duties, and privileges. Simultaneous adoptions therefore relatively to the general community are not likely to be numerous, nor can any custom to that effect be supposed to be general.*

In the case† of *Monemothonath Day* v. *Onauthnath Day*, a discussion arose both with regard to the simultaneous adoption and also with regard to a second adoption, living the subject of the first. No opinion was expressed by the Appellate Court, with regard either

* See 2 Macnaghten, pp. 181 and 182; Shamachurn, p. 779.

† 2 Ind. Jur., N. S., p. 24.

to the one or the other, but the Judge who tried the case after a protracted argument in reference to the validity of the second adoption, decided against it, holding that the law of the Bengal school did not differ in that respect from the law of Southern India, which had been finally declared by the Privy Council. He also ruled against the validity of the simultaneous adoption. The effect of this decision was, as I said before, neither weakened nor confirmed by anything that fell from the Appellate Court, before which the case eventually came. It has never, however, been questioned by any subsequent decision, and in the absence of any authority expressly in favor of a simultaneous adoption, there would probably be considerable hesitation in now disturbing it. LECTURE XII.

LECTURE XIII.

THE RIGHT TO GIVE IN ADOPTION.--THE QUALIFICATIONS FOR BEING ADOPTED.

Rules to be observed in adopting—*Kritrima* form—Right of the parents respectively to give in *dattaka* adoption—Mother's power to give her child—After the husband's death—Adoptive parents cannot give away their adopted son—The brother cannot give—No one but a parent can give—Neither an only nor an eldest son can be given—Madras ruling upon validity of adoption of only son—Bengal ruling upon the same point—Proprietary power of a father over his child—Is absolute when the extinction of his own lineage is provided against—Eldest Son—Second rule; A *dattaka* adoption must not import incest—General application of the rule—Sudras—Daughters—Brother's daughters—Equality of caste the only condition of eligibility for a *kritrima* adoption—Elder brother.

Rules to be observed in adopting.

HAVING now considered the rules of law which regulate the capacity of a Hindu to adopt or to give to his widow a power after his death to do for him that which he has omitted to do for himself, I pass on to the next division of the subject which relates to the qualification and capacity either to give, or to be given, in adoption.

Kritrima form.

I must premise, however, that, in the *kritrima* form of the ceremony, to which in general the only parties are the adopter and the adopted, the assent of the person adopted is necessary* if he has attained his majority, which con-

* Dhungopal Singh *v.* Roopun Singh, 6 S. D. R., p. 271.

sent must be given in the life-time of the adopter.* But where he is a minor, and therefore unable legally to give or express consent, the competence or legal ability to consent for him, and in effect to give him in adoption,† would rest in one or both of his parents, unless he has been abandoned by his parents, in which case he can himself consent so as to make the adoption good.

Right of the parents respecting to give in *dattaka* adoption.

Now as to the capacity to give a child in the *dattaka* form of adoption. According to Menu,‡ a father has absolute power to give, the mother being only able to do so with her husband's consent. Balambhatta, however, says that three cases are provided for with reference to the right to give a child in adoption ;§ and apparently his doctrine is that, although the right to receive in adoption is, as between the husband and wife absolute in the husband, it does not follow that he can assert the same superiority over his wife in respect of giving away the child, which equally belongs to them both ; but can only give away their child without her consent, if she be dead, insane, or otherwise incapable, unless the distress is very urgent. But besides the authority of Menu, for the father's absolute power in that respect, there is the direct authority of the Dattaka Mimansa, and the absence of any prohibition in the Dattaka Chandrika.‖ The first rule then is that the

* 1 Marshall, p. 95.

† 7 Sudder Dewanny Adawlut, 1856, p. 690. 2 Menu, verse 196.

‡ 9 Menu, verse 168:—" He whom his father, or mother *with her husband's assent*, gives to another as his son, provided that the donee have no issue, if the boy be of the same class and affectionately disposed, is considered as a son given, the gift being confirmed by pouring water."

§ Mitakshara, Chap. I., Sec. XI., verse 9, *note*.

‖ Dattaka Mimansa, Sec. IV., verse 13:—" The husband singly even and independent of his wife is competent to give a son;" for in the two passages cited in paragraph 11 (whom his mother

LECTURE XIII.

father has absolute power to give away his son, provided that he has more than one, without the consent of the mother.

Mother's power to give her child.

With regard to the mother's power to give, that appears from the text of Menu referred to above to be dependent upon her husband's consent. Vasishta* also ordained that a woman should neither give nor receive in adoption, unless with the consent of her husband. According to the Mitakshara,† the mother's power is said to be correlative to her husband's; and in a note the authority of Balambhatta is cited as confirmatory of that view. But it appears to rest on the authority of a text of Menu, the words of which, as cited, do not correspond with the original. But according to the Dattaka Mimansa, an exception is made in case of urgent distress: "during a season of calamity" the widow may give away her son, even though it be impossible to obtain the assent of her husband.

or his father gives, '*dadyat;*' his mother or father give, '*dadyatam*') the father is mentioned singly and unassociated with the mother; and there is this reason of Baudhayana found: "From the predominance of the virile seed, sons are regarded even as not produced of the womb." In the *Bharata* also a reason is found: "The mother is the fosterer; the son is of the father, he is as it were that very person, by whom produced." A passage of revealed law is likewise confirmatory "His-self is truly born a son."

Dattaka Chandrika, Section I., verses 31, 32.—"But by a woman the gift may be made with her husband's sanction, if he be alive; or even without it, if he be dead, have emigrated, or entered a religious order. Accordingly Vasishta: "Let not a woman either give or receive a son, unless with the assent of her husband."

Now if there be no prohibition even there is assent; on account of the maxim,—'The intention of another not prohibited, is sanctioned.' Yajnavalkya suggests the independency of the woman,—"He whom his father or mother gives, is a son given." Also in another place, "deserted by his father and mother or either of them."

* Dattaka Mimansa, Section I., verse 15.

† Mitakshara, Chap I., Section XI., verse 9.

LECTURE XIII.

After the husband's death.

The authority of Balambhatta, in the note above referred to, may be quoted in favor of the widow's power to give, after her husband's death. And also in the Dattaka Chandrika,* "by a woman the gift may be made with her husband's sanction, if he be alive; or even without it, if he be dead, have emigrated, or entered into a religious order." The absence of any prohibition by the husband, in any one of those three cases, is held to be equivalent to consent. The authority of Saunaka also may be cited for the doctrine that only in a time of trouble and difficulty is a man permitted to give away his son. But however this may be, the absence of distress on the part of the giver never invalidates the gift; and according to the Dattaka Mimansa,† the distress alluded to, may even be the distress of the adopter, meaning his destitution of male issue. The author of the Dattaka Chandrika‡ does not insist upon the distress of the giver, for he quotes, apparently with approval the text, "by one having several sons, such gift is to be anxiously made."

With regard to the power of a widow to give her son in adoption, without the consent and authority of her husband, it is necessary to attend to the ruling in *Debee Dial and another* v. *Hur Hor Sing*,§ in which case, after a long recognition by the adoptive family, of the son so given away by his mother, as a son duly affiliated, the Court nevertheless decided that the adoption was void *ab initio*. The circumstances of the case were these. The legitimate son and widow of a deceased Hindu sued, the report says, as his

* Dattaka Chandrika, Section I., verse 31.

† Dattaka Mimansa, Section IV., verse 21.

‡ Dattaka Chandrika, Section I., verse 29.

§ Select Reports (new edition), Vol. IV., p. 407.

LECTURE XIII.

heirs, in the Court at Benares, to recover property which had belonged to him at the time of his death. The defendant was his adopted son, adopted before the birth of the male plaintiff, and before the marriage of the female plaintiff; and he was by blood relationship his paternal uncle's grandson. He had lived with his adoptive father from the time of the adoption, had had the superintendence of his affairs, had been married at his expense, and at the marriage ceremony had been married by the officiating Brahmins as his son. Three objections were raised in this suit to the validity of his adoption: (1) that he was the only son of his father; (2) that he was given in adoption by his mother, after the death of his father, without any authority for such act; (3) that the prescribed ceremonies were not duly observed at the time of the adoption. It was in vain contended on his behalf, that when a mother, from the pressure of want, gave her only son to another person, on the special condition that her son thus given should perform the funeral rites, and inherit the estates of both his natural and adoptive fathers, the adoption was valid, and the adopted son was called a *dwyamushyayana.* For, notwithstanding the long recognition of the adoption, tending to raise a presumption of its legal validity, it was ruled, in accordance with the statement of the Pundits, that there is no precept in the shasters which enables a woman to give her son, even as a *dwyamushyayana* without authority from her husband. On that ground alone the adoption could not be upheld, without entering into the other important objections raised to its validity.

I have sufficiently referred to the texts, for the purpose of showing how the widow's power to give rests upon the earliest authorities, and I think that, notwithstanding the case just cited and the opinions of the Pundits on which it was based, Mr. Sutherland's statement of the law will probably be accepted as correct. He says, in his Synopsis, that the true doctrine to be extracted from the opinions of the sages is, (1) that the father may give away his minor son without the consent of the mother, though it is more laudable that he should consult her wishes; (2) that the mother generally is incapable of such gift while the father lives, except in case of urgent distress and necessity; and (3) that she may do so upon her husband's death, also in case of urgent distress and necessity, emigration, entering a religious order, becoming an outcast, or being otherwise civilly dead.

Adoptive parents cannot give away their adopted son.

No one but the natural parents can give a child in adoption. The adoptive parents cannot do so, for in the first place an only son is ineligible for gift; and, in the second, such gift would be inconsistent with the terms of the contract on which such parents received the child,—*viz.*, "as a son to themselves." The power of the adoptive parents over a child is in that respect less absolute than that of the natural parent. They can neither give such child away absolutely, nor can they give him as a *dwyamushyayana*. According to Mr. Sutherland, in his Synopsis,* "the same person cannot be adopted by more than one individual, except in the case of one nephew by several uncles, the whole brothers of his natural father. It may, however, be inferred, that a legal impediment would exist to the affiliation by an uncle of a nephew whom his father had given away in adoption as a '*Sudha dattaka*,' who retains no filial relation to his natural father." Sir

* Sutherland's Synopsis, Head II.

LECTURE XIII.

Thomas Strange* also considered that the exception thus referred to by Mr. Sutherland might be allowed. But Sir Francis Macnaghten† refers to a case pending in 1821 in the Madras Court, in reference to which, at the request of the Chief Justice of that Court, the Pundits of the Supreme and Sudder Courts of Bengal were consulted; and the reply received was that two men, whether brothers or not, could not adopt the same boy as a son; and that any attempt to do so must fail. Two brothers, it was said, cannot adopt the same person as a son, any more than two persons can marry the same girl. The decision proceeded upon that opinion, and was against the legality of several uncles adopting the same nephew. Mr. Macnaghten‡ approves of this view, and declares that the contrary opinion is due to a misconstruction of the text of Menu,—"if among several brothers of the whole blood, one have a son born, Menu pronounces them all fathers of a male child by means of that son." All that can be inferred from that text is that such persons need not adopt, but if they do not, their nephew can only succeed to their estate or perform their obsequies (in the absence of nearer heirs) in the capacity of a nephew, and not in that of a son.

The brother cannot give.

Further, the brother cannot give in adoption even though both the natural parents be dead. Brothers stand upon an equality, one has no proprietary right in, or authority over, the person of another. It was so decided in the case of *Mussamut Tarramonee Debea* v. *Deo Narayn Rai* and *Bishen Persad.*§ There the plaintiff claimed, as an adopt-

* Strange's Hindu Law, Vol. I., p. 86.

† Macnaghten's Considerations of Hindu Law, pp. 474, 476

‡ Macnaghten's Principles of Hindu Law, p. 77.

§ Select Reports (new edition), Vol. III., p. 516.

ed son, the estate of his adoptive father. The defendant, besides denying the authority of the adoptive mother to adopt a son to her husband, set up that, at the time of the alleged adoption, the plaintiff's father was dead, and his mother absent, and that the gift had been made by the plaintiff's brother, in the absence of all the relatives and also of the family priest. It was contended that such adoption was illegal, one brother not possessing any power to give away another brother in adoption. The Court accepted that contention as correct, and assigned it as one of the reasons for setting aside the adoption.

No one but a parent can give.

Further, the Madras High Court,* in 1864, held that, to constitute a valid adoption there must be a valid giving as well as receiving, and that where both parents are dead and there is no one to give the child, it cannot be received. No amount of ratification, it was said, can supply the essentials of sucha transaction. That case overruled the decision in *Veemaperval Pillay* v. *Narain Pillay*,† where it was held that though both parents were dead, a child might be given in adoption by his elder brother. It was overruled in deference to Sir Francis Macnaghten's opinion founded upon citations from Kullukabhatta Vachespati Misser and the Aditya Purana.

Neither an only nor an eldest son can be given.

The effective limitations however to the capacity of the parents to give chiefly depend upon what they have got to give,—that is to say, upon the qualifications of the child who is to be the subject of the gift. *First of all the child must not be an only son, either natural or adopted, nor an eldest son.* A man having an only son is disqualified,

* Subba Luvammai *v.* Ammakutti Ammal, 2 Madras Rep., p. 129.

† See Considerations of Hindu Law, pp. 186, 210.

LECTURE XIII.

according to the doctrine of Saunaka* and Vasistha,† from giving him in adoption, and if the precept be violated, the blame attaches both to the giver and to the taker. Nanda Pandita‡ ordains that a child can only be given by one having several sons; and therefore he adds this express prohibition: "He who has only one son is '*Eka-putra*,' or one having an only son; by such an one the gift of that son must not be made." The reason is that such only son is destined to continue the line of his own ancestors; and with this accords the doctrine of the Dattaka Chandrika, the object being, in both instances, to provide against an extinction of lineage. An only son, according to Mr. Sutherland, cannot become an absolutely adopted son, but he may be affiliated as a *dwyamashyayana*, or son of two fathers.

The rule, therefore, seems to be well ascertained and to be precise in its terms. But then the question arises whether the prohibition against adopting an only child applies both to the giver and the receiver, and extends to invalidate such an adoption when made. The gift may, for instance, be wholly improper and even illegal as regards the conduct of the donor. But when once it has been made and accepted, is it altogether a nullity, or does the adoption nevertheless take effect? Upon this subject the Courts of Madras and Bengal are at variance, as will be seen by the following decisions.

Madras ruling upon validity of gift of only son.

I give the Madras case first, namely the case of *Chinna Gaundar* v. *Kumara Gaundan*.§ The question in this

* Dattaka Mimansa, Sec. IV., verse 1.

† Mitakshara, Chap. I., Sec. XI., verse 11.

‡ Dattaka Mimansa, Sec. IV., verses 7 and 8.

§ 1 Madras High Court Reports, p. 54.

appeal was whether the adoption of an only son was, when made, valid according to the Hindu law. *Shumshere Mull* v. *Ranee Dibraj** was cited to show that, according to the law as current in Benares, the adoption of an only son was invalid, unless given and accepted on condition that he should be a *dwyamushyayana;* but Scotland, C. J., cited *Joymonee Dossee* v. *Sibbersoonderee Dossee*† to show that such condition will be inferred after the adoption has been performed; and according to *Pillay* v. *Pillay* and the case of the Rajah of Tanjore,‡ such an adoption, though improper or sinful, is not invalid. The Court seemed to consider that the adoption of an only son was void only from the orthodox theological point of view, and that they were justified in applying the maxim of *factum valet.* However blameable such an adoption might be in the giver, the selection they held to be according to Sir Thomas Strange,§ "finally a matter of conscience and discretion with the adopter, not of absolute prescription, rendering invalid an adoption of one not being precisely him, who, on spiritual considerations, ought to have been preferred."

Chief Justice Scotland proceeded:—"Referring to Mr. Justice Strange's argument, I may observe that it rests on the assumption that it is the birth or adoption of the son that delivers the natural or adoptive father from the danger of *put.* But surely this is erroneous. It is the son's performance of his father's exequial rites, not his birth or adoption that relieves the father from the danger in question. Would the father, after the birth or adoption

* 2 Sudder Dewanny Reports, p. 169.

† Fulton's Reports, p. 75.

‡ Strange's Hindu Law, Vol. I., p. 85.

§ *Ibid.*

LECTURE XIII.

of a son, be considered safe from *put* if those rites were not performed owing to the son's death, his loss of caste, or for any other reason. If the mere birth of a son were all that was required, it would hardly be laid down, as it is, that on the death of such a son the affiliation of another is indispensable. Adoption takes place according to Atri "for the sake of the funeral cake, water and solemn rites;" and according to Menu for these objects, and also for the celebrity of the adoptive father's name; but not for the sake of the supposed efficacy of the mere act of adoption. If, then, the saving virtue lies solely in the performance of the exequial rites, Mr. Justice Strange's doctrine of the total expenditure on the natural father of the efficacy of his son's birth, does not seem to warrant his conclusion. The adopted son may well perform his adoptive father's rites, and in certain cases, it appears, when he is a *dwyamushyayana*, those of his natural father also. It cannot then be said that the adoption "fails in its essential use," and is for this cause void. I may remark that the hostility shown in the shasters to the adoption of an only son arose, probably, from other than mere religious considerations. The true reason, perhaps, is furnished by Jagannatha,* who lays down the law thus: 'Let no man accept an only son, because he should not do that whereby the family of the natural father becomes extinct;' but this he goes on to say 'does not invalidate the adoption of such a son actually given to him.' On the whole, the case is concluded by authority; but I must say with all possible respect for Mr. Justice Strange that upon principle and reason I should have felt myself bound to decide the point in the same way."

* 1 Madras High Court Reports, p. 57.

The Bombay High Court have ruled in accordance with this* view.

Bengal ruling upon the same point.

But in the Bengal Presidency, notwithstanding the case cited by Sir C. Scotland from Fulton's Reports, a different ruling has been made. It is true that, in *Mussamut Tibdey* v. *Lallah Hurrololl,* † the validity of the adoption of an only son was upheld, but in that case the parties were Sudras; and the law applicable to the three higher *castes* is seldom concluded by the rulings which are considered effective for the maintenance of social order and religious principle amongst that degraded class. I refer to the case of *Rajah Opendur Loll Roy* v. *Ranee Bromo Moyee,* ‡ in which the plaintiff succeeded in showing that his ceremony of adoption had taken place as alleged, but it also appeared that he was the only son of his natural father. It was held that his title necessarily failed, and that it was beyond all controversy, that the adoption of an only son was prohibited by the Hindu Shasters.§ It was contended that the prohibition amounted to nothing more than a mere religious injunction, and that the violation of such an injunction could not invalidate the adoption after it had once taken place, but it was ruled that such contention was unsound, and that the religious and temporal aspects of adoption are wholly inseparable; and that the subject of adoption being inseparable from the

* Raje Vyankatra Anandrav Nimbalker *v.* Jayavantrav bin Malharra Banadiv, 4 Bombay A. C., p. 191.

† Sutherland's Weekly Reporter, 1864, p. 133.

‡ 10 S. W. R., p. 347; S. C., 1 B. L. R., A. C., p. 221; and see also *Nundrane* v. *Kashee Pande*, Select Reports (new edition), Vol. III., p. 310, which was a Tirhoot case, in which the *dattaka* (adoption) of an only child was held to be illegal.

§ Dattaka Mimansa, Section IV., verse 1:—" By no man, having an son (*Eka-putra*), is the gift of a son to be ever made;" and see Dattaka Chandrika, Section I., verse 29.

LECTURE XIII.

Hindu religion, all distinctions between religious and legal injunctions must be necessarily inapplicable to it. Neither the adoption of an only son, nor the adoption by a childless widow without the permission of her husband, can be justified upon the principle of *factum valet.* Both are invalid for the simple reason that they violate the injunctions of the Hindu shasters. The Madras case, which I have just referred to, was dissented from, and two cases in the Bengal Presidency cited, with approbation, by Sir William Macnaghten,* were approved.

The judgment in the case was delivered by Mr. Justice Dwarkanath Mitter; and is, doubtless, of the highest authority. But although the prohibitions are, in the matter of adopting an only son, so distinct as to justify their being extended to invalidate any adoption which takes place in defiance of them, it is nevertheless desirable that the distinction between religious and legal injunctions should not be lost sight of, and that the theory should not be too readily accepted that the religious and temporal aspects of any single doctrine or institution in Hindu law are altogether inseparable.

Proprietary power of a father over his child.

Such theory has been accepted by Courts of Justice with respect to that portion of Hindu law which confers rights, but not as a general rule with reference to that portion which imposes obligations. Prohibitions also which amount to a denial of legal right to do a particular thing are peremptory; but those which tacitly admit the right or capacity, but fetter the exercise of it, can only be regarded as dissuasive. The doctrine of *factum valet* only applies in the latter cases. If the texts quoted

* See 2 Macnaghten's Hindu Law, pp. 178, 179.

above, and the purposes for which Hindu law grants the right to give or receive a child in adoption, show that that right is not conferred in reference to an only son; there is no room for the distinction between law and religion. The proprietary power of a father over his child is a thing of positive law, and must be measured by the terms and policy of that law. A Hindu father has an absolute right to give away a son in adoption, provided he has more than one. If it could be shown by positive precept, or by an accepted text, that he has the right to give an only son also, a religious obligation not to exercise that right might possibly not be enforced. But it would be difficult to show that the power of a Hindu father extends so far over his only sons; such a power would be inconsistent with the whole spirit and teaching of Hindu law which attaches such infinite importance to the possession of a begotten son, and resorts to adoption because of the paramount necessity of obtaining male issue, by whatever means. It would require strong authority to prove that Hindu law enables a man voluntarily to reduce himself to that destitution which it forbids, and from which it so anxiously provides him an escape; and to make use of the institution, to exchange as it were his own offspring for the son of a stranger. The law which invalidates such an adoption stands on an entirely different footing from the supposed law which also invalidates any adoption, by reason only of the omission of a particular sacrifice. In such a case the right to give and accept a child and the eligibility of the child may be beyond question. The omission is to perform an act which ceremonial religion prescribes. The transfer of the child from one family to another is by law complete, but the *status* of the child in that family is

LECTURE XIII.

affected by the omission. He is to be held legally responsible for the omission of others to perform a religious duty, and deprived of his rights of inheritance, and reduced from a position of sonship to that of slavery, because others in the exercise of their undoubted rights failed in a purely religious observance. Such a rule is plainly subversive of justice, and is widely different in principle from the rule which invalidates the adoption of an only son, or of any other child in reference to whom there was no legal right to give, receive, or be given.

Is absolute when the extinction of his own lineage is provided against.

If it be true that a man has no more power of gift over his only son* than he has over his wife or any other relation; when does the right to give in adoption accrue? It appears that it only arises when the extinction of a man's own lineage is duly provided against. There is a precept in the Dattaka Mimansa† against the gift of one out of only two sons. But having regard to the texts and the policy of law, the right to give one of two sons cannot be denied, and the injunction of Nanda Pandita is, in the language of Mr. Macnaghten,‡ merely dissuasive, and not peremptory. Sir Thomas Strange§ also says that, in strictness, it is not sufficient for a man to have more than one son, before he gives in adoption; since, if having only two sons, he part with one, the death of the remaining one is not to be risked. But he adds that it does not appear that this ever prevailed as

* Dattaka Mimansa, Chap. IV., verse 5; As for another text of recorded law,—"In instruction the father is absolute over a son and son's wives, but not so with respect to the son, in sale and gift;" and the text of the Holy Saint: "Except a wife and a son other things may be given." These texts regard the case of an only son.

† Dattaka Mimansa, Chap. IV., verse 8.

‡ Principles of Hindu Law, p. 77.

§ Strange's Hindu Law, Vol. I., p. 85.

a rule, and that therefore if he have two, he may relinquish the younger. The selection of the younger one should be made apparently in deference to the author of the Mitakshara, who forbids the gift of an eldest son; "for he chiefly fulfils the office of a son, as is shown in the following text, by the eldest son, as soon as born, a man becomes the father of male issue." LECTURE XIII.

The eldest son, therefore, as well as the only son, cannot be given in adoption. Eldest son.

The Madras* High Court, however, have held that even assuming the prohibition against an only son to be valid, it does not extend to invalidate the adoption of an eldest or only son of a brother.

The last surviving son is not regarded as an only son, provided there be male issue living of the deceased sons. The father in that case is amply provided with male issue for all purposes, whether of performance of obsequies or of continuance of his lineage.†

An adopted son could never be given in adoption, since he will generally, if not always, be an only son; and where he is not so, it would be a violation of the contract on the faith of which his natural parents gave him away, to transfer him to another family, even if the adoptive parents had a sufficiently absolute property in him to enable him to do so.

Were it not for the authority of the Madras case to which I have referred, the rule against the adoption of an only, an eldest, or a previously adopted son, might be based upon the absence of any proprietary right over such child, involving the power to give him away. As it is I

* Indian Jurist, O. S., p. 105.

† Macnaghten's Hindu Law, Vol. II., p. 195.

LECTURE XIII.

have placed the rule as the first which affects the eligibility of the child. If the power to give him be conceded, then the acceptance of him will, according to the Bengal High Court, be absolutely prohibited, and according to the Madras Court, it will be left to the discretion and conscience of the adopter.

Second rule. A *dattaka* adoption must not import incest.

Secondly, the child must be one whom his natural mother might have borne to his adoptive father in a legal marriage, or whom his adoptive mother might have borne to his natural father in a legal marriage. The son, therefore, of a sister or any other female relative of the adoptive father, with whom he could not have legally intermarried, cannot be affiliated by him. In the language of the text* 'the boy must bear the reflection of a son,' which is described to be the capability to have sprung from the adopter himself through an appointment to raise issue on another's wife. Accordingly the brother, paternal and maternal uncles, the daughter's son and that of the sister, are all excluded, for they are all unfitted to have been begotten by the individual himself through an appointment to raise issue on the wife of another.

The necessary inference from this doctrine is that any adoption which imports incest, that is any child of a woman standing towards the adoptive father in the prohibited degrees of affinity, cannot be received by him. The principle of law which forbids it underlies the whole theory and practice of affiliation as it is understood amongst Hindus. Accordingly, there can be no question that the prohibition to adopt such a child,† whether explicit or in-

* Dattaka Mimansa, Section V., verse 16.

† See Dattaka Mimansa, Section II., verse 34; Dattaka Mimansa, Section V., verse 17; Dattaka Chandrika, Section I., verse 17.

ferred, is one of positive and peremptory character, and is not to be viewed as merely dissuasive, or of a nature importing such merely religious obligations as would make a man only responsible for its breach either in *in foro consientiæ* or to the spiritual authorities in the family or caste to which he belongs. In Bengal there was originally some hesitation in affirming this principle, and a Brahmin's adoption of a sister's son was in one instance declared to be valid. But in Sir Francis Macnaghten's Considerations of Hindu Law, * a work which was first published in 1824, there is a case referred to, in which the Supreme Court recognized the invalidity of any adoption by a man (meaning of course of the three superior castes), of a child whom he could not have begotten on his natural mother without incest; and also affirmed the further rule that he cannot adopt a child as his, by a particular wife, nor can she after his death adopt to him a child whom she could not have borne without incest to his natural father. Natural relationship is the foundation of the rule. The change is both of paternity and also of maternity, and if either the one or the other imports a prohibited connection, it violates an essential principle of a Hindu adoption. The adoptive father and the natural mother must have been in point of affinity capable of contracting a legal marriage; and so also must have been the adoptive mother and the natural father.

General application of the rule.

This rule binds all Hindus of the three superior castes according to all the schools of Hindu law which admit the *dattaka* form of adoption. In the Madras Presidency the question was raised, whether such rule

* Considerations of Hindu Law, pp. 166, 174.

LECTURE XIII.

extended to persons who were governed by the Hindu law prevalent in the Dravida country. It arose in the suit of *Narasaama* v. *Balasa Macharu*,* which was brought in the Zillah of Vizagapatam, by a Hindu widow, to recover the property of her deceased husband. She asserted the invalidity of the adoption of the defendant who was her husband's sister's son. The evidence as to the fact of the adoption and the performance of the necessary ceremonies was conclusive. The only question was as to its validity. The Pundits of the Sudder Court gave different opinions, one Pundit declaring that, among Brahmins, a sister's son cannot be adopted; and the other, that, in the Dravida country, such adoption is both sanctioned by law and recognized by custom. Sir Thomas Strange in his work on Hindu Law lays it down that emergency will justify this adoption among all classes, and that custom sanctions it in the Dravida country even without such emergency. Mr. Ellis too had given it as his opinion, that in practice the adoption of a sister's son by persons of all castes was not uncommon, and was not prohibited. It was admitted that there was no judicial authority upon the subject. The Court referred to Mr. Sutherland, who regarded it as a fundamental principle, that the person to be adopted must be one with the mother of whom the adopter could legally have intermarried; to the passage in Strange† which forbids such adoption by one of the three higher classes, and allows it to the Sudras; and to the Dattaka Chandrika, Section 2, para. 8, which defines the reflection of a son as "the capability to be begotten by the adopter through appointment and so forth." The Court considered it necessary

* Madras Reports, Vol. I., p. 420.

† Strange's Hindu Law, Vol. I., p. 84.

"to uphold a positive prohibition of the law when that prohibition is itself a logical deduction from the very nature of the subject to which it applies. The whole theory of adoption is a complete change of paternity." LECTURE XIII.

They said that an adopted son must be considered as one actually begotten by the adoptive father in all respects save in his incapacity to contract marriage in the family from which he was taken: a theory of relationship in the adoptive family which is the same as that which obtained in the Roman Law. They declared themselves bound to decide that the adoption of a sister's son by a Brahmin was void in the Andhra country as well as in Bengal.

The foundation upon which such prohibition rests is that the adoption of a son with whose mother the adopter could not have intermarried imports incest.* The same rule would hold good with regard to an adoption by a Brahmin widow. She could not adopt her uncle's son, inasmuch as she could not have been his mother without incest. The rule appears to be of general application, it extends over Madras, Bengal, and the North-West Provinces.

The application of a rule thus clearly laid down needs no comment. It is obvious that both the paternal and maternal uncles', sister's, and daughter's sons, and many other blood relations are included in the prohibition. Sudras.

With regard to the law on this point relating to the adoption of Sudras in the *dattaka* form, the author of the Dattaka Mimansa expressly permits them to give and receive sister's and daughter's sons. No doubt as to their capacity in this respect ever existed.

Unless the parties† belong to one of the three regener-

* Macnaghten's Considerations of Hindu Law, p. 170.

† See Nunkoo Singh *v.* Purun Dhun Singh, 12 S. W. R., p. 356.

LECTURE XIII.

ated castes, no objection grounded upon consanguinity between the adopter and the adopted would avail to invalidate the adoption. It is said* to be settled law that the adoption of a sister's son by a Hindu of the Vaisya caste is valid.

Daughters.

With regard to the affiliation of daughters (a subject to which the mention of daughter's sons naturally leads us) Mr. Macnaghten† says that though formerly the practice, it is now forbidden.

Brother's daughter.

An adoption, however, of a brother's daughter was declared to be legal by the Bengal Sudder Court in the case of *Nawab Roy v. Bhuggobutty Koonwur*,‡ and a condition made by her adoptive father, when giving her in marriage, that her first born son should be his *putrika putra* (son of a daughter) was valid, but that to entitle such son to succeed, the adoption of his mother must be proved. The case was discussed at some length. The suit was brought in the Patna Court by the husband of the alleged adopted daughter to recover the property of his wife's adoptive father, on the ground that such adoptive father had, at the time of the marriage, agreed with the plaintiff's father, that the first born son of the marriage should belong to him as his *putrika putra*. This adopted daughter was the natural daughter and only child of an elder brother of the adopter.

One defendant was the widow of the adoptive father above referred to; and it was alleged that the co-defendant who had taken possession of the property was the *kritrima* adopted son of the deceased. One of the Judges in his re-

* Ganpatroo Vireshwar *v.* Vithoba Khandabba, 4 Bombay A. C., p. 130.

† 1 Macnaghten, Chapater VI.

‡ 6 Sudder Dewanny Reports, p. 5.

corded opinion remarked that the answers of the Supreme Court Pundit declared the adoption of the plaintiff's son as *putrika putra* to be lawful, and that a person so adopted was on equal terms with an *ouras* (legitimate son) but that to render such an adoption legal it was necessary that the mother of the *putrika putra* should be herself adopted previous to the marriage. He did not however consider the adoption of the mother proved, and doubted its validity if it were. He referred the case to another Judge, who eventually referred it to a third, who raised the question, "Is the Dattaka adoption by a younger brother of an elder brother's daughter permitted by the shasters of the western country." The opinion of the Court was that such adoption was valid in Mithila. This opinion being in conflict with the opinion of the other Judges, it was referred to another Judge, who based a final order in the suit upon the opinion that the adoption of a daughter was allowable, that she may be, nay, ought to be, the daughter of a brother; that a *putrika putra* ought to be the daughter of a brother; that a *putrika putra* can succeed; but that to make a boy *putrika putra,* it is necessary that the adoption of the mother prior to marriage be proved. Such was the opinion which prevailed with the Court at that date (1835), but considering the proof defective upon the last point, the final decree was one dismissing the suit.

The rule does not apply to *kritrima* adoptions.

With regard to the law which prevails in the province of Mithila, that rests upon a different footing. The *kritrima* adoption effects no change either of paternity or maternity. The son so received is not transferred from one family to another. There is merely a temporary arrangement between the adopter and the adopted, with the addition of certain legal rights of inheritance and legal duties.

Accordingly a sister's son may be received in adoption, without violating Hindu law as interpreted by the doctrines of the Mithila school. In the case of *Chowdree Purmesur Dutt Jha* v. *Hunooman Dutt Roy*,* decided by the Bengal Sudder Court, the plaintiffs sued as heirs of a Hindu, who died leaving, beside the plaintiffs, a widow and a sister's son. The latter had been put into possession of his estate by an order of the Magistrate, he set up an adoption by the deceased in the *kritrima* form, by virtue of which he claimed to hold the estate. The widow was made a co-defendant with him, having recently colluded with him to uphold the adoption. The plaintiffs declared that it was against the Hindu law for a Brahmin to adopt his sister's son; the defendant replied that, according to the law as current in Mithila, the adoption of a sister's son after the *kritrima* form was legal and of frequent occurrence, although the adoption of such a relative after the *dattaka* form was admitted to be illegal. The opinions of the Pundits were as usual contradictory, but it was pointed out by one of them that there was a great difference between the *dattaka* and *kritrima* forms of adoption; that, according to the Mithila commentators, a *kritrima* adopted son might perform the obsequies of his natural father and mother, and that the adoption according to the *kritrima* form of near relations, and particularly of a sister's son, was valid and customary among the Brahmins and persons of high caste in the Mithila country. The text in the Dattaka Mimansa which prohibited the adoption by a Brahmin of his sister's son had reference merely to the *dattaka* form. The prohibition did not

* 6 Sudder Dewanny Reports, p. 192.

include the *kritrima* adoption to the validity of which equality of caste was the only thing essential. It was held that the rule in regard to a *dattaka* adoption which bars the adoption of a child of a mother within the prohibited degrees of marriage is not applicable to the *kritrima* adoption as practised in Mithila.

The Court referred to the case of *Ooman Dutt* v. *Kunhia Singh** where it was held that while a brother's son exists the adoption of any other child either in the *dattaka* or *kritrima* form is illegal,—a doctrine which accords with the Dattaka Mimansa,† and is expressly stated in the Dattaka Chandrika. Equality of caste was judicially declared to be the only necessary condition to the legality of the *kritrima* form of adoption, and the plaintiff's suit was accordingly dismissed.

Equality of caste the only condition of eligibility for a *kritrima* adoption.

In the case of *Ooman Dutt* v. *Kunhia Singh*, referred to in the above decision, the same principle had been affirmed in reference to the daughter's son. I may conveniently refer to it now, as it also expresses the rule of law relative to the age of a boy eligible for a *kritrima* adoption, and seems to recognize the principle that equality of caste is the only condition of eligibility for that mode of affiliation. It appears from the report that the plaintiff sued in the Zillah Court of Tirhoot as the adopted son of a man, who by blood relationship, was

* Select Reports (new edition), Vol. III., p. 192.

† 2 Dattaka Mimansa, Section II., verse 74.—"If no brother's son exist, another, even being the nearest relative, according to the mode mentioned, must be adopted."

Dattaka Chandrika, Section 1, verse 20.—"In respect however to this subject, it is to be observed that where a brother's son may exist amongst near kinsmen, he only is to be adopted. If a brother's son is in any manner capable of being a substitute, it is inferred that another is not to be adopted." See Principles of Hindu Law, p. 68.

LECTURE XIII.

his maternal grandfather. One contention of the defendant was that such adoption was repugnant to the shasters, and utterly unlawful, and the question ultimately raised was as follows:—If one of two full brothers joint in estate having no lineal descendants adopt, by the *kritrima* form, his own daughter's son, can such child succeed by virtue of his adoption? It was stated by the Pundits and held by the Judge that the adoption of the plaintiff in the *kritrima* form was not illegal either by reason of his having been ten years old at the time, or because he was the daughter's son of the adopter, or because he was the eldest son of his natural father.

Elder brother.

An elder brother can never be adopted by a younger one, even according to the Mithila School. That was decided by the Sudder Court in a suit brought in the Zillah Court at Tirhoot,* by two brothers, to recover a moiety of the ancestral estate. The defendant whom the plaintiffs alleged to be entitled to the other moiety, besides disputing the plaintiffs' claim upon other grounds, contended that in any event he was entitled to two-thirds of the estate. The plaintiffs were descended from the eldest of three brothers, and the defendant was the son of the second brother. The youngest brother had died without issue, but had, it was said, adopted the defendant's father as his *kurta putra.* The Pundit, when referred to, declared that an elder brother cannot be the *kurta putra* (adopted son) of a younger according to the doctrine of the Dattaka Mimansa, and that this was so, even though there were no younger brother to be adopted. The Court ruled in accordance with this answer.

* Baboo Runjeet Singh *v.* Baboo Obhye Narain Singh, Select Reports (new edition), Vol. II., p. 315.

LECTURE XIV.

THE QUALIFICATIONS FOR BEING ADOPTED.

Third Rule—One of a different Class cannot be adopted—Fourth Rule—Proximity of Sapindaship should determine the choice of a son to be adopted—A *dattaka* adoption cannot take place after marriage of the son to be adopted—But a *kritrima* adoption can take place at any time—What ceremonies performed by the natural father render the child ineligible—In Bengal adoptions should take place before the Investiture of the boy—Elsewhere, before his Tonsure—According to Jagannatha, before the proper age for Tonsure, *i. e.*, five years—The Courts have allowed considerable latitude as to age—So also with regard to the performance of Ceremonies—How far these Rules are directory and not imperative—Rules seem to be relaxed in favor of a near Relation—Proximity of kindred should be chiefly attended to in adoption—The celebration of marriage the only bar to adoption, except perhaps when the child is selected from a different *Gotra*—When selected from a different *Gotra*—*Dwyamushyayana.*

Two rules have already been enunciated with regard to the eligibility of a child for adoption, in addition to those rules which appeared to be more appropriately considered in reference to the legal power of disposition possessed by the parent. The subject must be pursued at greater length; for, although the prescribed ordinances of the shasters upon it may not be difficult to collect and arrange, there is considerable perplexity in distinguishing, either on principle or in reference to decided cases, between those rules which are essential to be observed in order to secure a valid adoption, and those the breach of which involves merely a religious or moral offence.

LECTURE XIV.

Third rule—One of a different class cannot be adopted.

The third rule to be laid down is that *one of a different class or tribe or caste cannot be adopted:* "should one of a different class be taken as a son in any instance, let the adopter not make him a participator of a share;* this is the doctrine of Saunaka;" and the author of the Dattaka Mimansa also quotes the authority of Menu and of the "chief of the saints" (Yajnavalkya), in support of the same doctrine. He rejects the interpretation that suitable qualities are a sufficient ground of equality, and insists that adopter and adopted must be equal in class. Katyayana lays it down that, if adopted sons be of a different class, they are entitled to food and raiment only; and according to the general consent of the earliest authorities, the filial relation of one of a different class, in default of obtaining one in the same class, is not absolutely denied; but he is regarded† merely as prolonging the line, and as entitled to maintenance only from the person succeeding to the estate.

The strict rule may even be extended to require that an adoption be made from the same special caste to which the adoptive parents belong, provided that such caste is recog-

* Dattaka Mimansa, Section II., verses 21, 22; Dattaka Chandrika, Section VI., verse 4.

† Dattaka Chandrika, Section I., verse 15.—Katyayana declares this: "If they be of a different class, they are entitled to food and raiment only." Saunaka only "If one of a different class should, however, in any case, have been adopted as a son, he should not make him the participator of a share; this is the doctrine of Saunaka. By Yajnavalkya also it is declared that one of the same class presents the funeral cake, and participates in a share; but the filial relations of one of a different class is not denied; and Yaska explicitly declares this: "A person of the same class must be adopted as a son. Such a son performs the oblations, and takes the estate; on default of him, one different in class, who is regarded merely as prolonging the line. He receives food and raiment only from the person succeeding to the estate."

nized by the custom of the particular country as distinct, though derivative, from any one or two of the four general castes.* Mr. Sutherland also, in his Synopsis, points out that marriage with one unequal in class is prohibited, and that therefore one of a different class, borne of a mother whom the adopter could not have married, is excluded from adoption. The rule under consideration, so far as it is a breach of the last rule, and so far as inequality of caste involves the incapacity of the natural and adoptive parents to intermarry, must be regarded as prohibitory; and an adoption, in defiance of it, would be void for the purpose of transferring a child from one family to another. According to Sir Thomas Strange† such an adoption has, in general, nothing but disqualifying effects:—"parted with by his parents, it divests the child of his natural, without entitling him to the substituted claims incident to an unexceptionable adoption. Incompetent to perform effectually those rites on account of which adoption is resorted to, he cannot inherit to the adopter, but remains a charge upon him entitled only to maintenance."

And even in the *kritrima* form of adoption, this condition is insisted upon and derives additional force from the circumstance that it is the one solitary condition imposed by law in that form of adoption,—*viz.*, that the adopter and the adopted should be of the same class.

No case has yet been decided in which the question of the validity of an adoption, in breach of this rule, has been determined. But there can be no reason for carrying the rule beyond the foundation on which it is apparently based,—*viz.*, the incapacity of the parents (who assume to contract

* Sutherland's Synopsis, Head II.

† Strange's Hindu Law, Vol. I., p. 82.

LECTURE XIV.

the adoption) to contract a valid marriage. If the rules which prohibit marriage between persons of different classes, be, as they have been held by the Madras High Court to be, of no weight at the present day, the same relaxation may safely be extended to adoptions in which persons of different classes are interested. The rule, at all events, is not one which, in the present day, it is useful or expedient to insist upon.

Fourth rule—Proximity of *sapindaship* should determine the choice of a son to be adopted.

The fourth rule* is, in accordance with the doctrine of Vasistha and Saunaka, that *the adoption of a son by any Brahmana must be made from amongst sapindas (the nearer being preferred to the more remote), and only upon failure of these may an adopted son be sought amongst those not so connected.* Of these latter the kinsmen, allied by an oblation of water (*sodaka*), should be preferred; and next in order, one of the same general family to the twenty-first degree; and then, on failure of all of these, a person of a different family may be at last resorted to; but even then the boy should be at least of the same tribe with the adoptive father. Although the principle of selection is thus rigidly laid down, the rule is, nevertheless, merely directory, and is only binding, if at all, in a religious point of view. The principle, according to Mr. Sutherland, cannot be regarded as vitiating the adoption of a remote where a near kinsman exists, or of a stranger where a relative exists.

Sir Francis Macnaghten† lays down the rule in these

* Dattaka Mimansa, Section II., verse 2. Saunaka has declared "the adoption of a son by any Brahmana must be made from amongst *sapindas* or kinsmen connected by an oblation of food; or, on failure of these an *asapinda*, or one not so connected, may be adopted, otherwise let him not adopt."

† Considerations of Hindu Law, p. 150.

words: "Brahmins should adopt sons from among their own *sapindas,* and on failure of *sapindas,* from among those not *sapindas.* Among *sapindas,* the brother's son is to be considered as the best. If a brother's son does not exist, a *sapinda,* who is also a *sagotra,* is to be chosen." If such is not to be found, a *sagotra* who is not a *sapinda;* and if such is not to be found, one neither a *sagotra* nor a *sapinda.*

According to the generally received rule of the shasters founded on the oft-quoted text of Menu,* the son of a whole brother has, in the absence of any impediment, a preferential right to be adopted. Proximity of kindred should, undoubtedly, determine the choice of an adopted son, but the law only interfered for the protection of the son of the whole brother. Even the only son of a whole brother has a preferential right, according to the Dattaka Mimansa,† to be adopted, of course as a *dwyamushyayana,* but at the present day it does not appear that even in provinces where the Dattaka Mimansa is the leading authority, and still less according to the law of the Bengal school, would the validity of an adoption actually made be affected by any disregard of this rule of selection, even though the interests of the brother's son have been passed over.

A *dattaka* adoption cannot take place after marriage of the son to be adopted.

The last of the rules which relate to the qualifications of a child for adoption refer to his age. It is not the number of years which have passed over his head which is of importance, so much as the progress which has been made in the process of regeneration in the natural family. The effect, however, of the initiatory ceremonies which have been per-

* 9 Menu, 182. "If, among several brothers of the whole blood, one have a son born, Menu pronounces them all fathers of a male child by means of that son; so that, if such nephew would be the heir, the uncles have no power to adopt sons."

† Dattaka Mimansa, Section II., verses 37, 38.

formed by the natural father is rather to modify the character in the eye of religion of the new relationship formed by adoption or of the heritable rights of the child in his new family, than to create an absolute bar to his adoption. This rule, however, is not allowed to be violated by any of the schools, except that of Mithila, that *the performance of the rite of marriage in the natural family, which in the case of the three higher castes is the last ceremony of regeneration, and in the case of Sudras is the only one, is an insurmountable bar to adoption.* A man who has once been married can never be affiliated.

But a *kritrima* adoption can take place at any time.

As respects the Mithila school I will merely refer to Mr. Macnaghten.* There is, according to that authority, no sort of restriction, except as to tribe. There is no limit as to age; no condition as to the performance of ceremonies. It has even been declared that a man may adopt his own brother or even his own father. But he, as well as his issue, continues after his adoption to be considered a member of his natural family; and he takes the inheritance both of his own family and that of his adopting father. Another peculiarity of this species of adoption is that a person adopted in this form by the widow does not thereby become the adopted son of the husband: and the express consent of the person nominated for the adoption must be obtained during the life-time of the adopting party. The relation of *kritrima* here extends to the contracting parties only; and the son so adopted will not be considered the grandson of the adopting father's father, nor will the son of the adopted be considered as the grandson of his adoptive father. He does not inherit collaterally, being ninth in the enumeration according to Yajnavalkya.

* Principles of Hindu Law, p. 75.

LECTURE XIV.

Passing now to the Dattaka form of adoption and the question of the proper age of the child, or rather of the progress which he has made, or ought to have made, in the family of his natural parents towards a state of regeneration, it must always be borne in mind, that the final act of affiliation having regard to the ceremonial prescribed, proceeds from the performance by the adopter of the boy's initiatory rites. And it is upon this principle that, under no circumstances whatever, can one whose marriage, which is the final or only ceremony of regeneration as the case may be, has taken place and been completed in the family of birth, ever be the subject of adoption. And upon the same principle it follows that that child is to be preferred as the most eligible subject of transfer from one family to another, and most capable of effecting all the religious purposes for which such transfer is sought, who is still wholly unaffected by any initiatory rites,—*i. e.*, whose process of regeneration has not even been begun.

What ceremonies performed by natural father render the child ineligible.

When we pass from the child who is absolutely unaffected by any initiatory ceremonies, we come to the first topic in the law of adoption, in which there was originally any serious division of opinion between the schools who recognize and prescribe the *dattaka* form. The Bengal school has adopted the doctrine of the *Dattaka Chandrika*, which is more liberal in this respect than the teaching of the *Dattaka Mimansa*, and relaxes the restriction which the latter authority places upon the qualification to be absolutely and completely transferred from one family, or from one father, to another. The difference between the authors of those two celebrated treatises arose, as Mr. Macnaghten points out, merely from a difference of a grammatical construction of the original text.

* Macnaghten's Hindu Law, p. 72, note.

LECTURE XIV.

But however that may be, it forms the subject of an important difference of law as it prevailed amongst the followers of the respective schools.

In Bengal adoption should take place before the investiture of the boy.

According to Devandabhatta,* whose authority prevails in Bengal, Menu must be accepted to mean that, through the extinction of his filial relation from gift alone, the property of the son given in the estate of the giver ceases, and his relation to the family of that person is annulled; therefore the adoptive father must perform the initiatory rites of the given son, which have yet to be completed; but those already performed by the natural father are not to be cancelled. He ought not to perform those rites which the natural father has already performed, but he may complete them if they have been neglected, even although the appropriate time of performance has passed; on account of the indispensable necessity of removing the taint of the seed and womb, and for the sake of preserving the order prescribed for the performance of the rites in question. Thence he concludes, as matter of law, that if the rite of investiture merely be performed by the adopter, the previous rites having been performed by the natural father, the filiation of the son given, as son of the adopter, is completed. Thus the investiture with the Brahminical thread in the family of the adopter, under the family name of the adopter, is a sufficient compliance with the rule which requires that regeneration should be effected in the adoptive family.

Elsewhere before his tonsure.

In the Dattaka Mimansa,† on the other hand, the rule is laid down as propounded in the Kalika Purana, that sons who have once been initiated, as far as the ceremony of *tonsure* inclusive, under the family name of the natural

* Dattaka Chandrika, Section II., verses 19, 23.

† Dattaka Mimansa, Section IV., verses 22, *et seq.*

father, cannot become sons of other men. The filial relation proceeding from initiatory rites is thus declared to be completed by the ceremony of *tonsure.* When it has once taken place in the natural family, it is irrevocable, and according to the schools which recognize this doctrine, a child so filiated cannot be adopted except as a *dwyamushyayana;* and even this effect will only be produced when he is under six years of age at the time of gift, and when his adoptive father repeats the performance of all the initiatory rites down to the ceremony of *tonsure*, having first performed the *putreshti*, or sacrifice, for male issue. The necessity of the sacrifice is that, strictly speaking, such a gift not merely does not produce the status of sonship, but imposes a servile condition in the adoptive family. This servile state is removed by the performance of the *putreshti*, and then the second filial relation is produced from the initiatory rites.

According to Jagannatha, before the proper age for tonsure, *i. e.* five years.

Jagannatha, in his Digest, still further restricts the qualifications or eligibility of the adopted child.* He insists that the performance of the initiatory rite of *tonsure* under the family name of the natural father is a bar to a subsequent transfer of the child. Further he insists that if the boy has completed his fifth year, and has thereby passed the proper age for the performance of that ceremony, he is also ineligible. He only allows of one instance, in which a boy initiated as far as *tonsure* can be affiliated in another family,—*viz.*, where the gift and acceptance of the child have taken place before the completion of the fifth year and before the performance of the ceremony, and then the natural father afterwards performs the *tonsure*. Then that, in that case, the

* Colebrooke's Digest, Book V., Chap. IV., Section VIII., verse 273, note.

LECTURE XIV.

adoption remains good, acceptance in a certain form being the efficient cause of filiation, and the ceremony of *tonsure* performed by the natural father is void.

This doctrine of Jagannatha, and the question thus raised of the eligibility for adoption of a boy above the age of five years, occasioned some perplexity in former* times. In the case of *Kerut Narain* v. *Musst. Bhoobunesree*, cited by Mr. Sutherland, and reported in the first volume of Select Reports, the question was settled for a time, and so far at least as regards Bengal, after the subject had for a long time occasioned considerable discussion. In a note to the report of the case, it is stated that it had often been agitated before the Supreme Government in former times, when it used to exercise judicial authority with regard to the succession to zemindaries, whether an adoption of a child above the age of five years was valid according the Hindu law of Bengal. The question was whether any authority imposed a positive limitation of age as essential to a valid adoption. The point first came for judicial decision before the late Sudder Court in 1806, when the daughter of a deceased zemindar sued to recover his estate, the defendant having been adopted by the widow of the deceased, in pursuance of his written authority, at the age of about eight years, with the usual legal ceremonies. It was decided that, according to the Bengal school, the adoption of a boy of above five years of age, although the selection be not laudable, is valid; provided the initiatory ceremonies (especially the principal one of *tonsure*) have been performed in the family of the adopter and not in that of the natural father.

The Courts have allowed considerable latitude as to age.

The Court thus, in the language of Mr. Sutherland,

* Select Reports (new edition), Vol. I., p. 213.

determined the following points as applicable to that province.* First, that adoption is restricted to no particular age; secondly, that one initiated as far as *tonsure* in the name and family of his natural father is incapable of adoption; thirdly, that the age of the person selected for adoption must be such as to admit of the ceremony of *tonsure* being performed in the adopter's name and family. These rulings, however, applied, if they be of any force at all, exclusively to adoption in the *dattaka* form, and are only of authority within the province of Bengal. The last two rulings, however, are wholly inconsistent with the doctrine of the Dattaka Chandrika, as quoted above, and doubtless would not now be accepted as law.

Moreover, this case must be read in connection with that of *Mussamut Dullabh De* v. *Manu Bibi*,† in which the natural mother of an adopted child, acting in the capacity of his guardian, brought a suit against his alleged adoptive mother, to establish his rights as heir to the defendant's husband. The child had been promised by his mother while still in the womb, if it proved male, and both father and mother gave the child for adoption shortly after its birth. Further, the child had been publicly constituted by the defendant the adopted son of her husband, with due solemnities, including a sacrifice for male issue. She, however, set up the defence, that at the date of the public ceremony he was an only son, his elder brother having died previously to the gift; that he had not been given by his father and mother; that at the time of the public ceremony his age exceeded five years; that his *tonsure* had been performed in his natural family; and that he

* Sutherland's Synopsis, Head II.

† 5 Sudder Dewanny Reports, p. 50.

had performed exequial rites in honor of his own forefathers. The admitted fact in the case was that, at the date of the public ceremony, the child's father and elder brother were both dead. It seemed to be considered that even if the ceremony of *tonsure* had been performed in the natural family of the adopted, at a time subsequent to the gift and adoption, and before the sacrifice to male issue, it was an indifferent act by a stranger possessing no effect whatever. Such a ruling would be in accordance with the opinion of Jagannatha quoted above, to the effect that the ceremony of *tonsure* performed in the natural family after a gift and acceptance of the child is null and void. It was further held (notwithstanding the rulings in *Kerut Narain* v. *Musst. Bhoobunesree*), that, in adoption, considerable latitude as to age was admissible, the only proviso mentioned being that the child, at the time he was given and received, was uninvested with the characteristic cord.

So also with regard to the performance of ceremonies.

Mr. Sutherland remarks that, although the author of the Dattaka Chandrika* has left it doubtful whether in his opinion the celebration of the *upanayana* by the natural father would be an insuperable bar to its re-performance by the adopter, and hence to adoption: yet, that it appears more reasonable to suppose that the celebration in the family of the natural father of so important a rite as the *upanayana*, or that the expiration of the secondary period prescribed for its performance, should constitute an impediment to the adoption of a son given, by precluding the celebration of the rite referred to in the family and name of the adopter, even though sacrifices and penances should be performed. If this rule may be regarded as correct, it

* Sutherland's Synopsis, Note XII.

follows that, throughout Bengal, notwithstanding the decision above quoted, any one can be given and received as a *dattaka* son, whose *upanayana* has not been performed; but that, when once it has been performed, or the time for its performance has finally passed, then the boy is no longer capable of being adopted. And the further limitation must, I think, be laid down, with regard to those schools which reject the authority of the Dattaka Chandrika, when it is opposed to that of the Dattaka Mimansa, that, if the child be over six years old, and has been initiated as far as tonsure in the natural family, he also is totally ineligible; nor can he, according to those schools, be received as a *dattaka* son, wholly transferred and separated from his natural family, unless he be under five years old, and the ceremony of tonsure has not been performed. LECTURE XIV.

Sudras.

In later years, the Court* regarded it as well established by the precedents, that the adoption of a Sudra boy (otherwise eligible), in Bengal, is permissible at any age previous to his marriage; as that of boys of the higher caste, is at any age before investiture with the thread (*upanayana*).

How far these rules are directory and not imperative.

None of the prohibitions, however, against adoption of a boy before marriage must be accepted at the present day as of actual binding legal validity, unless it be the rule which makes the investiture with the thread a bar to adoption; and it is at least open to doubt whether that rule is absolutely prohibitory in its nature. Upon this latter point,† Mr. Ellis, as quoted by Sir T. Strange, says, speaking of an adoption in Southern India:—" With respect to the ineligibility of a person for adoption, on whom the

* Ranee Nitradaye *v.* Bholanath Doss, 9 S. D. Dec., p. 553.

† Strange's Hindu Law, Vol. II., p. 104.

LECTURE XIV.

upanayana rites have been performed, it is much disputed: the more correct, *because the more reasonable* opinion would appear to be that he is eligible if of the same *gotra;* ineligible if of a different *gotra* from the adopter; for if of the same *gotra*, the *datta-homam*, though proper, is not necessary: if of a different *gotra*, the *datta-homam* is necessary, and it cannot be performed on one who, by the rites of the *upanayana,* has been definitively established in his natural *gotra.*"

And in 1859, it was held by the late Sudder Court* of Bengal, that the rule prescribing that adoption shall take place before the boy is five years old is directory only, and not imperative, and that the only absolute prohibition as to age is that, among Brahmins, a boy cannot be adopted after his investiture with the thread, which must occur not later than his sixteenth year; and that, among Sudras, the adoption must take place before marriage. Within that limit adoption may take place; the rule, however, as to the performance of the ceremonies of inauguration, of which the principal is tonsure, varying according as the boy to be adopted is a stranger or related to the adopting father. In the case referred to, the plaintiff was the nephew of his adopting father; and it had been held in a Madras† case, that an adoption is good, though the adopted boy should have passed his fifth year, and have undergone the ceremony of purification by tonsure, provided he be a *sagotra,* or descended in a direct male line from a common male ancestor, or that he be the son of a near relation on the paternal side of the adopter.

Rules seem to be relaxed in favour of a near relation.

"And this doctrine," the Court observed, "seems to be

* Ramkishore Acharj Chowdry *v.* Bhoobunmoyee Debea Chowdrain, Sudder Dewanny Adawlut, 1859, p. 254.

† Morley's Digest, Vol. I., p. 22.

assented to in a note by Mr. Colebrooke, appended to the case of *Kerutnarain* v. *Bhoobunesree.** After remarking on the supposed limitation of five years, Mr. Colebrooke observes 'in other provinces, and even in Bengal, if the adoption be of a near relation on the paternal side, no difficulty would occur; as the adoption of a brother's son, or other nearest male relation of the husband, would be unquestionably valid at an age much exceeding that specified. But in Bengal, where the adoption of strangers to the family is practised, the settled doctrine is that the boy's age must be such that his initiation, the principal ceremony of which is tonsure, may yet be performed in the adopter's name and family.' Under this view, there seems to be no doubt but that the plaintiff in this case, a nephew, was altogether eligible for adoption by the uncle, his adopting father. Whether, under any and what circumstances, a stranger can be adopted, after the ceremony of tonsure has been performed in his natural father's family; and whether that ceremony can and should be repeated, and if it can, what is the effect of its repetition,—are questions regarding which conflicting opinions may be gathered from the Hindu law text books." In an application for review of this judgment, it was contended that adoption must take place before the eighth year, that being the primary season for the rite of investiture. The Court† observed: "It was formerly contended that the adoption must be made before the boy to be adopted was five years old. The text was declared to be simply directory, and not imperative. Passing that year, it is now contended, that although an adoption may be made after a

* Select Reports (new edition), Vol. I., p. 215.

† Sudder Dewanny Adawlut, 1860, pp. 485-490.

LECTURE XIV.

boy has reached five years of age, it must be made before his eighth, or the expiry of the primary season, for the performance of the rite of investiture with the thread. On this point it appears that the Dattaka Chandrika is also directory, and not imperative; and notwithstanding the preference which Hindu lawyers have always shown for early adoptions, they have never restricted the adoption of any Brahmin in Bengal to any particular time, previous to the period before which the ceremony of investiture must take place, namely the sixteenth year."

Proximity of kindred should be chiefly attended to in adoption.

The question is not concluded by any decided cases. But looking to the manner in which the early authorities direct and minutely prescribe, with a force which only falls short of imposing legal obligation, the selection of a child to be adopted with special reference to proximity of kindred, it would be in accordance with the spirit of Hindu law, and, generally speaking, with the words of the *Dattaka Mimansa* and *Dattaka Chandrika*, if the restrictions (other than that of a marriage having been performed) with regard to adoption be limited in all the schools and in all the classes to the case in which a child passes from one *gotra* to another. To apply them to render the son of a brother or other near relative ineligible for adoption, may be to compel the adoptive father to resort to a different *gotra*, contrary to the express injunction of the shasters, and to the prejudice of his own relations and those who may fairly expect to succeed to his estate. Social convenience and the express directions of the Hindu law-givers point to encouraging and facilitating adoption within the *gotra* of the adoptive father; and if marriage alone, or the age of puberty, or majority, were regarded as the one insuperable bar to the adoption of a sapinda, and

The celebration of marriage the only bar to adoption, except perhaps when the child is selected from a different *gotra*.

the other restrictions were enforced solely with reference to a *bandhu*, or a stranger, it would be difficult to believe that the objects, social or religious, of a Hindu adoption would be frustrated. Those objects when once ascertained, together with considerations which regard the present convenience and well being of Hindu society, may surely outweigh the authority of any passage of a commentator, if any such be found. The clear written text of sages, whose maxims are received and held in reverence by Hindus, and shewn to be generally acted upon, must always prevail in deciding upon their laws and usages; but where sages and commentators are at variance, or where their language and meaning are doubtful, the most liberal interpretation of their precepts, which shall be consistent with the objects they had in view, and with those considerations of public policy which Courts of justice are in the habit of regarding, may fairly be resorted to in the exposition of Hindu law.

When selected from a different *gotra*.

And even with regard to the adoption of a child of a different *gotra*, it is a question of considerable difficulty and importance how far these rules, with respect to the age or regenerate condition of the child to be adopted, are imperative or directory. The whole system of adoption is, from a religious point of view, extremely mystical; and in a legal and social point of view, I have the high authority of the late Mr. Justice Sumboonath Pundit, for saying that it is one full of injustice. The binding force of some of the many rules which are prescribed, depends to a great extent upon the degree to which the religious and legal character of the system may be held to be separable in their nature, or in the eye of a Court of justice. From a consideration of the system as a whole (and it is one of the leading institutions of Hindu life), as well as of the course which the decisions have taken, and the doctrines which have been from time to time accepted upon the subject, I think that those characters are thus far inseparable, that the proprietary power of a parent over his child to give him in adoption, and the legal right to receive him, must be limited by regard to the religious purposes for which they are conferred. When the capacity to give and receive are established, then arises the question under what circumstances and in what manner may those rights be exercised. A number of perplexing rules are prescribed, and it is then that the necessity is imposed upon us of distinguishing between those which are imperative and those which may be disregarded in a legal point of view. In so doing, one consideration of moral justice ought at least to be attended to,—*viz.*, that the validity of the gift, and the validity of the acceptance of a child, should stand or fall together, and that one and the same act of adoption should not be held valid as regards his separation from one family, and invalid as regards his introduction to another.

To vitiate the acceptance of a child, given by a valid act, merely because some mystical ceremony has been omitted at or subsequent to the adoption, and to hold that his *status* of sonship and rights of inheritance are affected by the omission (the result, of which, in an orthodox religious view, may be to affect his regeneracy, or his capacity to perform exequial rites) seems to be inconsistent with the provisions of Act XXI of 1850, which provides that even an outcast and a pervert shall retain his rights of inheritance, though, of course, the capacity to discharge the religious duties annexed to them are gone. The civil and religious character of the act of adoption, when once the capacity of the contracting parties has been ascertained, may, as it seems to me, be fairly distinguished in laying down the legal rules which shall regulate its performance. And then, with regard to the eligibility of the child, that may, in a legal point of view, inasmuch as he is a merely passive subject of property and contract, depend upon the existence of proprietary power over him for purposes of gift. Undoubtedly that power ceases with his marriage; possibly also in the three higher castes, with the performance of the *upanayana*. In a religious point of view, the latter circumstance may be of the utmost importance, but it may be left to the conscience of the parties, consistently with the ordinary action of the Courts, in reference to matters of religion and conscience. The actual marriage and the attainment of majority are the important periods, in reference to this subject, in the eye of the law.

Dwyamushyayana.

I may conclude this subject, with a brief reference to the law relating to the *dwyamushyayana*. The essential element in this species of adoption is an agreement, express or implied, between the natural and adoptive fathers to this effect,—"this is a son to us both." If such child undergo the rite of tonsure by his natural father, and then be so adopted by a person of a different *gotra*, he becomes what is called *anitya dwyamushyayana*,—that is, incompletely son of two fathers, as distinguished from *nitya dwyamushyayana*, or absolutely son of two fathers. In the former case, according to Mr. Macnaghten, the connection between the child and his adoptive father endures only during the life-time of the adopted, the children of the adopted son revert to their natural family. According to Mr. Ellis,* some writers make a similar distinction

* Strange's Hindu Law, Vol. II., p. 122.

LECTURE XIV.

between *nitya datta* and *anitya-datta,* the latter being the name given to a son adopted in the *dattaka* form from a different *gotra,* after he has received the tonsure in his natural *gotra.* He also, it is said, remains, while he lives, in the *gotra* of his adoptive father, but his son returns to his natural one. This latter distinction, however, can only apply to Bengal; for, except in that school, the performance of the rite of tonsure by the natural father, at least in a different *gotra,* is a bar to a *dattaka* adoption; religion only conceding that such a child may, up to six years of age, become an *anitya dwyamushyayana.* The broad distinction between the *nitya* and the *anitya dwyamushyayana* is that the issue of the former* belong to the adoptive, and of the latter to the natural family.

But the law affecting *dwyamushyayana* is not now of much practical importance. A child at the present time is either absolutely transferred from one father or family to another, or his adoption is held to be altogether void; while all the mystical rules were attended to, which made the eligibility of the child for transfer, dependent upon ceremonial observances, a sort of compromise between inclination and religion was supposed to be effected by regarding the child as in some sort belonging to both families. Simplicity and common sense have a tendency ultimately to prevail, and the *dwyamushyayana,* except perhaps in the case of the only son of a brother, may be said to be abolished.

* Dattaka Mimansa, Section VI., verse 41.

LECTURE XV.

THE EFFECTS OF ADOPTION.

Effect of *Kritrima* adoption—Effect of *Dattaka* adoption—To whom an adopted son becomes Sapinda—His right of lineal Succession—Also of collateral Succession—Adopted son is related to adoptive mother and her ancestors—But not to such mother's co-wife—Adopted son inherits his adoptive mother's Stridhun—But not her ancestral Property—He does not inherit from a *Bandhu*—Adopted son does not inherit from his maternal relations, nor they from him—Maintenance of adopted son—Son adopted by a widow only inherits the husband's Estate, which is at the time of adoption vested in her.

Effect of *kritrima* adoption.

THE last point to be discussed in reference to this subject of adoption is the legal effects of the rite or contract upon the *status* and heritable rights of the adopted child. As respects the *kritrima* adopted son, I have already pointed out that that mode of adoption does not effect a transfer from one family to another. Accordingly* it has been held, that a son so adopted retains the right of succession and of presenting the funeral cake in his natural family, while he also acquires the same rights in his adoptive family. The son therefore of such adopted child can succeed to the estate of his natural father's brother.

Effect of *dattaka* adoption.

It is chiefly necessary to attend to those results which accrue when a valid transfer of a child has been effect-

* Mussamut Depoo *v.* Goureeshunker, Select Reports (new edition), Vol. III., p. 410.

LECTURE XV.

ed from one father to another, or from one *gotra* to another, by a complete *dattaka* adoption. Such a child ceases to have any connection with the natural family, or father, except so far as he is affected by the prohibition to contract marriage therein; and also by the days and seasons of mourning. He is incapable of performing the funeral rites of his natural father, and* ceases to have any claim upon the family or estate. It is said that the Dattaka son is prohibited from marrying not only within certain degrees in the family of his natural father, but totally in that *gotra.* He is bound to perform the exequial rites to his adopted father, and he is entitled to succeed to his estate, not merely lineally, but also collaterally, in the same way as he would have succeeded had he been a natural son. According to Mr. Sutherland, he also represents the real legitimate son† in relationship to his adoptive mother; and her ancestry are his maternal grandsires.

To whom an adopted son becomes sapinda.

Thus the sapindaship of the adopted son is the first question to be disposed of. First the consanguineal connection involved in that term. Secondly, the connection by the pinda or funeral cake. The sapindaship‡ arising from consanguinity cannot be broken; to that extent the

* Dattaka Mimansa, Section VI., verses 6 and 7.

Menu next propounds another rule:—"A given son must never claim the family and estate of his natural father. The funeral cake follows the family and estate; but of him who has given away his son the obsequies fail."

"The son given must never claim his natural father's family and estate. Thus the obsequies, that is the funeral repast, which would have been performed by the son given, fails of him who has given away his son."

Dattaka Chandrika, Section II., verses 18, 19; Sutherland's Synopsis, Head IV; Vyavastha Darpana, p. 887.

† Sutherland's Synopsis, Head IV.

‡ Vyavastha Darpana, p. 889.

relationship of the adopted child to his natural parent's family continues; but with regard to connection by funeral oblations the severance from the natural parents is complete. I will only quote upon this subject the text of Vrihat Menu: "Sons given, purchased, and the rest retain relations of *sapinda* to the natural father as extending to the fifth and seventh degrees." In the Dattaka Mimansa* it is explained that the meaning of this passage is, that a consanguineal connection only with the natural family, and not connection by the *pinda*, or funeral cake, remains. On the other hand, no consanguineal tie is formed with the adoptive family; the *sapindaship* which results from adoption is solely a connection by means of the *pinda*, or funeral cake. That connection, it will be remembered, extends to only three degrees, while the consanguineal tie extends to seven. When, therefore, we come to enquire what are the prohibitions as to marriage, and the rules as to days of impurity which affect the adopted son in his new family, they will extend only to the third degree,† that being the limit of the relationship formed by adoption. In‡ the adoptive family, the rules which regulate the son's oblation of the funeral cake, impurity on occasions of births and deaths, and disability to contract marriage, all stand on the same footing. It must, however, be recollected that this can only apply in all its strictness where the adopted son passes from one *gotra* to another. Whatever sanguineal connection there was originally with the adoptive family, will, of course, remain.

* Dattaka Mimansa, Section VI., verse 9.

† Dattaka Mimansa, Section VI., verse 32.—When a *dattaka* son passes from one *gotra* to another, there is no reciprocal impurity in the family of the natural father. See Dattaka Chandrika, Section IV., verse 1.

‡ Sutherland's Synopsis, Note xx., Dattaka Mimansa, Section VIII.

LECTURE XV.

It is said by Menu* that a son of any description must be anxiously adopted by a man destitute of male issue, for the sake of the funeral cake, water, and solemn rites, and for the celebrity of his name. The adopted son, therefore, provided† he is not displaced by a subsequently born legitimate son, performs the adopter's funeral obsequies, the sixteen *shraddhas*, commencing with the first and ending with the *sapindakarana*, the *ekoddista sharddha*, and the *parvana shraddha.*‡ This latter, however, he does not, like the legitimate son, perform on the anniversary of the day of death. He also presents oblations to the father and other ancestors of his adoptive mother only§, for he is capable of performing the funeral rites of that mother only. This duty is limited to that wife of the adopter‖ by whom he was received in adoption; if he were adopted by the husband alone, and not exclusively to any one wife, then he performs the *parvana shraddha* in honor of the ancestors of all such wives.

His right of lineal succession.

The right of the adopted son to succeed lineally in the family of his adoptive father is undisputed.

Also of collateral succession.

The right to inherit from his collaterals in the same family was first established in 1807 in the case of *Shamchunder* and *Roodenchunder* v. *Narayni Dibeh.*¶ The question submitted to the Pundits was "in the case of two adopted sons of a common adoptive father, can

* Dattaka Chandrika, Section I., verse 3.

† Dattaka Chandrika, Section III., verse 1.

‡ Vyavastha Darpana, p. 896.

§ Dattaka Chandrika, Section III., verse 17.

‖ Dattaka Mimansa, Section VI., verse 50.—The forefathers of the adoptive mother only are also the maternal grandsires of sons given, and the rest: for the rule regarding the paternal is equally applicable to the maternal grandsires of adopted sons.

¶ Select Reports (new edition), Vol. I., p. 279.

one, on the decease of the other, succeed to his property as his collateral heirs?" The answer was in the affirmative, and the Court decreed in accordance with it.

The question of collateral succession in its more general form,—*viz.*, to the estate of the collateral relations of the father, came on for discussion a few years later in the case of *Gourhurree Kubraj* v. *Rutnessuree Debia.** That suit, originally brought at Moorshedabad, was apparently decided by the Bengal Sudder Court in 1821, and arose in this way. On the death of a certain Rajah, his zemindary descended in equal moieties through two of his sons, the ultimate heir of each claiming through adoption. The question was raised whether, supposing an adoption to be valid, the person adopted is entitled only to the property of his adopting father, or whether he can claim also the property of his adopting father's family and collateral r elations. In the *vyavastha* of the Pundits delivered in 1807 in the case of *Shamchunder* v. *Narayni Dibeh*, the following text of Boudhayana was said to have been quoted: "Participation of wealth belongs to the son begotten by a man himself in lawful wedlock, the son of his appointed daughter, the son begotten on his wife by a kinsman legally appointed, a son given, a son made by adoption, a son of concealed birth, and a son rejected by his natural parents. Consanguinity denoted by a common family appellation belongs to the son of an unmarried girl, the son of pregnant bride, a son bought, a son by a twice married woman, a son self given, and a son of a priest by a Sudra." Although they said, Jimutavahana, Rughunandana and others, explaining the text of Devala cited in the Dayabhaga, have not reconciled the dispute with regard to the given son

* 6 Sudder Dewanny Report, p. 203.

LECTURE XV.

and the rest being heirs to collaterals or otherwise, yet it should not be, therefore, supposed that the given son has right of collateral succession. The Pundits attempted to reconcile it by laying down that the given son and the rest who are endued with good qualities, are entitled to succeed collaterally. In the present case, the Pundits declared that although it is the opinion of Jimutavahana, quoting the text of Devala, and adopting his order of enumeration, that the son affiliated in the *dattaka* form is not the heir of collateral relations, they, nevertheless, concurred with many previous *vyavasthas* which established the adopted son's collateral succession according to the law promulgated by Menu.

And in another case* the question raised was whether the daughter of an adopted son could inherit from her father's adoptive collateral relatives. The suit was brought at Dacca, and it was again for the third time urged that, by the Dayabagha, the adopted son is excluded from sharing with those of the blood; and that, even if he be not, his daughter has no right. It was held that an adopted son succeeds collaterally, as well as lineally, in the family of his adoptive father. Menu had so laid it down; and although Jimutavahana contended for a contrary doctrine, yet, being in opposition to Menu, his opinion, it was said, was not entitled to weight. The Court cited, with approbation, a *vyavastha* of the Pundits† to the effect "that a valid adopted son must be considered as a member of the *gotra* of his adopting father, and legally entitled to the property of his adopting father's *sapindas*. This opinion is conformable to Menu; and although it is the opinion of

* Lokenath Roy *v.* Shamasoondery, 14 S. D. Dec., p. 1863.

† Select Reports, Vol. VI., p. 203.

Jimutavahana, quoting the text of Devala, and adopting his order of enumeration, that the son affiliated in the *dattaka* form is not an heir of collateral relations (*sapindas*, &c.,) nevertheless, as many *vyavasthas* have been delivered in the Court, establishing the adopted son's collateral succession, according to the law promulgated by Menu, this opinion was delivered according to the same law." The Court, in ruling that an adopted son succeeds collaterally, as well as lineally, in the family of his adoptive father, expressly stated that the ruling was limited to succession to the property of *sapindas*, agnates to the adoptive father; with respect to *bandhus* or cognate relations, the ruling had no concern, the question not arising before them. This was the third case in which the Sudder Court, administering the Hindu law of Bengal, had disregarded the authority of the Dayabhaga.

And in later cases,* it has been held that, beyond all doubt, an adopted son succeeds collaterally, as well as lineally, to the inheritance within the family of his adoptive father.

Adopted son is related to adoptive mother and her ancestors.

The question left open in the third case, cited above as to the right of the adopted son to succeed to those who were not, by adoption, agnatically related to him, is the next one which presents itself for discussion. According to Mr. Sutherland, the *dattaka* adopted child represents the real legitimate son, not merely in his relationship to his adoptive father and his paternal ancestors, but also in relationship to his adoptive mother and her paternal ancestors. Such rule is founded on the authority, both of the Dattaka Mimansa† and of the

* Sumbho Chunder Chowdhry *v.* Naranee Debia, 5 S. W. R., P. C., p. 100. See also Kishen Nath Roy *v.* Hurreegobind Roy, 15 S. D. Dec., p. 18.

† Dattaka Mimansa, Section VI., verse 50.

LECTURE XV.

Dattaka Chandrika.* The former lays it down that the forefathers of the adoptive mother only are also the maternal ancestors of sons given. An adopted son, however, forms no relationship to his adoptive mother's maternal ancestors. The latter authority also lays it down that the *dattaka* adopted son presents oblations to the father and the other paternal ancestors of his adoptive mother only, for he is only capable of performing the funeral rites of that mother. Both authors, therefore, exclude all relationship of such child to the adoptive mother's co-wife and her ancestors.

It may here be remarked that, as a man's right to adopt is as respects his wives absolute, it follows that, if he adopts generally, that is, to himself, both or all his wives become, by virtue of that act, adoptive mothers. But there is no text or primitive rule of law which prevents a husband from joining one wife, to the exclusion of any other wife he may have with him in the act of adoption. Nor is there any rule which expressly permits it. So far as such a rule is recognized, it follows that that wife only who joins in the adoption becomes an adoptive mother. And further, with regard to a permission to adopt, it follows that that widow alone who has authority from her husband can become an adoptive mother; the co-widows have no relationship to the adopted child. Such would be the consequence of a rule of that kind, but it is questionable how far it is or ought to be recognized.

But not to such mother's co-wife.

With regard to the decisions of the Court upon the relationship of an adopted child to the wives of the adopter, and his title to inherit from and through his adoptive mother, or any one of his co-wives, there is first of all the

* Dattaka Chandrika, Section III., verse 17.

case of *Kasheeshuree Debea* v. *Greesh Chunder Lahoree*,* in which a Hindu adopted a boy as son to his second wife. The mother and adopted son survived the adoptive father, and then died. The first wife alleged that she was equally an adoptive mother, and claimed to succeed to the estate which had vested in the son. Her claim was dismissed, and it was held that the son's property would go, not to the stepmother, but to the next legal heir of the son, who, in the case before the Court, was the nephew. An adopted son, it was said, is son to both his father and mother, but only to that mother whose adopted son he is especially taken to be.

This case, therefore, is an authority for the proposition that the adopted son to one wife is no relation, or at least no heir, to the co-wife; and also for the proposition that such co-wife is not entitled to inherit from him; and that her husband's property having once vested in the son, her rights as widow to anything except maintenance are gone.

Adopted son inherits his adoptive mother's stridhun, not her ancestral property.

Now, with regard to the adopted son's right to inherit from his adoptive mother, that was, in the case of *Tincowree Chatterjee* v. *Denonath Bannerjee*,† limited to her stridhun, and expressly stated not to extend to the property which she had inherited from her father and paternal ancestors. The effect of such limitation is to deny to the adopted son a derivative title, through his adoptive mother, to the estate of her forefathers, although a natural-born son might, on failure of nearer heirs, have succeeded. The High Court, however, decided that an adopted son has all the rights and privileges of a son born. He is the

* Weekly Reporter (1864), p. 71.

† 3 Sutherland's Weekly Reporter, 49.

son of the father and of the mother, and he succeeds to the paternal property, and also to the stridhun of his adoptive mother, in the absence of daughters, as a son born would do. That portion of his adoptive mother's estate, which had come to her by inheritance from her father, it was said, would go to her father's heirs, and not to the adopted son. The reasons referred to were that such son passes into his adoptive father's family, but not into his adoptive mother's; and that, although he can perform the *shraddha* of his adoptive mother, he cannot perform that of her father, reasons which are inconsistent with the passages of the Dattaka Mimansa and Dattaka Chandrika, which I have quoted. Further, it was said that a son adopted by one wife can succeed to the co-wife's stridhun. The rule of law, however, referred to by the Court, in support of this proposition, apparently relates to the natural son of the co-wife, or the son adopted by the husband to both wives.

He does not inherit from a *bandhu*.

There would appear to be some inconsistency in these two cases. Mr. Macnaghten,* however, was of opinion that the adopted son's right of succession did not include succession to a *bandhu*. "For instance," he says, "if a woman, on whom her father's estate had devolved, adopt a son, with the permission of her husband, the son so adopted will not be entitled to such estate, on his adopting mother's death. It is not quite evident why a daughter's adopted son should be excluded from inheriting the estate of his adopting mother's father, while the son of an adopted son has an acknowledged right of collateral succession; inasmuch as the maternal grandfather is enumerated among the kindred

* Principles of Hindu Law, p. 78.

by all the Hindu legislators. But the reason is that the party adopted in the latter case becomes the son of a person whose lineage is distinct from that of the maternal grandfather." Although there have been conflicting judicial decisions, the opinion of Mr. Macnaghten appears to have prevailed over that of Mr. Sutherland as given above. A Full Bench of the High Court of Bengal affirmed the principle contended for by Mr. Macnaghten, and decided* that an adopted son cannot succeed to the estate of his adoptive maternal grandfather. I think it will be useful to extract from the judgment of Mr. Justice Shumboonath Pundit, delivered upon that occasion, the following passage:—

"No direct text of Hindu law has been shown distinctly ruling that an adopted son of a daughter can (after the death of his adoptive mother) succeed to the estate of the father of the latter, though, by adoption, the deceased, undoubtedly, had legally become his maternal grandfather.

"No case, either of Bengal or Behar, within the jurisdiction of any of the two Courts of this Presidency, or of any other Presidency, ruling the point, has been shown. Really, such a claim was not likely to be found to be so rare, if there was any foundation for it. The very fact of no case being found shows that the law on the point, as put down in all the English compilations of Hindu law (though not affirmed directly by any decision in a proper case), must have long been considered as settled, or else we should have found numerous cases in which the point now under discussion would have fairly been raised. It is asked by those who contend for the rights of the adopted

* Morun Moyee Debia v. Bejoy Kishen Gossamee, Suth. F. B. R., p. 121.

LECTURE XV. grandsons by daughters, why should they lose a particular line of inheritance altogether? The answer is simply this, that, in other respects besides this, such an adopted son is admittedly in a worse position than a son of the body.

"If, for instance, after the adoption of a son, a son of the body be born to the adopting father, the adopted son obtains less than he would have got if he also had been a son of the body; and is not, in many other respects, treated as the eldest son of his adopting father.

"The system of adoption is one full of injustice; and while the adopted himself becomes the cause of disappointment to others, he himself is not altogether exempt from the possibility of his rights of inheritance in one direction being curtailed entirely, just as well as in being adopted, he might be a loser of his share of a valuable ancestral estate by his being given away by his natural father, perhaps a rich man, for adoption in a family comparatively indigent and poor. If this right of an adopted son of a daughter had been ever recognized in Hindu law, then its rules regarding the rights of the daughters to succeed to their father would have been worded quite differently from the manner in which in all books they are expressed. Some allusion to an adopted son would necessarily have been made, just where barrenness and childless widowhood are described as bars to their right of inheritance. Allusion would also have been made where such expressions as 'capable of bearing children' are used. It is quite obvious that the present wording of the law on this subject is clearly inconsistent with the right of an adopted son of a daughter to succeed to the estate of her father. Besides, if an adopted son lose a part of his rights by a son of the body being born to his adopting parents, after his adoption, much more than an elder brother loses by the subsequent birth to his father of another son of the body, it is natural to suppose that the same difference which is observed between two such brothers, with regard to the estate of their fathers, adoptive and natural respectively, would reasonably be maintained with regard to their rights of succession to the estate of the father of their mother. No such provision is made when the right of succession of daughter's sons is specified in all text books and English compilations of Hindu law.

"Notwithstanding the amendment made by the late Sudder Court upon the doctrine of the Dayabhaga, to the extent of admitting the right of an adopted son to succeed collaterally, according to the doctrines of Menu (as explained by his best commentators) in the family of his adopting father, it may still be an open question whether, when two brothers, one an adopted son and the other the son of the body of his father, have to inherit as brother's sons, or brother's grandsons, the property of a kindred of their father, they take this estate in equal, or in the same shares, in which they had taken their father's estate. It is clear that the last mentioned argument is not conclusive if these brothers can, in the above case, succeed in equal shares; and in that case the omission of such distinction would be useless in both cases. We do not find that we can dispose of this question by stating, as a general principle, that one may adopt another as his own heir, and give him all his own property, but cannot be allowed through such an act to disinherit a *third* person from the estate of a *fourth* individual; because an adopting father may even now do so, when his adopted son may have a right to claim

LECTURE XV.

as a nearer kinsman the estate of a brother, or cousin, or uncle of his adopting father, to the prejudice of another kindred, who is distant by one degree in descent, and who might have succeeded to the same unopposed, if there had not been this adoption.

"The principal grounds upon which we think that the opinion of the English compilers of Hindu law against the right of an adopted grandson to succeed to the estate of his maternal grandfather is correct, are the fact of no direct texts acknowledging such a right being any where traced, and the absence among the reported cases of any suit in which the question directly arose. For aught we know, the case that we are now deciding might have arisen from a wrong understanding of the effect of the decision of 1859 upon this point of Hindu law, which however, it did not attempt to decide.

"From that decision it may be argued, that if the maternal relatives of the adopting mother stand in the position of those relatives that they would be to the son of the body of the daughter of their family, and if they have a right to succeed to the estate of this adoptod son, just as to that of a son of the daughter, why should the adopted son himself be debarred from claiming a similar right of inheritance himself to the estate of these maternal relatives?

"Such reciprocal rights are not however invariably any part of the Hindu system of succession. A man never succeeds his own daughter; and a husband is not invariably, to all kinds of his wife's stridhun property, her heir exclusively or jointly with others; and though to some stridhun of a stepmother, a son may be heir, she can never claim any inheritance from such a son of her husband."

The decision of 1859, referred to in this judgment, was to the effect that the relations of an adoptive mother inherit the property of her adopted son, just as they would inherit the property of her natural son.* This decision was upon a converse point to that decided by the Full Bench, and would probably not now be accepted as law; notwithstanding that rights of inheritance as pointed out by Mr. Justice Shumboonath Pundit are not always reciprocal, an adopted son, it may be laid down, does not succeed to the property of his *bandhus*, connected through his adoptive mother as their heir, nor do they succeed to him as his heirs.

And conversely the *bandhu* does not inherit from him.

If the rule of law is correct that a co-wife has no relationship to the wife's adopted son, and is not connected by the *pinda*, as was laid down in the case of *Kasheeshuree Debia* v. *Greeschunder Lahoorie*, she cannot succeed as his heir, nor can he have any rights of inheritance to her property, *stridhun* or ancestral. The decisions are not quite consistent, but it may be that the rule is erroneous, which enables a man, without any express permission of law, to affiliate a son to one wife, in exclusion of the others.

Adopted son does not inherit from his natural relations, nor they from him.

It is, however, quite clear that an adopted son loses all claim upon the family and estates of his natural parents. He has no title to succeed therein, either lineally or collaterally. Nor have the members of the family, which he has quitted, any title to succeed to the estate left by him or his heirs. They are entire strangers to his estate, ancestral or self-acquired. In Madras, an attempt was recently made by the natural relations of an adopted child to make out a title by inheritance to his property. It was in the case of *Srinivasa Ayyangar* v. *Kuppan Ayyangar*,† in

* Sudder Dewanny Adawlut Decisions, 1859, p.1091.

† Madras High Court Report, Vol. I., p. 180.

LECTURE XV.

which the plaintiff was brother to the natural father,—*i. e.*, the uncle by blood relationship of a deceased adopted son of a Hindu widow. That widow had mortgaged some property, and died before her adopted son. The plaintiff sued, as the rightful heir to her adopted son, who had died unmarried without issue, to redeem the property, and the question to be decided was, whether a member of the natural family can succeed to one taken out of the family by adoption. The Pundits in the Madras Sudder Court, as late as the year 1859, had given it as their opinion that, when an adopted son dies without issue, his natural heirs will succeed to property which he has inherited from his adoptive father. Such opinion had been rejected by the Court, who were satisfied that a gift made of one for adoption created an entire and irrevocable severance of him from his natural family. The High Court proceeded:—"We are of opinion that the above decision is founded upon a just appreciation of the principle of an adoption, whereby the son of one man ceases to be such in the eye of the law, and becomes the son of another man, inheriting thenceforth in his adoptive family, and having no more rights in his own family. If it would be a violation of that principle to allow a person adopted to return to his natural family, and take up their rights, it would be a still greater violation thereof to introduce to heritable rights, in the adoptive family, the natural kindred of the adopted person, who assuredly never had any part or title in the adoptive family, or in their possession.

"We observe further more that, in the Mitakshara, the great authority in this Presidency on the law of inheritance, no place has been given in the natural family for the re-introduction into the line of heirs of one taken out of that family by adoption, and none in the adoptive family for the admission of those in the natural family." LECTURE XV.

Where a son is born, after the parents have received a child in adoption, according to some copies of the texts of Katyayana, and according to the authority of Vasishta,* such adopted son takes a fourth share of the ancestral estate. The rule of law, so laid down, is accepted by the schools other than that of Bengal. They apparently follow the author of the Mitakshara.† The Bengal school, on the other hand, follows the teaching of Jimutavahana,‡ who, on the authority of a text of Devala, and other copies of the text of Katyayana, prescribes one-third.

With regard to the succession of sons who are adopted by disqualified persons, assuming such adoption to be valid, as it is nowhere authoritatively prohibited, such sons have no right to succeed to the estate of the adoptive grandfather; maintenance alone can be claimed by them according to the authority of the Dattaka Chandrika.§

Maintenance of adoptive son.

Maintenance also is frequently assigned where the ceremony of adoption is by any reason invalid for the purpose of creating affiliation, but nevertheless sufficient to effect the separation of a child from his natural parents. The Madras High Court assumed the existence of such a rule to be correct in a case‖ decided in 1862, but the next year the same Court held that there was nothing in Hindu law which would warrant a claim to maintenance, where there

* Dattaka Chandrika, Section V., verses 16, 17.

† Mitakshara, Chap. I., Section XI., verse 24.

‡ Dayabhaga, Chap. X., verse 7.

§ Dattaka Chandrika, Section VI., verse 1.

‖ Ayyavu Muspanar *v.* Niladatchi Ammal, Madras High Court Reports, Vol. I., p. 45.

LECTURE XV.

was no valid adoption* notwithstanding the authorities which they referred to, which were Mr. Strange's Manual, ss. 120 and 197; Strange's Hindu Law, Vol. I., p. 82; Dattaka Chandrika, Sec. I, clauses 14, 15, and Sec. 6, clause 4. The case was one, however, in which it was claimed that an invalidly adopted son could transmit to his widow and heir a right to be maintained out of the estate of his alleged adoptive father.

Son adopted by a widow only inherits the husband's estate which is at the time of adoption vested in her.

It appears also that a widow who exercises a power to adopt, after her husband's estate has vested elsewhere than in herself, cannot confer on her child any rights of inheritance, but only, if any thing, a title to be maintained out of the estate, or at least by herself. The case in which such adopted son was held to be without any title to succeed to the estates of his adoptive mother's husband is an extremely important one, as it shows conclusively that it is only the last full independent owner who can give a permission to adopt, which shall be valid to all purposes including those of inheritance. If a Hindu neglects to adopt, the widow of his father may repair the omission so far as the obsequies of her husband and his ancestors are concerned; but the ancestral estate which would have been answerable for those charges is gone.

A Hindu† being the owner of considerable estates in Bengal died in the year 1821. He left surviving him a widow, and an only son who succeeded as his heir; being at the time of his father's death about four years of age. The son attained his majority and married. In August 1840, he

* Bawani Sankara Pundit v. Ambabay Ammul, Madras High Court Report, Vol. I., p. 363.

† Mussamut Bhoobun Moyee Debia v. Ram Kishore Acharj Chowdhry, 10 Moore's Indian Appeals, p. 304; S. C., 3 Weekly Reporter, P. C., p. 15.

died at the age of 24, leaving no issue, and thereupon his widow became the heiress of his property, both ancestral and self-acquired. Immediately upon the death of this only son, an instrument was set up by the widow of the father and the widow of the son, purporting to be the last will of the son. By this instrument, power to adopt a son was given to the younger widow, and in December 1843 she professed to exercise the power and adopted a boy. Upon this a quarrel arose between the two widows, and the mother alleged and proved that the supposed will of her son was a forgery. She in her turn set up an instrument called an *onoomutteeputro,* or deed of permission, by which she alleged that a power to adopt a son had been given to her, by her husband, in his life-time, under which she adopted a boy as the son of her late husband, who accordingly sued the younger widow and her adopted son to establish his rights and recover the property. The case came before the Privy Council on appeal by the younger widow, as representing her own rights, and the rights of her adopted son, as well as on a cross-appeal by the adopted son of the mother, who complained that the decree in his favour ought to have included the self-acquired, as well as the ancestral property of the last deceased owner.

The Privy Council confined the discussion in their judgment to the single question whether the power which the father's widow professed to exercise was at that time capable of execution. In the year 1811, on March 30th, the father had executed an *onoomutteeputro* in favour of his wife. In 1819, two years after the birth of his son, he executed the instrument which his widow professed to act under, which was held by the Privy Council to be a deed of permission to adopt. It was in these words, addressed

LECTURE XV.

to his wife: "Prior to the birth of a male child from your womb, I had executed in your favour an *onoomuttee-putro* on the subject of your receiving an adopted son; subsequently by the will of God you have given birth to a male child, still, having regard to the future, I have again given you permission. If, which God forbid, the male child of your body be non-existent, then you will adopt a son from my *gotra* or from a different *gotra*, for the purpose of performing mine and your *shraddha* and other rites, and for the *sheba* of the gods and for the succession to the zemindary and other property, on which, if the adopted son be non-existent, which God forbid, then you shall, according to your pleasure on the failure of one, adopt other sons in succession to avoid the extinction of the *pinda* (funeral cake or offering); that *dattaka* son shall be entitled to perform your and my *shraddha* and that of our ancestors, and also to succeed to the property." The deed did not in express terms assign any limit to the period within which the adoption might be made. The natural son might have left a son; that son might have died, leaving a son who might have attained his majority in the life-time of the father's widow; but it could hardly have been intended that, after the death of several successive heirs, a son should be adopted to the great-grandfather of the last taker, when all the spiritual purposes of a son would have been satisfied. The natural son himself had probably performed all the spiritual duties which devolved upon him as a son; he had succeeded to the ancestral property as heir; he had full power of disposition over it; he might have alienated it; he might have adopted a son to succeed to it; he might have defeated every intention which his father entertained with respect to the property. On his death, his widow succeeded as heir, and would have excluded his natural brothers if he had had any. It would be singular if a brother of the natural son, made such by adoption, could take from his widow the whole of his property, when a natural-born brother could have taken no part at all. Moreover, the adopted son, as such, takes by inheritance and not by devise. The rule of Hindu law is, that in the case of inheritance, the person to succeed must be the heir of the last full owner. In this case the natural son was the last full owner. His widow succeeded as his heir to a widow's estate, and on her death the person to succeed will again be the heir, at that time, of her husband. Supposing that his mother should be that heir, then, the question of an adoption by her would stand on quite different grounds. By exercising the power of adoption she would have divested no estate but her own, and this would have brought the case within the ordinary rule; but it cannot be argued that by the mere gift of the power of adoption to a widow, the estate of the heir of a deceased son vested in possession can be defeated and divested. The case of *Rykant Monee Roy* v. *Kisto Soonderee Roy** was decided in pursuance of the ruling of the Privy Council in *Bhoobun Moyee Debia* v. *Ramkishore Acharjee.* A Hindu, with his father's consent, gave his wife permission to adopt a son in the event of the death of his natural son. That natural son lived to succeed to the ancestral estate and died, leaving a widow who held possession till her death; and then the property reverted to her husband's mother as his next legal heir. She

* 7 Sutherland's Weekly Reports, p. 392.

LECTURE XV. thereupon took advantage of the permission given her by her husband, and adopted a son who succeeded to the ancestral property. It was contended that he was not entitled to succeed as son to her husband, for that husband had died before his father; nor could he succeed as the brother and legal heir of her natural son, as his adoption did not take place till after that natural son's death. Moreover, at the time of the adoption, the adoptive mother held possession of the property, not as the widow of her husband but as the heir of her natural son. The case differed from that before the Privy Council, inasmuch as the adoption in that case took place, living the natural son's widow, while in the case now under consideration it occurred after her death. In both cases the adoption was held to be good, but in the former case the Privy Council held, that the adopted son of the mother could not divest the widow of the natural son, he having been the last full owner of the estate. But whether such natural son died unmarried, or in any other turn of events his mother should become his heir, then, if that mother exercised her husband's power of adoption, her estate would be divested by the son so obtained, whether that estate came to her immediately from her husband, or as heir to her natural son. The dictum in the Privy Council, and the judgment of the High Court in this case, finally decide that a widow does not lose the right to exercise the power of adoption because her husband's estate has, after his death, vested in his son, and then devolved upon her in succession to him. She retains that power, and if she exercises it, her adopted son acquires all the rights belonging to that character, and can divest her of her estate; but his right does not extend to the prejudice of any other person in whom that estate may, in the events which have happened since her husband's death, have legally vested. Lecture XV.

INDEX.